This book is published to accompany the television series entitled *People's Century*, which was first broadcast in September 1995

Published by
BBC BOOKS
an imprint of
BBC Worldwide Publishing

BBC WORLDWIDE LTD
WOODLANDS
80 WOOD LANE
LONDON W12 0TT

First published 1995

ISBN 0 563 37024 6

EDITED AND DESIGNED BY
B·C·S Publishing Ltd,
Chesterton, Oxfordshire

PRINTED AND BOUND IN
GREAT BRITAIN BY
Butler & Tanner Ltd,
Frome, Somerset

COLOUR ORIGINATIONS
BY
Fotographics,
London-Hong Kong

JACKET PRINTED BY
Laurence Allen Ltd,
Weston-super-Mare

Set in Bembo and Futura

ГОД
ПРОЛЄТАРСКО
ДИКТАТУРЫ
ОКТЯБРЬ 1917 – ОКТЯБРЬ 191

PEOPLE'S CENTURY 20th

From the dawn of the century to the start of the Cold War

Godfrey Hodgson

BBC BOOKS

Contents

Foreword

by

Dr J.M. Roberts

MOST HISTORY IS NOT WRITTEN IN WHAT WE might call a democratic mode. It is not about 'ordinary people' – people like us. This is both understandable and defensible. Individual decisions by remarkable individuals, or those taken by people in power, can make big differences to the lives of the rest of us: the course of the Second World War – and therefore the lives of millions of people – might have been wholly different if Hitler had not decided to go to war formally with the United States. Somewhat less dramatically, individuals have also shaped our cultures decisively: the world's history would have been very different without Confucius, St Paul, Isaac Newton and many, many others. Much time and attention has been given by historians to distinguished men and women and to the things they did, and rightly so.

But there is a sense, too, in which history cannot but be concerned with the lives of anonymous millions, as well as those of the great shapers of events. Why do we think that individuals such as those mentioned in the last paragraph are historically important? It is because they have had a great impact on the lives of huge numbers of their fellow human-beings. History is the story of what has been done by and made a difference to human beings. The more of them that have been affected, the more historically important the events, influences and decisions that shape the story are. That is how historical importance is measured; I know of no other way.

Perhaps this has become more obvious during the present century. Not only have there been more people on whom its events have played, sometimes with terrible effect, but much more is known about them than is known about their predecessors in more distant times. More important still, a number of processes have been going forward – some political, some technological, some economic – all of which have tended to give large numbers of people a more active role in events, or at any rate the illusion of one. More and more countries have, for instance, at least formally become democracies, with elected governments. That has meant that politicians have had to posture and bribe, placate and persuade more potential supporters in more countries than ever before. The world has grown richer in this century, too (if it had not done so there would probably be fewer people alive today than there were in 1900). As more people have had access to some wealth, they have come to matter more as consumers; whole industries have grown up to supply what they could be persuaded to buy. In many parts of the world mass education has become available for the first time in this century, and that has had incalculable effects on wants, the way people see those wants, and their visions of what may be possible.

When the television series on which these books are based was devised, it was hoped that it would bring to a large audience (another creation of what we aptly call 'mass' communications) a historical emphasis that would show just what was this unique new feature of the twentieth century. Even if the involvement of 'peoples' in history in a new way was already foreshadowed before 1900, its mass character is clearer than ever as the year 2000 approaches. Huge numbers of men and women have been caught up in processes that transform their lives. Sometimes the outcome has been welcome; sometimes – perhaps more often – it has been the opposite of what they would have wanted.

Much has had to be left out in telling this story, as there is so vast a canvas to cover. But what follows is, I believe, a stimulating, thought-provoking and suggestive impression of the history of the first century that can be seen in the perspective of mass participation: our own.

Introduction

THE PEOPLE YOU WILL meet in this book are not, for the most part, people you will have heard of. It belongs not to the giants – to Lenin or Hitler, Mao Zedong or Gandhi, Roosevelt or Churchill – but to the men and women who lived in their shadows, who fought in their wars, voted in their elections, worked in their factories, died for their mistakes. These are the voices of men and women who saw what they saw – horrible or exhilarating – with their own eyes; who experienced the tragic drama of great events, as actors or victims or eyewitnesses, in their own lives; or who lived through the slow but almost equally dramatic transformation of everyday life. They were not all innocent bystanders or passive sufferers: we have recorded the voices of guards as well as prisoners, villains as well as victims, and the great majority who were neither one nor the other.

You might expect to find these people's stories strung like beads on the narrative of the century's great events. Instead, we have given the main thread of the chapters over to what might be called the 'little histories' of our witnesses, and to the context in which they led their lives. We have used the boxed features to provide the framework of 'big history', and also to explain some of the byways of the century's activities: how Mickey Mouse cartoons are made, why trench warfare is so murderous, what drives governments into wars they do not want to wage. The chapters are arranged thematically as well as following a broadly chronological sequence, so you may follow a story through several decades to a chapter's end, and at the beginning of the next chapter cut back some years to pick up a new theme.

All human beings are at the centre of their own universe, so there are as many true histories of the twentieth century as there are people who have lived through it: some twelve billion of us, at a rough calculation. We have attempted to hint at the sheer variety of their experience. And we have allowed our eyewitnesses to tell their stories as they saw them, in their own terms and in terms of their own attitudes and beliefs, with neither judgement nor hindsight. We hope to have demonstrated what it has felt like to be alive in this century, rather than to pass judgement on how its great events may come to be seen, or to predict what the future may bring.

Age of Hope

THE TURN OF THE CENTURY

THE TWENTIETH CENTURY made a dazzling entrance at the Paris Exhibition of 1900. Special trains brought people from all over France and other European countries, to a display designed to show what the new century might hold. Millions of visitors were whisked along moving walkways, carried high above the stands, and plunged into displays from far-flung corners of the globe that heralded a future in which their work and leisure would be transformed.

Raymond Abescat was nine years old when he visited the exhibition. 'It really opened my eyes to everything that was going on around us outside Paris, seeing all those stands – stands of every nationality. I was able to compare what was going on in England, in Germany and so on. It gave me the urge to travel.'

One of the highlights of the exhibition was the Palace of Electricity, with its hall full of lamps, generators and motors, and its grand façade lit up at night. Raymond Abescat remembers, 'At home we used oil lamps and candles – we didn't have electricity....For me the electricity stand, which was about as wide as the Champs de Mars and brightly illuminated by all those lights – that was the most impressive sight of all.'

As the new century dawned in Russia, the young Alexander Briansky joined the celebrations in the port of Odessa, where he lived. 'The streets were illuminated. There were fireworks, drinkers. Nobody stayed at home – crowds of people were on the street....The twentieth century gave everybody some kind of specific hope.'

The hope went beyond a desire for material progress in a world characterized by deep social inequalities. Democracy, literacy and good health were privileges still denied to many. The struggle for emancipation, education and better working conditions accelerated as the century unfolded and people struggled to control and change their lives. In the years to come some of humanity's most cherished hopes and greatest dreams would be fulfilled, but many people would be confronted by horror beyond their worst nightmares.

DAWN OF THE CENTURY *The cover of a song published to herald the new century, decorated with symbols of progress.*

The old order

'The Queen is dead' blazed newspaper headlines all over the world. It was January 1901. Queen Victoria, British monarch, empress of India, ruler of half a billion people and a quarter of the world, had reigned for sixty-four years. At her funeral tens of thousands of mourners watched silently as the gun carriage bearing her coffin passed by. Two emperors, two kings, twenty-four princes and thirteen dukes followed it.

The crowned heads who followed Victoria's coffin between them governed most of the world. The major European powers had established empires far beyond their own borders. Nearly three-quarters of the world's people lived under foreign rule, and not only in Europe but also in Africa, Australia, the Far East, India and North America indigenous peoples had been subjugated.

The century dawned on a society based on privilege and obedience, on simple certainties and prejudices. In Britain only men with some wealth and over a certain age were able to vote, while women in Germany could not go to university. American factory owners could fire their workers simply on suspicion of joining a union. Elaborate social codes determined relations between the sexes and between people of different rank. It was a world built on Victorian notions of hard work and thrift, and it looked as though it would endure for ever. Donald Hodge grew up in a small English village at the turn of the century. He remembers how people were expected to touch their caps to show respect to their social superiors – the squire, the vicar and the doctor. He also recalls his childhood conviction that nothing would change. 'It was going to go on. We were the greatest democracy in the world, and we felt a kind of pride in our empire.'

Confidence in the established order was echoed in Japan. Mohei Tamura, who grew up in the town of Maebashi north-west of Tokyo, remembers that at the beginning of the century 'People worshipped the emperor as God'. He believes it was this devotion to the emperor that united the nation. 'I think that was why the Japanese soldiers were so brave. We, the ordinary people, had the same feelings. Everyone remembers the time when the emperor

DRESSED TO KILL *in India. Hunting was one of the familiar sporting activities that Europeans continued to pursue throughout their empires. Hunting clothes were hot and uncomfortable to wear in tropical climates, but Western traditions were rigidly maintained.*

Toys for teaching

JIGSAW PUZZLES *were originally designed as a way for children to learn geography, and they became extremely popular in the early 1900s. Piecing together pictures such as this one, which shows King George V in royal regalia at the centre of imperial activities, taught children about the extent and influence of the British empire.*

A SOLEMN SPECTACLE (LEFT) *Crowds line the pavements and rooftops to catch a glimpse of Queen Victoria's funeral procession through the London streets. Her death marked the end of an era. Within just two decades, most of the people riding behind her coffin had lost their crowns.*

NATIVE LABOUR (ABOVE) *A group of Malagasy, the people of Madagascar, pause with their French overseer in their construction of a new railway. France had greatly extended its empire by the early 1900s, ruling much of west and central Africa as well as lands in Indochina and South America.*

THE NEW JAPAN *Millions of Japanese citizens flooded into the growing industrial towns to find work in the new factories. By 1900 Japan had left feudalism behind, and had launched into a programme of modernization that soon rivalled economic development in the West. Coal, iron and steel production all expanded rapidly, the textile industry flourished, and Japan's decisive victory in the war with China in 1894–95 demonstrated the power of its army and navy. In the West Japan's emergence was viewed with admiration and disquiet.*

died; people from all over the country gathered at the front garden of the Imperial Palace and cried bitterly.'

The rise of Japan, the one country in Asia modernizing itself successfully, was regarded with some suspicion in the West. Mohei Tamura remembers that when Japan invaded China in 1894 the Europeans had been quick to defend their own interests. 'Russia, Germany and France were worried about the power Japan might possess after the invasion, so they interfered, forcing Japan to compensate China.' But Japan still made considerable gains. In 1904 war broke out between Japan and Russia. Japan's victory, after destroying the Russian fleet in the straits of Tsushima, was widely celebrated. 'We were ecstatic about the outcome, and held a great festival that lasted for three days,' recalls Mohei Tamura. 'Because of the great victory over Russia, we had no fear of foreigners. We felt that Japan was the land of the gods and would therefore never lose a war in the future.'

Japan's success brought confidence and pride to its people.

HATRED UNLEASHED
(RIGHT) *The Boxer Rising was characterized by the violent killing of foreign missionaries and traders by Chinese nationalists. The Chinese regarded the establishment and control of railways and telegraph services by Westerners as economically exploitative, and zealous Christian missionaries threatened the traditional social framework.*

In many other countries there was good reason to fear foreigners, and to hope for change. In China Guo Jingtong remembers how people felt about the way their Manchu emperors had allowed Westerners to penetrate the country. 'The foreigners wanted to control us. They burned down our historical sites and bullied our China. In any decent-sized village or town they set up Catholic churches. The Church paid the Chinese who were prepared to convert.' In 1900 long-standing resentment at Western intrusion exploded into a violent rebellion known as the Boxer Rising. Both Europeans and Chinese Christians were killed by Chinese nationalists, and foreign legations in Peking were besieged. It took a large international military force to reimpose control.

White masters also exercised control over African peoples. In the newly formed Union of South Africa, Bob Ngwenya grew up working on a farm in the Orange Free State. 'The Boer was the king. Nothing else. He could do whatever he wished. They told us that blacks were nothing – and we accepted it.' Dorah Ramothibe also grew up on a Boer farm. 'They used to punish us. They'd make us lie on the table and whip us – even the men. Our fathers weren't happy about the way we lived. But there was nothing we could do, there was no alternative. So we had to stay.'

The United States had escaped from European colonization and tended to criticize European governments for their empires, but minorities within their own country were also oppressed. By 1900 most American Indians had been forced to live in designated reservations. There were concerted efforts to make them conform to the government's vision of what proper Americans should be. Indian children were forced to go to government schools, most of which were more like army camps: they were given uniforms and made to drill or set to work. They were ordered to speak only English, and were punished for talking in their own language.

Slavery had been abolished in the United States at the end of the Civil War. But thirty-five years later a comprehensive system of segregation still kept black people quite separate from the whites. Equality existed only in theory; blacks were not allowed to use the white man's restaurants, buses, railway carriages or schools. John Morton Finney, whose father had been born a slave, was eleven years old in 1900. He remembers that segregation

"We couldn't talk our language, we got punished for that, and if we did they took you and they whipped you…they forced us to go to school….We had already been here before the white man ever came, we've suffered for five hundred years."

HARRY BYRD

HOPI INDIANS *in Arizona, which had been taken from Mexico by the United States. As settlers moved westwards after gold was discovered in California, fierce Indian resistance to the incursions of the whites onto their traditional lands was crushed. Centuries of European migration greatly reduced the population of American Indians, who were expected ultimately not to survive at all.*

patiently in the Register Room on Ellis Island on arrival in the United States after their journey across the Atlantic. Yetta Sperling and her family had endured a rough ten-day voyage in an overcrowded ship. She recalls their reception by the authorities. 'Every family was put in a cubicle, with bars like a prison. We slept in it that night.'

CREATED EQUAL *Liberty and the pursuit of happiness still seemed to be remote aspirations for most blacks in the United States. John Morton Finney learned when he was still very young that 'the blacks had nothing, and the only way they could survive was to work for the whites'.*

was not the worst thing that blacks had to face. 'There was no limit, it extended to everything. In many places black people could not even go to the polls to vote, though the law said they had a right to do so. If they did they could be killed, shot down or beaten to death.'

In Russia the hardship took a different form. Like black American slaves, the peasants had been liberated from serfdom in the 1860s, but by the early twentieth century their lives had changed little. The Russian monarch, the tsar, was venerated with almost religious fervour, and the great landowners still effectively controlled the lives of the peasants, who endured grinding poverty. Sergei Butsko grew up living in primitive conditions in a hut; eight of his brothers and sisters died from dysentery, and the whole family had to work for the local nobleman. 'All the tools were wooden. Almost everything was made by the family itself. The floor was earth....We had a loom where we used to weave all our linen for clothes.' For Sergei Butsko and for millions like him all over the world, the new opportunities that the twentieth century offered were still far out of reach.

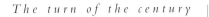

A NEW LIFE IN THE NEW WORLD

'**G**IVE ME YOUR TIRED, YOUR POOR, your huddled masses yearning to breathe free.' This invitation, inscribed on the base of the Statue of Liberty in New York, welcomed millions of European immigrants to the United States in the first two decades of the twentieth century.

Potential immigrants, many of them young, were drawn by the advertisements placed abroad by employers and by the managers of steamship and railroad companies. Most people went in search of work, particularly those living in southern and eastern Europe, where the industrial development that had brought jobs to people in northern Europe was slower to develop. There were other reasons to seek a new life: to escape persecution, to avoid military conscription or to regain religious freedom. By 1920 a third of eastern Europe's Jewish population – many from Poland and Russia, where anti-Semitism was increasing – had migrated, 90 per cent of them to the United States.

Nellie Gillenson was the tenth child born to Jewish parents in Galicia, Austria. 'We had a poor life,' she remembers. 'My mother and father had to worry every day about our food....There was no way of making a living.' After a traumatic parting from her parents, who she never saw again, she sailed to the United States with her sister. Her spirits soared when they arrived there safely. 'When I made my first step on the ground of America I felt like I wanted to kiss it, and I said "God bless America" even then.'

By 1910 a third of the poulation of the twelve largest cities in the United States was foreign-born. While some of the immigrants returned to Europe, unable to adjust to the new country and new way of life, the great majority learned a new language and new skills, and also brought their own habits and experiences from Europe with them. Surrounded by their fellow immigrants, they set up new communities that were not the same as those they had left behind nor exactly imitated the American way of life. Many immigrants did enjoy more freedom than they had ever known, with the chance to work, live and worship as they pleased. Nellie Gillenson remembers, 'We felt that we were welcomed. They let us go wherever we wanted to go. They let us live the way we wanted.'

YETTA SPERLING (RIGHT) *was still a child when she sailed to join her father, who had migrated to the United States to avoid compulsory military service in the German army. Shipping lines offered advice to 'every intending emigrant to Canada or the United States' (RIGHT). Those who made the journey were given a medical inspection as they embarked (ABOVE) and when they arrived. Only healthy immigrants were allowed to stay.*

FLIGHTS OF FANCY
(OPPOSITE) *became a reality when Louis Blériot flew across the English Channel. Jeanne Plouvin (BELOW) was among the crowd watching him take off.*

STRIKING OIL (BELOW) *meant big business in the rapidly growing economy of the United States. Both industry and the internal combustion engine relied on oil for fuel.*

New idols

Technology, the fruit of science, was the great new force expected to transform people's lives. Many people had moved from the land to the cities since the nineteenth century, and it was there that the promise of the new century was felt the most strongly. 'In a city like Chicago,' says the American Elmie Steever, then a young girl, 'everything was modern. We had modern equipment, we had running water, we had bathrooms and the houses were well heated or cared for. And of course we didn't have those conveniences in the country – we couldn't have.'

Before 1900 people travelled by horse, bicycle, boat and train, but most often on their own two feet. The new century pioneered and popularized other means of transport. In 1900 the first electric tram appeared on the streets of New York. The first rigid airship, the zeppelin, was launched in Germany, and the first French underground railway, the Metro, opened in Paris. The new vehicle that had the most immediate impact was the motor car.

It was still an event to see a car when the first aircraft were also being built. In December 1903 the Wright brothers achieved the first controlled, powered flight in a heavier-than-air machine, a biplane, on a beach near Kitty Hawk, North Carolina. Then the French aviator Louis Blériot stole the limelight when he flew in a single-winged craft from Calais to Dover in 1909. Jeanne Plouvin, a young French girl, was there. 'When we knew that Blériot was going to leave, all the children in the district – everyone, from the smallest to the biggest – gathered in a field along the road. We heard him start to move forwards and begin to take off. Everyone clapped and waved, everyone shouted "Bravo!"....There was immense joy when we heard he'd landed on the cliffs of Dover.'

The inventions and new conveniences rapidly followed one another. People could get to work more quickly, and work faster when they were there. They could travel more and learn more, earn and spend more money. One of the most dramatic domestic changes came when electricity was introduced. For Elmie Steever, 'It was very exciting when we got electricity into the church, and the man just touched a button and the church lit up. It was just beautiful. Then of course they had electricity in the stores, and a few put it into their homes. My first experience with an electrical appliance was an iron. I thought it was the most wonderful thing to stand there and just iron, and not have to keep your irons on the stove, and keep the fire going to keep your irons hot.'

Another change came when the telephone was introduced. Jean Eloy was growing up in Paris, and his family thought it was a 'marvellous, magnificent invention....You had to turn the handle again and again until the operator finally deigned to answer.' He recalls his father's impatience when he had to wait for a response. 'When my father's shouting got too much, she'd get her own back on him by not putting him through.'

As a young woman Elmie Steever worked at the telephone exchange in Stromsburg, Nebraska. She recalls how long it took for people to get used to the telephone. 'People were supposed to look in the directory, find the number and give that number to the operator. But lots of times people just picked up the telephone and said "Give me Mr or Mrs so and so".' There were at first so few telephones that operators could memorize their numbers.

Technology was increasingly able to establish links across the world as well as between individuals. In 1901 the Italian scientist Guglielmo Marconi transmitted the first transatlantic radio signals; only two years later regular radio news services were set up in New York and London.

WINDOW SHOPPING (RIGHT) *Electric lighting installed by shopkeepers to light up their window displays at the beginning of the century was many people's first experience of electricity. In the industrialized world the range of goods on offer in the busy shopping districts was matched by the numbers of city dwellers able to afford them.*

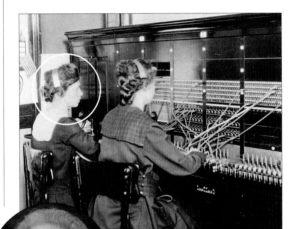

MAKING THE CONNECTION
*Elmie Steever worked shifts with a
team of women at the Stromsburg
telephone exchange. 'It was busy every
minute, there was just no let-up at all...when your shift
changed you had your headset on, and as the girl slid out to
the right, you slid in behind her. There was never a pause.'*

SELLING THE NEWS *was
an increasingly competitive
business in the early
twentieth century. As
education helped more people
learn to read, many of them
became eager for information
and gossip. The tabloids
offered headlines in large
print and stories of foreign
atrocities, and promoted the
latest fads and crazes.*

The age of the masses

For many of those who led privileged and protected lives, the most dramatic – and threatening – aspect of the new century was the growth of the new industrial class swelling beneath society's civilized and apparently stable veneer. For the twentieth century was to be the age of the masses.

There were now more people alive than ever before, and they were multiplying fast. Millions of people were on the move, drawn to the cities in the search for work. Industrialization in Europe and North America had created a new demand for factory workers, clerks and labourers. On trains, in cafés and parks, at seaside resorts, concerts, theatres and spilling over the streets there were crowds of people. Rural communities, closely knit and in many countries still based on feudal relationships, were in decline. The urban population was on the rise.

The press and later radio encouraged political awareness. The typical newspaper of the nineteenth century, which was densely written and highly informative, was read by very few. It was being superseded by the new tabloids: the *Daily Mail*, the *New York World* and *Le Petit Journal* were among the newspapers that were designed to be read by millions. They included photographs, which helped to sell copies and gave the public a new familiarity with prime minsters and presidents; advertisements alerted readers to the possibilities of life with more money. The new journalism, deliberately aimed at the new industrial class, gave them a more conscious sense of society and their position in it.

As people's expectations rose, so did their demands. And with each new gain they rose further. Strikes and protests were not a twentieth-century invention, but the extent and variety of the new organizations that led them was new. And for every benefit or reform granted to one person in the nineteenth century there were ten times as many people with ten times as many demands in the twentieth. Many people's working life began in childhood and ended only when they died. Edith Corcoran worked in a New York knitting mill from the age of fourteen. 'When I went into the mill, everyone was much older than me. It was a lifetime thing. There was no retirement. You worked until you couldn't get to your job any more.' Arthur Whitlock was born in London in 1891. He too remembers the advantages of the rich. 'I only had an elementary education because in those days education belonged to the upper classes. You either had to find the money to go on to that further education, or it was impossible.' At the age of fourteen he found work at the prestigious Army and Navy Stores. Although he enjoyed his work – he was a telephonist and messenger boy – he was aware that all the employees were vulnerable. 'There was really no security in employment. If a customer complained, you were likely to get dismissal at a moment's notice.'

Minnie Way had begun work in a Scottish jute mill at the even younger age of twelve. She remembers how common the strikes were. 'They would go down the street singing: "We are out for higher wages/As we have a right to do/But we will never be content/Until we get the ten per cent/For we've a right to live as well as you".' Most industrialized countries were swept by strikes in the early years of the century. From 1900 to 1905 half a million American workers were fired each year because of their involvement in unions and strikes; Belgian workers paralysed the country in 1902, demanding electoral reform.

WAVES OF WORKERS *at the Belfast shipyard where the* Titanic *was under construction; more than 11 000 workers were employed to build the world's largest passenger liner. The ship's advanced safety features did not prevent disaster: as the* Titanic *crossed the north Atlantic on her maiden voyage in April 1912, she struck an iceberg and sank.*

ARTHUR WHITLOCK (ABOVE) *found that changes in retailing such as the mail-order catalogues were not matched by better job security for employees: 'There was no redundancy or anything like that,' he recalls.*

NEW INHABITANTS
thronged the streets of large cities such as New York at the turn of the century. It was in the world's cities that political upheaval and social change began.

ROWS OF CLERKS
(BELOW) *maintained the accounts and kept records up to date. As industry expanded, the need for administrative staff grew. Employment in offices was highly respectable; while men became clerks, educated women found work as shop assistants or typists.*

In many countries working people were already organizing themselves politically and campaigning for change. The German Social Democratic Party had been set up in 1875 when two workers' parties combined. It received only 500 000 votes and gained twelve seats in the Reichstag, the German parliament, at its first election; by 1912 it was the largest parliamentary party. Across Europe, new workers' parties were established on the German model. The British Labour Party was formed in 1900, and by 1906 there were twenty-six Labour members of parliament.

There were some who would not wait for peaceful change. Anarchists, ultra-nationalists and secret revolutionary societies were

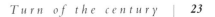

WOMEN VOTE FOR CHANGE

'I WAS ASKED IF I WOULD AGREE TO BE CHAINED to Buckingham Palace gates and I said yes....I would agree to anything if it would help women.' Gertrude Jarrett worked in a British pottery factory; she was determined to help the Suffragette movement in its struggle to gain women the vote, even if it meant violent and sometimes dangerous demonstration.

At the beginning of the twentieth century women's lives were changing as more women went out to work, not only in factories but as typists, clerks, bookkeepers and postal workers. There was a growing demand for teachers and nurses. As more women gained financial independence, their social status improved. But economic power was not matched by political power. In 1900 the only countries in which women could vote were New Zealand, parts of Australia and the state of Wyoming in the United States.

Mounting pressure to grant women the right to vote had been growing in the United States and in Europe. In the United States the campaign for women's suffrage had at first been linked to the movement for the abolition of slavery, but although black Americans had gained voting rights after the Civil War, women had not. However, by 1915 a further fifteen states had followed the example set by Wyoming.

In Britain the first effective women's movement was launched in 1903: the Women's Social and Political Union. The suffragettes, as they became known, led a campaign to bring the issue of women's rights to the fore. Their tactics included public speeches, protest marches, civil disturbance, heckling politicians, and hunger strikes by demonstrators when they were imprisoned.

As women's associations became established in other countries, from France to India, the suffragette movement gained an international perspective. Women in Germany were denied the right to join any political organizations until 1907; that year, Finland became the first European country to give its women the vote. Suffrage was granted in Norway in 1913, Denmark in 1915, revolutionary Russia in 1917 and Canada in 1918. In some countries it was the First World War that precipitated a change in attitude, as women proved the value of their skills and resilience in a time of crisis. British women over thirty were granted the right to vote in 1918; postwar reconstruction brought voting rights to women in Austria, Czechoslovakia, Germany and Poland. In 1920 the right to vote was extended throughout the United States.

VOTES FOR WOMEN
(RIGHT) *American suffragettes take to the streets to publicize women's right to gain a public voice. Gertrude Jarrett remembers how in Britain, 'If it got too rowdy the police would come and move us off. We still used to say what we thought....I believed that women were equal to men and should have a say in things.'*

prepared to stop at nothing, and assassinations were reported in the newspapers almost as regularly as were strikes: the king of Italy, the president of the United States and the head of the Russian secret police were all killed by an assassin's bullet or bomb.

Socialism was also on the march in eastern Europe, and in Russia unrest and dissatisfaction led to revolt in St Petersburg in January 1905. Alexander Briansky remembers, 'People hoped the tsar could make their lives better, and would force capitalists to do something for the people, to ensure that they were not so oppressed....After 1905, when thousands of women and children had been killed, revolutionary ideas began to penetrate deeper into the people.'

Beyond Europe and the United States, it was even more difficult to achieve change. When the Herero people rebelled against their German masters in South-West Africa, the Germans responded with a massacre that killed several thousand. Other movements were beginning that would grow during the century, and eventually triumph. In South Africa blacks began to organize to press for peaceful change. Dorah Ramothibe was at one of the early meetings in the Orange Free State: 'We also wanted to be treated all right. We also wanted to live a better life like the white people, and have money and to be paid for the work we did, instead of being given a piece of bread.' In 1912 the various local groups merged to form the African National Congress. 'Just after the formation of Congress there was light, there was hope.'

In the years before the First World War, all the seeds of the twentieth century were sown. They included anti-Semitism, mass propaganda, government repression, and in the Boer War the first concentration camps for civilians, alongside democracy, equal rights and peaceful prosperity. Schools, mass literacy, newspapers and new communications were used to build up the power of the state: people taught to read and vote were also taught to obey. By 1914, poised on the brink of a war that would shatter the old world for ever, the masses who demonstrated for greater freedom were being marched to their deaths with barely a murmur.

POVERTY IN PUBLIC
Poor families gathered in the back streets of many of the world's cities and towns, where industrialization brought wealth to a few but continued poverty and hardship to many of those who sought work in them.

THE WORLD OF LEARNING (ABOVE)
Education was seen as the key to the future. Those who had access to the schoolroom, girls as well as boys, would become part of a better educated and better informed workforce who would learn to demand change rather than just enduring it.

WAR GAMES (RIGHT)
A gymnastic display demonstrates the fitness of young Frenchmen. Their mettle, and that of young men all over Europe, would soon be tested in a real war.

2

Killing Fields

THE EXPERIENCE OF THE FIRST WORLD WAR

EARLY ON THE MORNING OF 1 July 1916, just as the first waves of British soldiers climbed out of their trenches and advanced towards the German lines, the German troops scrambled out of their deep bunkers and opened fire. The British troops were heavily laden with the ammunition, grenades, rifles and barbed wire that they would need when – or if – they reached the German lines. Even under heavy fire these well-disciplined men continued to walk steadily forward across no-man's-land, to almost certain death. A German gunner remembered: 'We were surprised to see them walking...we just had to load and reload. You didn't have to aim, you just fired into them.'

The British soldiers had been told that the huge artillery barrage would already have killed most of the Germans, and that those who had survived it would have been buried alive. One battalion was told: 'You can slope arms, light up your pipes, and march all the way to Pozières before you meet any live Germans.' They had also been told that the Germans' barbed-wire defences would all have been flattened. But neither assurance was true. The men of many battalions were trapped by uncut wire entanglements, then raked by machine-gun fire. The men had been betrayed by poor planning and muddle; they were, as one German said, 'lions, led by donkeys'.

This was to prove one of the most gallant and disastrous days in the history of warfare – the first day of the battle of the Somme, in northern France. In a war characterized by the remorseless slaughter of young men, it achieved a dreadful fame as the day on which there was the heaviest loss of life. In the four-month battle more than a million soldiers were killed or wounded.

The First World War was to sweep away empires, to cripple both the victorious and the defeated nations, and to leave a dangerous legacy of hate. It brought the United States into Europe, and ended European world supremacy. In 1914 going to war seemed like an adventure; by 1918 it had become a nightmare.

GOING OVER THE TOP *This photomontage of battlefield images captures the experience of the war.*

For king and country

The mood in which the world went to war in 1914 was one of naive patriotic fervour. It was your duty to serve your country. In four years of combat, sixty-five million men from more than twenty countries were called up. At first they did this with real enthusiasm. Margarethe Stahl, who worked in the press section of the German war office, saw the soldiers march through the streets of Berlin in August on their way to the front. 'There were flags everywhere, flowers everywhere. People were throwing flowers at the soldiers, and they had flowers in the muzzles of their rifles. They were given cigarettes and chocolate. Their mothers or wives ran along beside them and everyone was singing.' Carl von Clemm, who was in the German artillery, remembers how it felt: 'It is normal all over the world with young fellows who see the war as just an adventure, and it is patriotism and it is partly to get decorations...and you get away from family and so on, you are all of a sudden on your own at eighteen or nineteen, which is great.'

In Vienna and in St Petersburg there were the same excited scenes. And also in Paris, where, as Hermine Venot-Focké remembers, everyone 'really believed that the French army would perform miracles; that it would reach Berlin in forty-eight hours – no more than that.' They too left with flowers in their rifles.

In Europe, only Britain did not impose compulsory military service (conscription), but many young men were eager to join up. One of them, Norman Tennant, was excited because he had already enlisted in the Territorial Army and had a uniform. 'The atmosphere was certainly electric,' he recalls, 'but it seemed almost unbelievable because we thought that it really couldn't affect us, not in this country, we were well protected, we'd got a good navy....The country was overrun by volunteers, in such numbers that I don't think the government could deal with them for a long time.' Walter Hare joined up because he thought the country was 'worth fighting for and we

ACCOMPANIED BY THEIR FAMILIES, *French reservists eagerly make their way to the station following the mobilization call. Military service was accepted as something required of all able-bodied men. Their sense of duty continued to make men respond to being called up as older age groups were drafted to replace the young men who had been killed or wounded in battle.*

Come and fi and Co in the

YOU A AT · T ENLIS

AN ENLISTMENT POSTER *urges British men to do their duty and join the army. At first Britain relied on the patriotism of its citizens to volunteer for military service, before the compulsory call-up was introduced.*

THE WORLD GOES TO WAR

SIX GREAT EUROPEAN POWERS dominated most of the world at the beginning of the twentieth century. Years of diplomacy had established a fragile balance of power between them. Germany's rise to power alarmed its neighbours, particularly France; the alliance between France and Russia and the Anglo-French entente were an attempt to ensure that Germany could not dominate Europe. Feeling threatened by these three great states, Germany tried to strengthen its position through its alliance with the Austro-Hungarian empire and Italy. All these powers were rivals in industrial and military importance at home and abroad, so European stability was easily threatened.

The Balkan states of southeast Europe were of particular interest to the European powers. In the second half of the nineteenth century some Balkan provinces of the Turkish Ottoman empire – Bulgaria, Montenegro, Romania and Serbia – gained their independence. Bosnia and Herzegovina, two more Ottoman provinces, came under Austro-Hungarian rule. As their lands bordered the Balkans, both Austria-Hungary and Russia were closely involved with events in this unstable region. Russia encouraged the Balkan League (Bulgaria, Greece, Montenegro and Serbia) in its attempts finally to expel the Turks from Europe. In 1912 and 1913 two wars reduced Turkish territory in Europe to a toehold, and increased the lands owned by the members of the league. Serbia almost doubled in size; the upsurge of nationalism that followed found expression in a desire to 'free' the Serbs' fellow Slavs living under Austro-Hungarian rule in neighbouring Bosnia.

On 28 June 1914 the heir to the throne of Austria-Hungary, Archduke Franz Ferdinand, and his wife Sophie paid a state visit to Sarajevo, provincial capital of Bosnia. The Bosnian Serb extremists who assassinated the royal couple that day lit the fuse that led to world war. There was a tense pause, while Austria-Hungary sent a humiliating ultimatum to Serbia. Serbia was unable to meet all the Austrian demands; their counter-proposals were also regarded as unacceptable. On 28 July the Austrians prepared for war against Serbia.

It might have stopped there. But Russia was committed to come to Serbia's defence, and at once mobilized its troops. Germany felt obliged to make war on Russia if Austria was attacked, and believing that France would come to Russia's aid, invaded Luxembourg and Belgium and declared war on France. Britain had long promised to guarantee Belgian sovereignty, and entered the war against Germany. Lastly, Austria-Hungary and Russia went to war with one another. The system of alliances designed to keep the peace among powerful states had taken years to establish; it took only a few days for them now to lead to war.

ARRESTING THE ASSASSIN (RIGHT) *Gavrilo Princip, the Bosnian Serb nationalist who killed Archduke Franz Ferdinand, was one of a group of young extremists who were opposed to Austro-Hungarian rule and sought freedom for Bosnia to unite with Serbia.*

THE GREEDY BRITISH SPIDER *traps the whole of mainland Europe in its web – a German view of British intentions. Both sides used propaganda as an extra weapon of war, depicting the enemy as barbarous and evil. False stories were leaked to newspapers, and film, the newest art, was also used to spread myths about atrocities perpetrated by the enemy.*

ought to do our bit towards fighting for it. But we weren't fighting for king and country because we'd never met the king. I think it's because there was a war on and everybody felt that was something we could do. There was an army opposed to us and we didn't want them to get into England, and we thought the best way to stop them was to keep them where they were, in France.'

Everyone believed that the war would be over quickly, and that they were in the right. As Carl von Clemm says: 'We believed God was on our side, and we had it on our belts: "*Gott mit uns*"....After the shots at Sarajevo, we definitely thought that we were being attacked...the fact that the Austrians started their mobilization...the encirclement of Germany was being talked about...we certainly didn't feel we were out of a clear sky attacking others, we felt we were defending ourselves and I was very anxious to be a normal patriot and help defend my country.' Hermine Venot-Focké recalls: 'We didn't think that the war was going to be so long and so cruel.' She explains that the French regarded the Germans as 'uninvited guests who were depriving us of the joy of life, who were taking our men – our fathers, our brothers – and we resented them for it'.

A GERMAN TROOP TRAIN *at a station in Berlin prepares to take soldiers to the front in France. Chalked on the wagon is the boast* Auf zum Preis-schiessen nach Paris *– 'Off to Paris for a shooting prize'. Like their opponents, the Germans expected the war to be a brief and victorious one.*

War by timetable

Plans for mobilization in the event of war had been made by each of the European powers some years before. In every country mobilization was like a gigantic machine. Once it was switched on it simply poured men into their units and shipped them off to the front by train with the speed and efficiency of a factory production line. In the first month after war had been declared in August 1914, nearly sixteen million men were mobilized.

The speed of mobilization generated its own momentum. In Russia, with its millions of peasant soldiers, it was so vast a movement it could not be stopped once it had started. The same was true in Germany: when the Kaiser suggested that the march to the west be called off, he was told that there would be chaos if any attempt was made to stop the 11 000 trains that were carrying men, horses, supplies, artillery and ammunition. During the first six days of the war the German regular army of 70 000 men was augmented to nearly four million. Britain's war plans were detailed in the 'War Book'. Copies were kept in army depots and police stations; it took just a telegram to put the plans into motion. In one week 80 000 men and their horses were shipped to France. Horses presented a particular problem. They took much longer to train than the men, were difficult to load onto ships, and their oats and hay took up twice as much space as ammunition or food rations for the troops.

Outmanned by the Germans, France turned to its overseas empire to make up the numbers. Half a million soldiers went to fight in Europe from the French colonies in Africa, and another 150 000 volunteered from Indochina. Britain made a similar appeal. More than 300 000 Australians volunteered. 'It was the thing to do,' for Edward Smout, who left Sydney with the Australian Medical Corps for the Western Front in 1916. 'We were very loyal to Britain, and apart from that, if you had stayed a year or two longer you would have got a white feather from the girls.' Others volunteered from Canada, New Zealand and South Africa.

AN APPEAL TO SPORTSMEN *in Australia made the war seem like an adventure. Soldiers from Australia and New Zealand, as well as from other British colonies, fought for the Allies in Egypt, Mesopotamia, Palestine and most notably Gallipoli, where they suffered terrible losses in the unsuccessful attempt to inflict a major defeat on Turkey.*

FRENCH COLONIAL TROOPS *from Africa on a route march during training. All the major combatant countries looked to their overseas territories to contribute to the war effort, so both the impact of the war and the conflict itself extended far beyond the boundaries of the states that had started it.*

ALBERT POWIS (ABOVE) *joined the US Marines to fight in the Europeans' war. Fresh American troops arriving in France were keen to 'clean this goddamned thing up and get it done with', as he recalls.*

NEWLY DRAFTED US TROOPS (BELOW) *queue up to receive their equipment. American soldiers were told that their participation in the war was essential to the future of democracy.*

India contributed 1.3 million soldiers and labourers to the war effort, including 100 000 men who were shipped to France to fight on the Western Front. Cha Kunga volunteered to join the Indian Labour Corps. 'I wanted to fight in the British government's war. I wanted to see Western countries for myself. We were told they were healthy places.' But this was his first experience of very cold weather. 'I'd not seen snow before. It was unbearable. Some people just froze up and had to be carried away. We put on four layers of clothing, then a big coat on top of that. But with all these clothes on we couldn't work very fast.'

In 1917 the United States joined the war. The immediate reason was the threat to American lives, shipping and trade posed by the German submarine campaign. But the United States also changed the purpose of the war: it was presented as a crusade for democracy. Many of the four million young Americans who were drafted were also keen to go. Albert Powis was one of these. 'I guess I was patriotic,' he recalls. 'Every time I heard the band play a good marching song I'd have cold chills run up and down my back! We were fighting because they said that if the Germans whipped the English and the French they'd be over after us next. We knew the Germans wanted to rule the world. So we were fighting because they'd sunk our boats and we were fighting for injustices the Germans had done.'

With little idea of what they would have to face, the troops leaving New York harbour laughed off their fears. One of them was infantryman Tela Burt. He remembers coming up on deck and seeing the Statue of Liberty. 'One comic said, "Can you hear what that statue is saying?" They said no. "It's saying, 'That's your ass, big boy! That's your ass. You ain't never coming back!'"'

Like Tela Burt, a substantial number of the American soldiers were black, but they were often not trusted to fight; he had to stay behind the lines to help bury the dead, and 'never knew what the hell I was fighting for. I'd never heard of democracy before. All I knew was I liked the uniform and I wanted to be in the army.'

AN AMERICAN TROOPSHIP *arrives in Europe. The United States stayed neutral for as long as possible before becoming involved in the war. From 1917 the huge quantities of modern equipment, weaponry and ammunition, as well as the millions of extra men available to fight, turned the tide of war in the Allies' favour.*

A new kind of war

Few of the millions of soldiers converging on the battlefields knew how warfare had been transformed in recent years. They were ill-prepared for the reality of the front line. Walter Hare recalls his training with derision. 'It wasn't a scrap of good. I learned how to salute officers, which seemed to be the main thing in the army. I learned to slope arms and present arms, which you can't do in a muddy trench. I fired five rounds before I went out to France. I never saw a grenade, never saw a machine gun.'

The machine gun was born of the technology of the industrial revolution; it could be described as a machine tool of death. The counter to it was a tool of far more ancient date: the shovel. Both were to prove crucial to the character of the war. The battles of the early months demonstrated that the only defence against artillery bombardment and machine-gun fire was to dig a hole.

THE MACHINERY OF WAR

ECHNOLOGY TRANSFORMED military tactics during the First World War. New combat strategies were needed: cavalry could not charge against artillery fire, and infantry advancing in line towards machine guns proved suicidal as men were mown down in their thousands. In the early part of the war all sides used the Maxim machine gun. Capable of firing 600 rounds a minute, they were heavy, needing two or three men to operate them. Recognizing the need for mobility, the British introduced the Lewis gun, which could be carried and fired by just one man. Towards the end of the war the Germans developed the Schmeisser machine pistol, the first one-man portable sub-machine gun.

Deadly though the machine guns were, the worst injuries were inflicted by artillery fire, whose shells left huge craters in the landscape or exploded in the air, scattering deadly shards of steel – shrapnel.

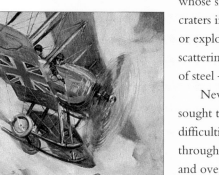

New ways were sought to overcome the difficulties of advancing through barbed wire and over broken ground under fire. The most promising innovation seemed to be the tank. Introduced by the Allies in 1916, its initial success was in shocking German troops. But these slow, heavy vehicles were unreliable and often broke down, and their primitive tracks proved no match for the mud and shell craters of the battlefield, where they became easy prey for the German field guns.

Submarines were introduced for the first time in the challenge between Britain and Germany for supremacy at sea. With its naval fleet bottled up by the British blockade of the North Sea, Germany's retaliation took place beneath the waves. It was Germany's unrestricted use of the *Unterseeboot*, the U-boat, against merchant shipping as well as warships that brought the United States into the war in 1917.

Aircraft were another innovation. In 1914 they were new and untried but were soon adopted by all the main combatants. Their initial role was reconnaissance and helping to direct ground artillery. As both sides increased their air forces, dozens of aircraft fought for control of the skies above the battlefield. The aircraft brought another kind of terror. For the first time there were bombers and airships that began to threaten not only the troops and transport of the enemy, but their families and homes far away from the war zone.

Pilots were seen as glamorous heroes, but it was generally hard to maintain the romantic myths of the chivalry of war. Some of the new weapons were used in a way that was despised: U-boats, for example, were used against unarmed and neutral shipping, and the Germans viewed the use of armoured tanks as lacking in honour. There was one more new and terrible category of weapon: gas. Poison gases, first used by the Germans and soon adopted by the British and the French, added a new dimension to the horror of war.

THE NEW WEAPONS *both shaped the character of the war and were shaped by it. Powerful artillery pieces could fire enormous shells over great distances (ABOVE); aircraft brought a new dimension to the battlefield (LEFT); and tanks were developed as a new device to break the defensive conditions of trench warfare (BELOW).*

The battles were more like long sieges, as both sides established elaborate defensive positions and tried to inflict maximum damage on the enemy's defences only a few hundred yards away.

By the end of 1914 the Western Front ran for hundreds of miles, from Switzerland to the English Channel. It was not to move more than 16 km (10 miles) either way for the next three years. The opposing trench systems were not single lines, but webs of frontline trenches, support trenches and communications trenches, wired with telephone lines, protected by belts of barbed wire, and studded with gun pits and dugouts. The Germans dug the most elaborate trench systems, strong enough to survive heavy bombardment. German trench lines were often better established than the Allied lines, with concrete machine-gun emplacements scattered at intervals. All trenches ran in zigzags, both to minimize the effects of a direct hit and to prevent a successful storming party from firing along the trench at the defenders.

The troops mostly huddled in the trench, keeping their heads below the parapet and peering through spyholes in steel shields. They stood on the firestep only at the dangerous moment just before dawn, when on sentry duty or before going 'over the top' to assault the other side's trenches. The fire, support and reserve trenches were all linked with communications trenches. Telephones, radios, runners and carrier pigeons, and in the German army dogs as well, were all used for communicating. Light railways were sometimes laid to bring in the vast quantities of food, stores and ammunition needed by densely held sectors of the front.

The trench war, with millions of men who rained millions of shells and tens of millions of bullets at each other, was a battle not only between two great armies, but also between the new industrial might of the two great alliances. The general staffs had to cope with military logistics on an unprecedented scale. In the logistical contest, in spite of the scale and efficiency of German industry, Britain and France had the advantage, for behind them they had the growing productivity of American steel mills and ordnance factories as well as their own. The contribution made by American industry was to be decisive in the outcome of the war.

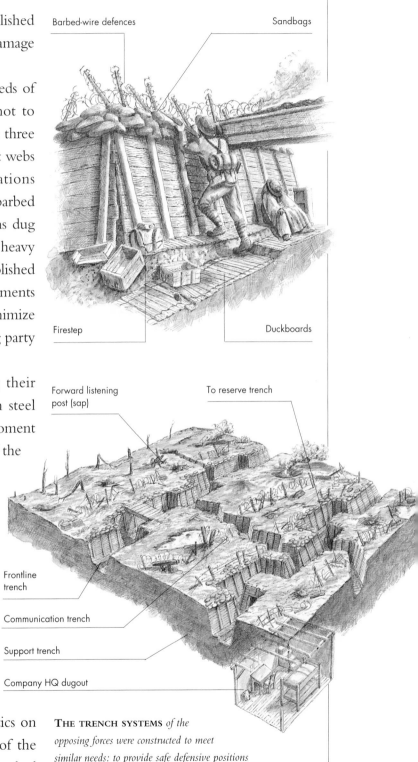

Barbed-wire defences   Sandbags

Firestep   Duckboards

Forward listening post (sap)   To reserve trench

Frontline trench

Communication trench

Support trench

Company HQ dugout

THE TRENCH SYSTEMS *of the opposing forces were constructed to meet similar needs: to provide safe defensive positions over long periods for the troops stationed at the front. Trench warfare took place not only on the Western Front but also on the Eastern Front in the conflict between the Germans and Russians, and in the Balkans between Austro-Hungarian and Serb forces.*

BRITISH TROOPS RESTING *in the trenches. Some parts of the front were quiet for months at a time. There were long days of boredom and discomfort, when in these cramped conditions the men just waited – waited for their next meal, waited for the post, waited for orders.*

A MOMENT OF RELAXATION *for Ernst Weckerling in a German dugout. He remembers periods when 'No food could get through to the front, and nothing to drink. We used to take the water from the machine guns, but then the guns weren't usable any more. We had very good discipline. Whether an order was pleasant or unpleasant, we just had to carry it through, we had to follow it. We just fulfilled our duty.'*

Life in the trenches

The Germans were relatively well equipped in their underground quarters, which often contained kitchens, hospitals, electricity and a water supply. 'They were better organized and harder working than we were,' concedes Marcel Batreau, who was in the French infantry. 'We were an offensive army whereas they wanted to hold on to what they'd got. They'd built tunnels which we saw when we advanced. They were really cushy.' It was different for the Allied forces. 'Our trenches were miserable little scratchings,' remembers Norman Tennant. This deliberately enforced the British commanders' view of the duty of the British soldier in the face of the enemy. A soldier able to take refuge in a trench or dugout might want to stay in it rather than join in an attack.

The German soldiers, however, envied the Allied troops' food supplies. Carl von Clemm helped to capture a British trench. 'The English had so many cigarettes, Player's Navy Cut, and it was wonderful they had so much condensed milk, it was sheer luxury.' The Germans were so hungry that if the troops passed a dead horse, within ten minutes there would be nothing but the bones left. Horse meat was specially welcome to accompany 'barbed wire', as the German army's issue of dried vegetables was called.

Karl Henning Oldekop remembers that there was plenty of turnip and potato soup, but 'the best things, like meat, the English had and we didn't.' The Germans ate a sort of dripping that was so disgusting they called it 'ape fat'.

When the Americans joined in the war, they did not dig trenches. 'They were too dirty,' explains Albert Powis. 'Every time it rained your latrine would overflow, and the rats that went in there were as big as tomcats.' Trench life was indeed unhygienic, and the soldiers were plagued by lice. This was humiliating as well as annoying. Edward Smout found that the steam laundry that cleaned his uniform failed to kill their eggs. They had to be burned off with a cigarette. His recipe for getting rid of lice was a mixture of jam and sulphur. He kept this secret, so the lice would move on to his neighbour.

Lice, dirt, heat, cold, rain, mud, rats, foul smells, days of boredom punctuated by periods of intense fear – this was life in the trenches. Conditions were so unpleasant that the troops were rotated regularly between the front line and the reserve trenches. Censorship prevented soldiers from telling their families how bad life was. Even if their mail had not been censored they would have found it difficult to describe how they felt. Marcel Batreau saw his

DREAMS OF HOME
(ABOVE) *were a source of comfort for men at the front. There was a brisk trade in sentimental postcards. It was often difficult both for the soldiers and for their loved ones at home to be honest about how they felt or the real conditions of the war. Not only was soldiers' mail censored, but to protect their families and try to maintain morale they often just wrote cheerful platitudes. Their relatives and friends did the same for them. This card was written to the Englishman Walter Hare at the front by his mother.*

NORMAN TENNANT (BELOW) *filled periods of inactivity by sketching. He explains the idea for this sketch: 'The listening patrol would be sent out to get as close as possible to the German trenches and pick up information from Germans talking among themselves, and one just thought of a German chomping away.'*

mother when he went on leave, but he never told her of the really horrible things he had to endure. When he was at the front he would just write on a postcard, as he did on 17 September 1918, after years of horror: 'Dear mother, I'm in very good health and I hope the same can be said of everyone at home.' Another French soldier, Henri Auclair, was once so thirsty that he lapped water like a dog – from a crater with three dead bodies in it. He can still remember wishing, 'If only I could be dead by tomorrow'. Yet when he wrote to his mother he would invariably write just *RAS* – *Rien à signaler*, 'Nothing to report'.

On leave from the trenches, men wanted to forget the war, not to describe it, and many of them took to alcohol to keep them going. 'I was nineteen years old,' says Ernst Weckerling, a German infantryman. 'You cannot describe how terrible it was. Sometimes we found alcohol and just sat and drank together. Then it was easier to bear.' The American Albert Powis recalls: 'After battle the officers would tell us: now go out and get drunk and forget it. So that's what we'd do. We'd go out and we'd get into the cafés and we'd get drunk and have a good time….That's what they wanted us to do – forget the battle and get ready for the next one. After the war I had a problem – I'd come damn near being an alcoholic.'

Tela Burt found he was specially popular among civilians. 'The French people seemed to like black people, the blacker the boys were, the more they would go for them. We taught them a lot of dances and they liked our music.' Seventy years later, he still keeps a picture of a French girl he met on leave.

TELA BURT (ABOVE) *discovered that being a black American in Europe made him popular – at least with the women. He played Dixieland jazz in a forty-two piece band to entertain fellow American soldiers.*

AN AFTERNOON'S PEACE (RIGHT) *at this fashionable French café offered a rare chance for officers of the Allied forces to leave behind the horrors of the front line. For the other ranks the village bars also provided a chance to relax and enjoy local hospitality.*

THE MAIN THEATRES OF WAR *surrounded the territories of the Central Powers. In the early months it was a war of movement, with the German invasion through Belgium into France in the west, and the Russian advance into Germany and Austria-Hungary in the east. But the new tactics developed in response to new weaponry led to the stalemate of trench warfare and high casualties. Many people were killed in the campaign by German and Austrian forces against the Serbians and their allies in the Balkans. The Italians also endured appalling casualties in the mountainous region near their border with Austria-Hungary.*

THE LOST GENERATION

THE TRUE NUMBER OF LIVES *affected by the war will never be known. Some countries kept accurate records of military casualties; for others they can only be estimated. These figures are chilling enough. No detailed records of civilian casualties are available, but there were probably as many civilian deaths – in excess of thirteen million people – during the war as a result of starvation, disease and military action. The influenza epidemic that swept the world in 1918–19 claimed another twenty million lives.*

Allied forces	Total mobilized	Deaths	Total casualties
Belgium	267 000	13 716	93 061
British empire	8 904 467	908 371	3 190 235
France	8 410 000	1 357 800	6 160 800
Greece	230 000	5 000	27 000
Italy	5 615 000	650 000	2 197 000
Japan	800 000	300	1 210
Montenegro	50 000	3 000	20 000
Portugal	100 000	7 222	33 291
Romania	750 000	335 706	535 706
Russia	12 000 000	1 700 000	9 150 000
Serbia	707 343	45 000	331 106
USA	4 355 000	116 516	323 018
Total	**42 188 810**	**5 142 631**	**22 064 427**

Central Powers			
Austria–Hungary	7 800 000	1 200 000	7 020 000
Bulgaria	1 200 000	87 500	266 919
Germany	11 000 000	1 773 700	7 142 558
Turkey	2 850 000	325 000	975 000
Total	**22 850 000**	**3 386 200**	**15 404 477**

Alliances

▨	Allied countries at outbreak of war
☐	Countries joining Allied forces
▨	Central Powers at outbreak of war
☐	Countries joining Central Powers
☐	Neutral countries

Major battles

* ✳ 1914
* ✳ 1915
* ✳ 1916
* ✳ 1917
* ✳ 1918

Ypres · Passchendaele · Messines Ridge · Neuve-Chapelle · Loos · Arras · Mons · Cambrai · Somme · St Quentin · Amiens · Chemin des Dames · Cantigny · Montdidier · Belleau Wood · Château-Thierry · Argonne · Verdun · St Mihiel · Marne · Paris · FRANCE · BELGIUM · GERMANY · LUXEMBOURG · Schelde · Rhine · Meuse · Mosel · Somme · Oise · Seine · front line 1916 · Armistice line Nov. 1918

Furthest German advance 1914 · Armistice line November 1918 · Furthest Russian advance 1914–15 · Armistice line December 1917 · NORWAY · GREAT BRITAIN · SWEDEN · DENMARK · North Sea · Baltic Sea · St Petersburg · Riga · Moscow · London · NETHERLANDS · BELGIUM · LUXEMBOURG · GERMANY · Berlin · Paris · Brussels · Jutland · Tannenberg · Gumbinnen · Masurian Lakes · Warsaw · Brest Litovsk · Kiev · Lodz · Cracow · Limanowa · Gorlice · RUSSIA · SWITZERLAND · FRANCE · Vienna · AUSTRIA-HUNGARY · Odessa · Vittorio · Caporetto · Asiago · Isonzo · Piave · Belgrade · Bukovina · Sebastopol · ITALY · Rome · Sarajevo · ROMANIA · Bucharest · MONTENEGRO · SERBIA · BULGARIA · Black Sea · Sofia · Vardar · Doiran · Constantinople · ALBANIA · Monastir · Salonika · Gallipoli · GREECE · Dardanelles · TURKEY

FRENCH TROOPS AT VERDUN (ABOVE) *listen cynically to an officer reading out a message from their commander, General Pétain. Of the 330 infantry regiments in the army, 259 were involved in the siege. One unit was told: 'You have a mission of sacrifice… on the day the Germans choose they will slaughter you to the last man, and it is your duty to fall.'*

THE TERRIBLE REALITY *of the war (OPPOSITE) is depicted in this painting, Hell, by a French artist, Georges Leroux. The dead and the living are both in danger of drowning in the mud-filled shell craters on a night lit only by the exploding shells bursting all around them.*

Going into battle

By 1916 soldiers were caught in a deadly war of attrition, as each side tried to wear the other down. The two major offensives of that year on the Western Front provide vivid examples of the character of the war as a whole. The great German effort to end the stalemate took place at Verdun in northeastern France. The Germans were convinced that if they could cripple the French army, Britain would also be defeated. They intended to 'bleed the French army white', and came close to success. Preparations moved with secrecy and speed, until by the beginning of February 1916 more than 1200 German guns were in position for an assault along a front less than 13 km (8 miles) long. The bombardment was heavier than anything the soldiers had experienced before, but the French high command was determined that this important fortress-city must not be surrendered, whatever the cost.

As French reinforcements were strengthened with their big guns, it was the Germans' turn to endure the terrible bombardment of the artillery. 'It was hell,' says Ernst Weckerling, who was pinned down in a shell crater. 'The air was full of smoke and fumes from the constant firing of the French guns. The crater I was in was so deep that the breeze couldn't blow the fumes away. The air was so bad that we were parched with thirst and breathing was very difficult.' He remembers with disgust the awful task of removing his dead comrades' belongings. 'I had to find the ID tags on their chests and remove them. I felt like a butcher sometimes as I rummaged around in all that blood. On some corpses the whole torso had been flattened by mortars, and pieces of flesh were hanging off everywhere.'

At Verdun, as at many other battles, the fighting was often so fierce that there was no opportunity for the dead to be buried. Marcel Batreau describes vividly how 'the rats would start eating their faces. First they'd gnaw at their lips and their noses, then get into their coats and start eating the rest.' The soldiers used their dead friends as duckboards. 'We had to jump from corpse to corpse,' he recalls. 'If we stepped in the mud on either side, we'd get stuck. We had to use the dead face-down because if we stepped on their stomachs our feet would sink in. It was disgusting. It was terrible. We were surrounded by death.'

"I knew I'd been hit...and when I sat up and looked at these other chaps, they were deadly still, every one of them. They weren't moving a muscle. I was the only survivor."

WALTER HARE

Flower of remembrance

THE POPPY *was the first plant to emerge from the mud of the Flanders battlefields. Its blood-red flowers became a potent symbol of those whose lives had been lost where the flowers now bloomed.*

The Somme offensive was launched by the Allies at the beginning of July. It was partly intended to make the Germans divert forces from Verdun, and was also the French and British attempt to end the stalemate and drive the Germans out of France. The plan was to concentrate a massive artillery barrage on just one section of the German lines near the river Somme. One and a half million shells were taken up to the gun batteries in preparation.

As the guns thundered and the shells exploded above their heads, the Germans stayed in their deep dugouts. After 20 000 tonnes of shells had rained down on the German positions during the seven-day onslaught, the British prepared to attack. Fresh troops waited to rush through the gap they expected to have opened up in the German lines. Some 100 000 soldiers set out. But their commanders were wrong. The barrage had failed; it had neither demolished the barbed-wire entanglements nor destroyed the German positions. As the British advanced towards the enemy lines, the German gunners simply mowed them down.

Walter Hare managed to get to the German lines. 'I kept going, I got to the German barbed wire, I got through that all right, and jumped into a German trench. We stayed there all that day and the following night, with no food, no water, dead short of ammunition. One of our chaps contacted headquarters, then came forward to us and said, "I've got orders for you. You've got to retire to the trenches you left as best as you can, get back as best as you can." So I finished up there, where I left. I think there were 230-odd casualties and we never gained a yard of ground. I'd lost a lot of my pals...and we needed them. I thought how stupid it was.'

The experience was similar for the German soldiers when they were ordered to go over the top. Karl Henning Oldekop recalls: 'You felt it was your duty to advance with the others, not to leave them in the lurch. You only feel fear when you hear enemy mortars whizzing right past you, and then without thinking you automatically throw yourself down on the ground.'

Twenty of the sixty British battalions committed to the first wave of that attack on the first day of the Somme offensive were cut to pieces by machine guns in no-man's-land, the devastated area between the lines. Others were killed by artillery or in the hand-to-hand fighting in the German trenches. Machine guns and

GERMAN TROOPS (ABOVE) *at the Somme defend their trench against the enemy with hand grenades and machine guns. Despite the dreadful effectiveness of these weapons, some of the advancing soldiers still came through.*

GOING OVER THE TOP
(BELOW) *was a perilous scramble out of the trenches and into the dangerous territory between the lines. Many soldiers were killed or mortally wounded before they even reached the enemy's positions.*

artillery gave an overwhelming advantage to the defence, especially a defence as well dug in as the Germans. One German regiment lost 280 out of 3000 soldiers that first day on the Somme; the British division attacking them lost 5000 out of 12 000. German losses over the whole period, however, were also great.

After the repulse of the first British attack, the generals kept up the offensive for several months after it had become plain that a breakthrough was impossible. Between July and November there were over one million casualties; 380 000 soldiers lost their lives. The heroic sacrifice achieved little or nothing, except marginally to relieve pressure on other fronts. The entire operation penetrated at most 8 km (5 miles) into the enemy's lines.

The worst casualties of all were caused by shells. Shrapnel shells released lethal pieces of flying metal; high explosives could tear off limbs or head, or even destroy a man's body completely. When shells were fired in your direction, there was nowhere to run to. Norman Tennant describes how it felt. 'The only thing you could do would be to drop flat on the ground and stay there...and wait for the shell which was going to hit you...they seemed to get closer and closer until you thought, the next one's going to get you, my lad, you've had it this time. And it came over and burst and it didn't get you and you were so grateful for that.'

But he also recalls the horror. 'Things were dropping out of the air, unspeakable things. Once, a book, with a hole torn right through the middle of it. One arm, part of a body, dropping. A man had been blown to bits and I just saw this remnant falling through the air.'

WALTER HARE *on leave in England with his girlfriend. He was wounded in the battle of the Somme and taken prisoner. Looking back on the war, he says: 'It meant three years of my life were wasted.'*

YOUR COUNTRY NEEDS YOU

THIS WAS A NEW KIND OF WAR, one in which civilians were mobilized. In previous wars, people caught in the track of fighting armies endured famine, disease and barbarous cruelties; this was the first time states mustered all their resources for war.

As more and more able-bodied men went off to fight, the people who remained at home had to devote their entire energies to the war effort. For the first time, civilians were as important as troops, women as important as men. Several civilians were needed to keep each soldier in the field supplied with equipment, ammunition and other essentials.

The shortage of men meant that women were needed to take over jobs they had never done before. Throughout Europe women ran public transport, did clerical work and operated machines in munitions factories. They worked not only in their traditional roles as nurses and cooks, but also as plumbers, electricians, shoemakers, farmhands, undertakers and even police officers. Their lives were hard; they often worked twelve-hour shifts, seven days a week, and were paid less than the men for doing so.

Before the war, women had already begun to work in paid jobs in large numbers. In France, for example, women made up 35 per cent of the labour force in 1914; the figure rose to 40 per cent during the war. The greatest change came in the kind of work that women undertook. Old prejudices were challenged as women proved that they could succeed in highly skilled, traditionally male occupations – as doctors and engineers, for example.

All the wealth of the combatant countries was diverted to one end. People were encouraged to invest in the nation as an act of patriotism by buying war bonds, loans to help their government meet the huge costs of war. Bonds were seen as an alternative to raising taxes; it was assumed by both sides that when the war was won, the enemy would have to pay reparations in compensation.

Everywhere, food was scarce and prices were high. Food rationing was introduced. Germany and Britain were both heavily dependent on imported food, and the war threatened their vital supplies. 'People's kitchens' sprang up in cities as governments struggled to keep their people fed; food riots became common as the hardships increased. In Britain more than 800 000 hectares (2 million acres) of pasture were ploughed up to grow cereal crops, and growing vegetables in allotment gardens became a patriotic activity.

In Germany one observer said, 'The whole empire is being turned into a field,' yet Germans were driven to use ersatz (substitute) foods that were more ingenious than nutritious. After the potato harvest failed in 1917, the Germans had to endure the 'turnip winter' – there was almost nothing else to eat. By this time many Germans and central Europeans were seriously undernourished, while in Russian and Polish cities many people were close to starvation.

Coal was in short supply, and the private use of electricity was restricted. The lack of food and warmth, the fear and loneliness drove many people to seek other forms of comfort. 'Drink is doing more damage than all the German submarines put together,' said the British prime minister, David Lloyd George. Britain and Germany introduced alcohol licensing laws, and in France alcoholic drinks could be bought only at mealtimes.

There were few opportunities to forget the war, though in the cities the need for escape was met by music halls and the cinema. The most chilling reminders were brought daily by the casualty lists carried by the newspapers. The thousands of names listed represented the lives of sons, brothers and husbands killed, wounded, captured or missing in action. Every family dreaded the arrival of a telegram bearing news of another life sacrificed in this terrible war.

WOMEN AT WAR *Women took over the jobs of the men who had gone to fight, directly contributing to the war effort in munitions factories. They worked in many previously male civilian activities, as well as nursing the wounded.*

THESE WOMEN ARE DOING THEIR BIT

LEARN TO MAKE MUNITIONS

Treating the wounded

As a stretcher-bearer collecting the wounded from the battlefield, Edward Smout saw more than his share of terrible injuries. 'You were frightened, there was no doubt about that. I was, I think everyone was...I lost weight, I became nervous. I was a complete nervous wreck and so I got leave...nobody understood shell shock. Looking back at it now,' he reflects, 'I feel it more than when I was there because you develop, not a callousness but...a certain indifference towards it because you couldn't carry on otherwise.'

Those who survived the perilous journey back across no-man's-land were treated behind the lines. The wounded were taken first to the field dressing station, where their injuries were assessed and they were given one of three different coloured tags, according to the type and seriousness of their wounds. Slightly

THE STRETCHER-BEARER (ABOVE) *was often in as much danger on the battlefield as the comrades it was his job to rescue.*

THIS DEVASTATED LANDSCAPE (BELOW) *had been a pleasant wooded valley set in fertile French countryside before the war.*

wounded men were moved to the casualty clearing station; the general hospital dealt with more serious cases; and soldiers with the worst injuries of all went to the big base at Etaples and then on to England. There were no painkillers except chloroform pads and morphia, and they were only for the seriously wounded. A very big shrapnel wound would be stitched, bandaged and tidied up before the patient was taken away. A shattered arm would not be amputated, but the man would be marked with an urgent tag.

Edward Smout reflects: 'Our two doctors at the field dressing station…I would say they learned more surgery in forty-eight hours than they would have learned in twenty years at home.'

Major surgery was undertaken at the general hospital. An exhausted surgeon recorded his day: 'The operating room starts at about 8.30 a.m., and four tables are going steadily until one o'clock at night. We've done 273 operations in four days.' One badly wounded British soldier was comforted by a young French-woman. 'He was hoping for his mother,' Hermine Venot-Focké remembers, 'which was of course quite impossible. He must have felt someone beside him, because he stretched out his hand, which I took in mine. I thought, "He's waiting for his mother, and I'm going to give him the kiss he's waiting for." I kissed him, and he died. I never found out his name, but I never forgot him.'

Max Nathanovich Kleinman was in the Russian imperial army on the Eastern Front. Poorly led, the peasant armies of the tsar suffered terribly. The inadequate army medical services were supplemented by private hospital trains run by the great ladies of the court, who were more willing than skilful. He was taken to one of the trains after being wounded in the chest; he was also infested with lice. 'The nurses came from upper-class families,' he explains. 'They were all white-skinned, pretty blondes, wearing headscarves. One could enjoy looking at the nurse, but she was afraid to come close to me as the lice were running all over me, so it was up to the male nurses to do the dirty jobs.' These genteel nurses were also not permitted to treat wounds inflicted below the soldiers' waists.

Dying for freedom and honour

A MEMORIAL PLAQUE *was given to the family of every Briton killed in the war, including nurses and other civilians as well as members of the armed forces, to remind them of the value of their loved one's sacrifice.*

BLINDED BY GAS, *soldiers support each other as they shuffle painfully forward. Both sides used poison gases, first chlorine and then phosgene. Many victims of gas attacks died by drowning in the fluid that collected in their lungs. Later mustard gas, which blistered the skin, was also used.*

TREATING THE WOUNDED (ABOVE) *was a seemingly endless task. While the battle rages, at this field dressing station behind the lines orderly rows of injured men await transport. Their destination will depend on the severity of their wounds.*

BEYOND THE CALL OF DUTY?

THE MEN WHO FOUGHT in the First World War experienced a new level of human endurance, both in the scale of the war and in the conditions in the trenches and on the battlefields. Harsh measures were taken against soldiers on both sides who could no longer bear the sights and sounds of death all around them. Some three hundred British soldiers were court-martialled and shot. One of them, Private Arthur Earp, was suffering from shell shock when he was found in June 1916 crouching in a dugout when he should have been in an attack. The court's recommendation that he should be shown mercy 'owing to the intense bombardment which the accused had been subjected to and on account of his good character' was overridden. The only choice for soldiers was between probable death if they went forward, and certain death if they went back.

In most armies there were mutinies as well as individual protests. On the Western Front the French had suffered the most. Those who had survived the bloodbath of Verdun were sent into an assault on the Chemin des Dames in spring 1917. Once again the infantry were hurled against strongly fortified positions. An advance of only 548 metres (600 yards) resulted in 120 000 French casualties. Some units began to bleat like sheep as they passed senior officers. 'We are men, and not beasts to be led to the abattoir to be slaughtered,' they objected. At the end of April one unit mutinied, and then disaffection spread through two-thirds of the French army divisions. Of the 3000 mutineers sentenced, 600 were to be executed; only about fifty executions were carried out.

On the Eastern Front, where more than two million Russians had been killed, discipline completely collapsed in the chaos following the fall of the tsar. Mikhail Abramovich Rosental was in the artillery. He remembers: 'It was chaos. The people who were supposed to give us logistical support ran away first. We began to go hungry. We were all very dirty....At the end of the war there were few people left who could give orders. Our division didn't exist. We were very happy that we were free to run away.' There were defections in the Austro-Hungarian infantry, and mass surrenders in Czech units.

Morale in the German army remained high; it was the navy that became disaffected. There were hunger strikes because food on board naval vessels was so poor. In June 1917 the crew of the *Prinzregent Luitpold* mutinied; two of the leaders were executed. In October 1918 the crews of the German fleets at Wilhelmshaven and Kiel received orders to sail into battle. Some refused to weigh anchor; others refused to return to their posts. Rebellion and insubordination spread rapidly through the fleet. The officers might have been prepared to launch a final attack as a display of honour, but the men made it clear that they had had enough.

A SENTENCE OF DEATH (BELOW) *was passed on Arthur Earp, who had disobeyed orders at the front. The plea for mercy was rejected by the British commander in chief, Sir Douglas Haig, who wrote: 'How can we ever win if this plea is allowed?'*

"I didn't feel like fighting any more, there was no one to fight for when Nicholas gave up the throne. **"**

MIKHAIL ABRAMOVICH ROSENTAL

RUSSIAN AND GERMAN SOLDIERS (ABOVE) *on the Eastern Front after Russia's withdrawal from the war in December 1917. After the fall of the tsar earlier that year, one of the promises that brought Lenin to power in the Soviet Union was that he would make peace with Germany and end the Russians' suffering. In the chaos surrounding the revolution in Russia, military leadership and organization disintegrated. The starving troops felt abandoned by their leaders, and no longer knew who or what they were fighting for.*

BURYING THE DEAD (OPPOSITE) *French soldiers near Reims in July 1918 identifying some of their dead comrades, who fell in one of the last major battles of the war. Many soldiers did not have the dignity of burial.*

The war ends

As the war dragged on, the atmosphere increasingly became one of exhaustion and despair. The Germans were given new hope when the Russian tsar was overthrown in March 1917. When the United States declared war in April, the German leaders knew that they must deploy as many troops as possible on the Western Front before the Americans arrived. As the Russian armies disintegrated, German troops were transported from the east to help those in the west. But the American declaration of war had given the Allies fresh hope too, and they held on despite war weariness, mutiny and the desperate desire for the war to end.

At last, in the summer of 1918, it began to dawn on the German general staff that the war was lost. Europe's reserves of manpower may have been almost exhausted, but now there were also four million Americans under arms, two million of them in Europe. By October 1918 the German generals had had enough. They marched their armies under perfect discipline back to the fatherland. Many Germans found it hard to understand why their armies, which they believed had not been beaten in battle, had capitulated. It felt more like betrayal than defeat.

Flanders, Ypres, Tannenberg, Gallipoli, Isonzo, Verdun, the Somme: these and many other less notorious places were the killing fields. The mud, fear, pain, death and futility there set new standards for what was imaginable in the scale and intensity of human suffering. The people of every nation that fought in the First World War experienced dreadful slaughter. For everyone involved the war had been an unparalleled catastrophe. Sixty-five million men, many of them hardly more than boys, spent up to four years in discomfort, misery and terror. Nearly nine million of them died. Every one of the sixty-five million represented a job unfilled, a family deprived, a woman husbandless, children fatherless. Each of the nine million deaths inflicted a bitter tragedy on a wife, a mother, a friend. For most of those who waited for the men who did not return, the war was the worst thing that had happened in their lives. The men who did come back brought with them their injuries, their nightmares, their rage, their new contempt for once revered authority – and their determination that it must never be allowed to happen again.

3

Red Flag

COMMUNISM COMES TO RUSSIA

IT WAS AT NINE O'CLOCK ONE autumn evening in 1917 that three blank shots were fired from the battle cruiser *Aurora* over the river Neva in Petrograd (as St Petersburg was then called). At this signal the Red Guards moved in to take the Winter Palace. The great wave of unrest spreading through the Russian capital was about to break into revolution.

Alexander Briansky was one of the guards. 'When the *Aurora* fired everyone rushed forward shouting "hurrah". I was at the front, I ran up the stairs and stumbled into a big hall where there was a detachment of officer cadets with their rifles at the ready. I shouted to the defenders, "Throw down your rifles!" and they threw down their weapons as if to order. They'd seen how angry we were.' There was confused scuffling. A few shots were fired along the corridors and staircases inside the enormous building, and some nervous telephone calls were made between the opposing sides.

Ministers of the Provisional Government, which had ruled Russia since the tsar's abdication eight months earlier, were hiding from the danger of bombardment in a back room of the palace. One of the men leading the operation to take control in Petrograd suddenly burst in and announced to them: 'In the name of the Military Revolutionary Committee, I declare you under arrest.' The ministers were taken across the Neva to the fortress prison of St Peter and St Paul.

This supreme moment of the revolution was an almost bloodless coup d'état, an anticlimax. One eyewitness described it as little more than a changing of the guard. Nevertheless, what took place that night was a turning point, perhaps *the* turning point of the twentieth century.

The communists who had seized power promised change, liberation and equality for the oppressed Russian people. Alexander Briansky, like many others, was full of hope. 'I thought the future of Russia would take a different path: the people would be free, and there would be work without exploitation.' But before long the very people the revolution sought to liberate would become victims of the new system.

STORMING THE WINTER PALACE *A dramatized portrayal of the moment of revolution.*

War and revolution

It was war that frayed the fabric of autocratic rule in Russia and paved the way for the revolution. First the Russians were humiliated in 1904–5 in the war against Japan. In 1914 Russia entered the First World War as France's ally against Germany. This enemy was both more deadly and closer at hand. Many Russian soldiers were sent into war without weapons. Hurled at German machine guns by aristocratic officers using obsolete tactics, sometimes ordered to charge armed only with bayonets and hand grenades, the soldiers responded with courage that exposed them to fearful casualties: well over a million men were killed, more than four million were wounded (of whom 350 000 died of their wounds), and a further two and a half million were captured. The soldiers' hardships were compounded by inadequate supplies, and disease spread among both the fighting men and those supporting them behind the lines.

Life was also very difficult for the civilian population. So many men had gone to the war that both farming and industry were crippled. By January 1917 the transport system had broken down, and the bread and fuel needed by people in the cities failed to reach them. Tens of thousands of workers, already politically aware and made increasingly restless by revolutionary propaganda, were out of work or on strike.

Alexander Briansky remembers those times. 'We lived very badly. It got so bad one day there wasn't even a piece of bread,' he recalls. He decided that he would join the revolutionaries. 'There were many reasons: hatred for the tsarists, the shooting of ordinary strikers, this endless war that didn't show any mercy to people.'

Driven to desperation, huge crowds came out onto the streets to demonstrate. When garrison officers tried to restore order, the soldiers proved reluctant to fire on civilians. In late February, when the last few strands of authority snapped, the government lost control of the capital. In March Tsar Nicholas abdicated, and authority was passed to a Provisional Government.

A SOLDIER COMES HOME
Some fifteen million Russians fought in the First World War. Many of those who survived had only further hardships to look forward to when they returned home. For them, the revolution offered a new alternative to despair.

REVOLUTIONARY GUARDS *on patrol in March 1917, waiting with fixed bayonets for any challenge from the tsarist forces in the streets of Petrograd.*

THE FALL OF THE TSAR

'TO THE EMPEROR OF ALL THE RUSSIAS belongs the supreme and unlimited power. Not only fear, but also conscience commanded by God Himself, is the basis of obedience to this power.' This declaration in the Fundamental Laws of Imperial Russia describes the absolute rule of the Romanov tsars, under which the Russians lived for nearly three hundred years.

From the middle of the nineteenth century there had been some gradual changes. In 1861 serfdom had been abolished – two years before the emancipation of slaves in the United States. Until then, many of the peasants had also been little more than slaves of the great landowners, labourers tied to the land where they worked. Russia's long-established feudal structure did not easily yield to change, and for most peasants conditions did not improve much; their life was often still very harsh.

Improvements in farming took second place to industrial development. In the late nineteenth and early twentieth centuries the Russian economy began to grow. People left the land to seek work in the towns. Here too life was hard, but many city workers learned to read, and as they came in contact with new ideas discontent began to spread.

In January 1905 a procession of workers presented a petition for political reform to the tsar, Nicholas II. Soldiers fired on the demonstrators; at least two hundred of them were killed that day, which was remembered as Bloody Sunday. There was turmoil elsewhere, too. Workers went on strike. Peasant mobs burned landlords' houses and seized their land. In Odessa the crew of the battleship *Potemkin* mutinied. Russia seemed to be on the brink of anarchy. In October the tsar reluctantly made some concessions. He signed a manifesto that agreed to grant civil liberties, including freedom of speech and assembly, to the people. It also established an elected assembly, the Duma, with some administrative power.

This was in effect Russia's first constitution. The new prime minister, Baron Peter Stolypin, recognized the urgent need for modernization. He encouraged a 'dash for growth' financed by foreign investment, carried out land reform in the hope of giving peasants an interest in improving their land, and improved the education system. Stolypin was assassinated in 1911; with his death Russia's chance to make a peaceful transition into a modern state perhaps disappeared.

The pace of change seemed to be too slow. Many political groups were opposed to Nicholas's government, and with the outbreak of war in 1914 the unrest grew. Over the next few years, as soldiers were killed in their thousands and civilians suffered further hardships at home, strikes, riots and rebellion increased. The Duma was ordered to dissolve, but instead set up the Provisional Government. The tsar, finally realizing that he had lost control, abdicated in March 1917. The monarchy had ended.

TSAR NICHOLAS *in captivity with his wife and children. After the abdication they were imprisoned in the town of Ekaterinburg in the Urals. But the tsar still posed a threat to the revolutionaries, who felt he could provide a focus for anti-Bolshevik resistance, and one night in July 1918 he and his family were shot by their guards.*

LEADING THE PEOPLE

ENIN, LIKE MANY OTHERS among the best-educated and most socially aware Russians of his generation, had long despised the tsarist regime, and sought new, radical solutions to his country's problems. He had become a revolutionary in 1890 at the age of twenty, after his brother had been hanged for his part in a conspiracy to assassinate the tsar. Born Vladimir Ilyich Ulyanov, Lenin took his name from the river Lena in Siberia, where he was exiled in 1897.

For thirty years Lenin's life was punctuated with danger, periods of imprisonment and exile. He studied and then practised law before moving to St Petersburg, where he was prominent in a revolutionary group. Lenin's ideas developed from those of Karl Marx, the nineteenth-century German philosopher. Marx declared that change had to come through struggle rather than gradual development, and that progress required the overthrow of capitalism to make way for socialism. Lenin saw imperialism as the last stage of capitalism, and this led him to call for world revolution. The armies of the First World War should not fight each other, but turn their rifles on their own officers and the ruling classes.

In a series of powerful pamphlets Lenin developed and explained his ideas. Insisting that the revolution should be led by professional revolutionaries, he opposed democratic voting out of fear that the votes of workers and socialists would be swamped by those of millions of peasants still in favour of monarchy. His later policies towards the peasants continued to reflect this mistrust of them.

From 1900 to 1905 Lenin lived in Switzerland. He returned to Russia to take part in the l905 revolution, but was again forced into exile. In March 1917, learning of the fall of the tsar, Lenin knew his time had come. The Germans, hoping to undermine their enemy's war effort by contributing to its unstable political situation, permitted Lenin to cross Germany in a sealed train on his way back to Russia. On his return he threw himself into coordinating the revolution.

Lenin brought new hope to millions of angry and frustrated Russians. He offered a new vision to people who had suffered a long history of oppression – to the soldiers exhausted by war, to the peasants who knew only work and poverty, to the city workers whose lives seemed to be a new kind of serfdom. He assured these voiceless people that their voice would at last be heard.

SPREADING THE REVOLUTION *Lenin believed that the revolution in Russia would ignite similar upheavals throughout Europe, setting the scene for the overthrow of capitalism and imperial rule everywhere. Many shared his belief, and waited with joy or dread for world revolution.*

LOOKING TO LENIN
Alexander Briansky (ABOVE AND RIGHT) *fought for the changes promised by Lenin (seen in the foreground of this photograph). 'I loved Lenin,' he explains, 'because he struggled for peace against blood-letting of any kind.'*

'Peace, land and bread'

Now a new contest began, between the Provisional Government and the revolutionary soviets, the councils of workers' and soldiers' representatives. The most powerful of these was the Petrograd soviet, led by Leon Trotsky. One young Russian, Valentin Astrov, reflects how many people felt at that time. 'There seemed to be no other way out of the crisis than going over to the soviets. The bourgeois would never be able to cope with the difficulties that were facing the people. I decided that's what I would struggle for.'

In the early years of the twentieth century there was a bewildering number of political groups, each of which claimed to offer the best alternative to absolute rule by the tsars. Among them were the Bolsheviks, a group of extreme socialists led by Lenin, who wanted a radical new system of government. After many months of political ferment, Lenin's conviction that the time for revolution had come took the Bolsheviks to the centre of the Russian political stage.

Under his leadership, the Bolsheviks' victory was sealed by the 'changing of the guard' at the Winter Palace. Karl Rianne, like Alexander Briansky, took part that autumn day in 1917. 'There were 90 000 of us, and when we arrived in Petrograd we were all sent to different areas. We were told to occupy the telegraph and the post office. There could have been blood spilt, but thanks to Lenin's orders we managed to cut all the means of communication of the Provisional Government in the Winter Palace in good time.'

That evening Lenin made an excited speech to members of the revolutionary soviets at the Smolny Institute, once a finishing school for the daughters of the nobility. Now its wooden floors echoed not to silk slippers in the waltz, but to the heavy boots of factory workers and peasant soldiers. He promised that the oppressed masses would themselves form the government. A new workers' state must be created. The war must be ended. Workers in Europe would come to the help of their Russian brothers. Landed property would be abolished, and the land given to the peasants to win their cooperation. 'Long live the worldwide socialist revolution!'

The slogan of the hour was 'Peace, land and bread'. It was a formula that would bind together behind the tiny clique of

The party card

EVERYONE WHO JOINED *the Communist Party had a party card – even Lenin. Between 1917 and 1921 three quarters of a million people became members; by 1940 there were almost two million. At first membership was a matter of patriotism, but it became increasingly necessary for those with political or social ambitions, and came to symbolize access to a ruling elite.*

FIGHTING FOR COMMUNISM *The people of Russia helped the revolutionary leaders to establish Bolshevik rule. Detachments of Red Guards were formed among many groups of workers* (BELOW). *But White armies resisted; a White army officer drew this sketch of a fellow Cossack with the two peasants he had just taken prisoner* (RIGHT).

CELEBRATING THE FIRST YEAR *of the 'dictatorship of the proletariat'* (OPPOSITE). *In this anniversary poster a worker and a peasant stand together triumphantly at the gate leading to the prosperous future world, the symbols of the power they have overthrown lying at their feet. The tools of their trade – the hammer and the sickle – became the emblems of the new Soviet Union's national flag.*

Bolshevik leaders the three great forces that would build a new Soviet society: peace for the soldiers, land for the peasants, and bread for the city workers. 'The ideals of the revolution inspired very many people. It seemed that life would open up in all its fullness and beauty,' explains a painter, Boris Smirnov-Russetsky. 'We believed that socialism was the path that would take our country to prosperity, to a new more complete form of society.' What Ella Shistyer, a member of the Communist Party from 1918, liked was 'the promise of a happy, classless society in the future, in which everyone would enjoy all the good created by the society.'

In the meantime, Russian soldiers demanded an end to the fighting that continued to claim lives in the war. Lenin gave them the peace he had promised by concluding the Treaty of Brest-Litovsk with Germany, though it was peace at a price as the terms further damaged the Russian economy. But the time for peace at home had not yet come.

Opposition to the revolution led to three more years of fighting, this time in a bitter civil war. In addition to their usual hardships, people who had already endured a foreign war were now exposed to the terror unleashed both by the Bolsheviks (the Reds) and by their opponents, the Whites, who were fighting to put an end to the revolution and to restore the monarchy with help from abroad. There was growing international involvement in Russia's revolutionary struggle. Troops of a dozen nations fought and pillaged their way across Russia, adding to the suffering. By December 1920 a further million people had lost their lives.

Taking revolution to the countryside

In this unpromising, even desperate time Lenin pushed ahead with his revolution. In March 1918 he moved the capital to Moscow as Germany threatened Petrograd. The Bolsheviks put themselves at the head of soldiers and urban workers. In Moscow and then in other cities and towns they took over shops, factories and other property, and set up revolutionary institutions, including the Red Army and, from the start, a secret police – the Cheka.

The most crucial test of the revolution was to come in the countryside. Lenin believed that the rural population were natural

ГОД
ПРОЛЄТАРСКОЙ
ДИКТАТУРЫ.
ОКТЯБРЬ 1917 – ОКТЯБРЬ 1918

'reactionaries' who would have to be taught to become good communists – whether they liked it or not. Everything depended on 'the dark people', as the peasants were called. Still making up four-fifths of the population, the peasants suffered for the most part in silence. Often with little or no education, and living in an enormous country with poor communications, they could know almost nothing about the world beyond their village or district. The revolution had to be brought to them.

The Russian peasantry had traditionally 'repartitioned' their land at intervals, reapportioning it so that no one would hold the best land permanently. However, much of the best land still belonged to the rich landowners. For the peasants, the revolution simply offered hope of a new and bigger repartition, in which the landlords' property would also be redistributed. In fact even before the 1917 revolution this 'grand repartition' was under way. Groups of peasants had been taking matters into their own hands, and seizing the estates of great landowners.

For the Bolsheviks land policy was a matter of tactics: Lenin knew that it was essential to win the peasants to his cause if the revolution was to endure. At the same time he was convinced that class struggle must be brought to the villages, and that class antagonisms were needed to help spread the revolution. To this end, Lenin invented new distinctions among the peasants, setting the poorer ones against their wealthier neighbours, who were labelled 'kulaks'. The word *kulak* means 'fist', and was used in a derogatory sense to imply greedy money-grabbing. Although it was not a term that the peasants used among themselves, the Bolsheviks adopted it as though it denoted an established class of society.

Force was also used against the peasants. From 1918 the Bolsheviks sent armed gangs to confiscate the harvest; the peasants fought back fiercely. Propaganda was used: special trains were sent to remote areas to demonstrate the achievements of the new state. At the same time, the rural population continued to be harassed, while inflation eliminated their savings. Decrees were ruthlessly enforced, and resistance mercilessly punished. Even in the early years after the revolution, the Russian people were being forced as well as led into Lenin's new world.

PEASANT PROSPERITY
Not all the peasants lived on the brink of starvation; some fared much better. But the wealthier peasants were also to suffer, as scapegoats in the communists' campaign to bring class struggle to the Russian countryside.

ENEMIES OF THE PEOPLE
(BELOW) *A revolutionary cartoon issued during the civil war reminded the Russian people who their traditional oppressors were: the aristocracy, supported by the capitalists, the Church and the rich peasants (the kulaks) – all typically depicted as fat, smug and greedy.*

Spreading the news (ABOVE) *Crowds flocked to hear the new messages of hope, possibility and achievement brought by the trains from the bureau of agitation and propaganda – Agitprop. Through plays, films and leaflets the ideas of communism were spread to the people in a very effective propaganda campaign. In a country where so many people could not read or write and had little access to the world beyond their own village, the impact of the Agitprop activities was enormous.*

The New Economic Policy

By 1921, when the civil war came to an end, the Communist Party (as the Bolsheviks were now known) emerged victorious, but the economy was in ruins. As a result of the war, and during the subsequent famine, millions of people had perished, and in many parts of the country the peasants were literally in arms against food requisitioning. Then a dangerous mutiny erupted in the Kronstadt naval base, once a citadel of revolutionary fervour. It was violently crushed. As a result of the unrest, however, Lenin made a tactical shift by introducing the New Economic Policy. He abandoned 'war communism', with its almost military conditions of work, replaced food requisitioning with a money tax, and allowed a degree of private enterprise, especially in retail trade. In the middle 1920s the people of the new Soviet Union were at last given a breathing space.

This was a time of hope and excitement. The ideals of the revolution were brought to the people: factory workers would take control and make decisions, and profit would be abandoned. The new benefits would come from hospitals, housing, schools. 'For a large number of people, perhaps the majority, it wasn't the

لوچ بلند!

A CHANCE TO LEARN
One of the major changes in the early years after the revolution took place in education. These Uzbek women were among the millions, both adults and children, who for the first time could now learn to read and write. For Anastasia Denisova, one of those who taught them, 'The revolution gave me complete freedom, independence. We all went to school. The majority were illiterate beforehand and now it was obligatory to be educated.'

'BOOKS – INTO ALL FIELDS OF KNOWLEDGE'
An enthusiastic message encouraging literacy as the doorway to learning.

ideology that was so important as the promise of a better life,' explains Lev Razgon, who was a young communist at the time. 'For most people this gave colour to their daily, ordinary, difficult, often unbearable existence.' Hopes rose as real change suddenly seemed possible. Literacy was one of communism's main aims: learning to read offered new possibilities to the millions of people trapped at the bottom of society. Before the revolution many people could not read or write, and among the peasants few had even seen a book. A campaign was launched to make lessons available to all, in every village.

Anastasia Denisova was seventeen years old in 1924, and worked in a local literacy programme. At first the men said, 'No, you can't teach us anything, you are too young'. But they soon changed their minds. One pupil was a woman who could not go to the class because she had to look after her baby, so she was taught at home. 'She held her baby in one arm and wrote while she rocked him. She studied so keenly. I'll remember that for ever – that striving for knowledge, for enlightenment. It was immense.'

This was a particularly exhilarating time for women, as new laws were passed to give them equality with men. They had the same opportunities in education and in work. Ella Shistyer taught Muslim women in Uzbekistan, one of the southern republics that had been incorporated into the new Soviet Union. 'At the same time as teaching them to sew we told them about equality,' she explains. 'They were real slaves....The revolution brought these Uzbek women into the world. It gave them the opportunity to get education and culture.' It brought Ella Shistyer herself new opportunities: 'The revolution gave me the right to feel equal with any man. It gave me the right to work, to study as I wanted.' She decided to become an electrical engineer. 'I didn't want just to draw up plans, I wanted to build an electric power station. That was my mission, and I achieved it.'

People who remembered life in the old Russia – unjust, poverty-stricken and illiterate – felt things were really improving. Lev Razgon remembers, 'There wasn't political freedom, but there existed cultural freedom. In the middle 1920s there were years of extraordinary blossoming, a renaissance of culture, triggered by the revolution.' There was a wave of artistic and musical experiment as young artists and designers put their creativity to work for the Party. The painter Boris Smirnov-Russetsky was one of them. 'We were carried away by a feeling of freedom – freedom to create, freedom of opportunities to work in whatever direction, whatever form we wanted,' he explains. 'That's how I understood communism – as the development of a new consciousness in people, a consciousness that would allow people to see all that was going on around them more broadly and more deeply.'

Izo Degtyar, a violinist, experienced the revolution as an orchestra with no conductor. In the 1920s he played in a Moscow orchestra in which the musicians were all regarded as equals, and made decisions collaboratively. 'If you didn't like something, you all had a vote. For instance, if you couldn't hear the clarinets, you told them the truth: "You're behind", or "You're not coming in on time. Who's in favour? Who's against?" This wouldn't happen in an orchestra with a conductor. It was a real innovation.'

Tatiana Gomolitskaya worked with the Moscow Theatre of the Proletariat. It was led by Sergei Eisenstein, who later became a great film director. 'All the actors were workers and peasants,' she says. 'We had very little to eat, but we didn't think about it. We were working for the future. The aim of the theatre was to bring culture to the people, and of course propaganda.'

New art for the people

'BEAT THE WHITES WITH THE RED WEDGE' *urges this civil war poster by El Lissitzky. The art movement known as Constructivism used new materials – plastic, glass and steel – to reflect the challenge of the times. It encouraged Soviet citizens to gain a new way of thinking for a new way of life.*

MASSACRE ON FILM *A woman flees with her injured child in a scene from Sergei Eisenstein's famous film,* The Battleship Potemkin. *The cinema was important to revolutionary Russia. Newsreels and feature films brought new ideas to the people, reflecting the hopes and opportunities communism offered, and celebrating its achievements. Films were an effective tool for propaganda, and film-making an exciting way to contribute to revolutionary fervour.*

"I loved Stalin from my whole heart. I would work enormously long hours and I gave all my strength, all my soul into this. "

ELLA SHISTYER

THE NEW SOVIET WOMAN *was encouraged to work on equal terms with the new Soviet man. Ella Shistyer, seen here with the team she led, contributed by qualifying as an electrical engineer. She also helped other women, both by her example and through her work as a teacher.*

Mobilizing the people

During the 1920s the ideas of communism polarized politics and society around the world. In Europe and also in the United States, where democracy was struggling against alternative ideologies in the post-war years, many people were excited by the 'Soviet experiment'. Boris Smirnov-Russetsky firmly believed that 'Russia would show the path for other countries'. But people also felt threatened by the uncertainty and cruelty of revolution. Many ordinary citizens in democratic countries were afraid that their world might be invaded by godless thugs who believed in free love and common property.

Such fears in the West were matched by the attitudes of the rulers of the Soviet Union. With the Cheka, Lenin had recreated the secret police of the tsar, and despite all his promises of equality he ruled the Russian people with full party authority. When he died in 1924 he left the tools of control in a one-party and one-ideology state. Armed with this legacy his successor, Joseph Stalin, assumed supreme power and immediately set out to protect his dictatorship and that of the proletariat from potential enemies at home and abroad.

After Lenin's death many of the revolution's aims remained unfulfilled. Stalin was convinced that to make communism work in practice, and to defend the Soviet Union in a hostile world, a powerful modern economy needed to be created as quickly as possible, so he launched the first Five-Year Plan (1928–33). The Soviet Union was fifty, perhaps even a hundred years behind the industrialized countries and had to catch up. 'We must make good this distance,' he declared, 'or we shall be crushed.' So he took a traditional peasant society, just beginning to modernize before the setbacks of war and revolution, and hurled it into a programme of breakneck industrialization. The production of pig iron, coal, steel, electricity and machinery rose remorselessly.

To storm these heights, Stalin called for a 'new Soviet man', and the people responded enthusiastically to the call. For Tatiana Fedorova, who worked in construction, it was like something out of a fairy tale. 'Stalin's greatest achievement was that he united the people,' she explains. 'Wherever the Party called you, everywhere there was a response from the heart. Stalin set a task: build this or

BUILDING THE FUTURE

IT WAS CALLED the Magnetic Mountain because of its vast deposits of iron ore. In 1929 it drew thousands of people to a desolate corner of the Urals. They were inspired by Stalin's decision to build a huge steel works. Industrialization was to liberate the people. One volunteer, Valentina Mikova, remembers why she went: 'My heart summoned me to the great construction site of socialism.'

The plans were modelled on those of the United States steel plant in Gary, Indiana. But Magnitogorsk was built by hand, as Valentina Mikova explains. 'One takes the earth, and throws it to the level above. The second person throws it to a third, the third to a fourth, up five or six levels. That was how we got the earth out of the trench. Then it was taken away in wheelbarrows.' Working in sub-zero temperatures, many people died.

After 1930 the volunteers were joined by at least 20 000 kulaks sentenced to forced labour. They lived separately, under police surveillance. But one of them, Mikhail Arkhipov, still remembers that in spite of the hardship and the shame, 'we caught the enthusiasm, we too were fanatics'. After three years it was finished, the biggest steelworks in the world, a monument to Stalinism – and to the ideals, beliefs and suffering of the people who built it.

MOVING THE MOUNTAIN *It took only three years to complete the Magnitogorsk steel works, though they were largely built by hand. Thousands of men and women lived at the site, inspired by their belief in Stalin and his drive to turn the Soviet Union from a backward agricultural country into one of the greatest industrial powers in the world.*

build that, and thanks to the fact that young people believed him, trusted him, this enthusiasm made it possible. Remember this was a country where people were illiterate, lived in virtual darkness, wore birch-bark shoes.'

The heroic productive feats of these workers, who came to be called Stakhanovites after a particularly successful coalminer, were publicized until they became the equivalent of film or sports stars. Tatiana Fedorova led a team of Stakhanovites who helped to

ALEXEI STAKHANOV *(in the foreground) with a group of his fellow coalminers. They were hailed as heroes for their hard work in the cause of Soviet industry. They helped to transform their country into a leading industrial power in little more than a generation.*

build the magnificent Moscow Metro. 'No one forced you to do it,' she says, 'everyone wanted to be a Stakhanovite. It is very hard to explain, but it was a time of enthusiasts. Everyone was trying to do the best for the motherland. It was such a good time. There wasn't much to eat, we weren't well dressed, we were simply very happy.' They felt they were making an important contribution.

The achievements of Soviet society in the 1920s continued into the 1930s. Workers who kept out of trouble were rewarded with paid vacations, free medical care, and for the lucky ones there was improved housing. Even sceptical Western visitors were impressed, as they compared the energy, idealism and achievements of the Soviet Union to the stagnation and hardship that economic depression was then inflicting on people in the West. Charlie Nusser was one young American profoundly influenced by the contrast. 'In the Soviet Union they were advertising for workers – that really struck me because I was out of high school and had no job and millions of others had no job.' Inspired by this example, he decided to turn to communism. 'Stalin was leading the country in a very difficult period to build socialism....I felt he was leading in the proper direction.' After a visit to the Soviet Union one American journalist, Lincoln Steffens, wrote in a letter to a friend, 'I have seen the future; and it works'.

Collectivization and famine

The land of hope that these Western visitors saw was in reality quite different for the people of the Ukraine and southern Russia, who now experienced the worst famine ever recorded outside China. In 1932 Stalin set out to complete the process Lenin had begun in the countryside, where peasants were still farming their own land and had largely remained outside the communist system. He moved to bring them into it by collectivizing agriculture.

Stalin blamed the kulaks, the better-off peasants, for the grain shortages and for opposing his plans, and adopted a ruthless policy towards them. Izrail Chernitsky, who was a member of the Komsomol, the communist youth movement, was among those who carried out Stalin's orders in the Ukraine. 'If Stalin decided to start dekulakization to start creating collective farms then it was what we needed. I thought it should be done, so I didn't think

COMMUNISTS OF THE FUTURE *From the beginning, the communists sought to mould the minds of Soviet children. All ages were catered for: the youngest groups of children were known as Little Octobrists; nine- to fourteen-year-olds were called Young Pioneers, and through political education and recreation were prepared for joining the Komsomol, the All-Union Leninist Communist League of Youth. Membership of these organizations was essential to get on in life professionally and politically, and an important step in being admitted to membership of the Communist Party.*

about my feelings towards these people.' One of his tasks was to prevent anyone leaving his local village meetings who might then warn kulaks that they were in danger of being eliminated. Thousands of people died in exile in Siberia or were shot.

The peasants' agricultural equipment was requisitioned by the state, and the land was taken over to be farmed collectively, in large units. The poorer peasants were also targeted, and many resisted by killing their livestock in protest. Piotr Shelest, also in the Komsomol, took the machinery, horses and cattle from the peasants. He remembers their responses well. 'Some cursed their fate, others gave statements, there were those who even helped us. We asked them, "Do you want to go into the collective farm?" Several agreed and transferred their possessions to the collective farm – cows, horses. Some of them went very angrily. There were episodes when the father murdered his son because he had told the brigade that there was more. It was a very hard struggle....The elimination of the kulaks was to do with changing the social status among the peasantry. They did everything to put the brakes on giving up their meat or their products. That's why they were liquidated.' Like Izrail Chernitsky, his faith in Stalin and in the system prevailed. 'I was convinced that this was necessary and my feelings were on the side of action.'

Izrail Chernitsky went to one kulak's house with his commission. 'They had just built a very big new house and they lived well, were quite rich. There were no men at the house. The head of the commission said to the women and children, "No hysterics! Nobody's to leave the house. Put your valuables, earrings, rings on the table." I'd never seen so many valuable things. They made a list of goods in their house and they were told not to touch these things any more because they were to be taken by the state. The next morning people would come and take these

PERSUADING PEASANTS *of the advantages of new farming methods was no easy task. Thousands of meetings and rallies were held to try to convince them that working on large-scale collective farms would benefit them. Any resistance to the changes was brutally suppressed.*

POVERTY AND PLENTY
Reality for this ragged band of undernourished children (ABOVE) *was a very different experience from propaganda that reported well-stocked granaries* (RIGHT) *and a wide choice of food and other goods in the shops during the years of famine. Many children died of starvation and disease; many of those who survived were orphaned when their parents succumbed.*

things and in one or two days all these people were taken to a railway station to be transported to Siberia...or perhaps to be killed.' But, Izrail Chernitsky remembers, 'Everyone lived with the hope of a radiant future. And apart from that, we really trusted the Party. If Stalin said "Do it", then it was necessary.'

In a year of poor harvest, some 12 per cent below average, the government increased its demands of food by 44 per cent. It took all the grain, including what was being kept as seed to sow for the following year. The result was famine. While exports of grain and other farm products actually rose, over five years some seven million people died. As a child Pelagaya Ovcharenko was a victim of the famine. She remembers the terrible hunger. 'I would climb a cherry tree and would eat cherries, green cherries. My body swelled up, and I survived eating only grass and leaves. That was all my food.' One day three men came to the house with a cart. One of them looked after the horses, while the others piled up bodies on the cart. 'They threw on my mother. Then they

ON STALIN'S FIFTIETH BIRTHDAY in 1929 *Pravda* broke all its own rules and published a full-page portrait of Stalin. For five years he had been general secretary of the Communist Party. Now he became the *vozhd*, the 'power', the 'boss'. To celebrate his seventieth birthday, Stalin's portrait was suspended from an invisible balloon and transfixed by spotlights, shimmering in the sky over tens of thousands of worshippers in Moscow's Red Square. In the intervening twenty years Stalin had ruthlessly eliminated all rivals, real or imagined, and deported millions of prisoners to the labour camps under the Gulag system. He had also become the icon of a quasi-religious cult.

Born Joseph Vissarionovich Djugashvili, the son of a shoemaker in the Georgian mountains and intended for the priesthood, Stalin attained an almost divine stature for many ordinary Russians. He was accorded the ancient religious epithet of 'Father of the People'. Painters in the different Soviet republics gave him the features of their own people – Georgian, Kurdish or Uzbek. Kazakh mothers crooned:

> *Go to sleep, my Kazakh babe,*
> *Knowing hands will care for you.*
> *Stalin peers from out his window,*
> *Keeping our vast land in view.*

Stalin established his revolutionary legitimacy by persuading people that he had been Lenin's chief collaborator, even creating a false 'historical memory' by doctoring photographs. Every school, office, factory and collective farm in the land had his picture on its wall, and he used hoardings, newspapers and radio to propagate his image.

No flattery was too great. He was called 'the greatest man of all time'. Cities were given his name: Stalingrad,

Stalino, Stalinabad, Stalinsk. Climbers carried his bust to the top of peaks named after him. The veneration that many people genuinely felt for Stalin reached back into both religious and monarchical tradition. Many prisoners refused to believe that he had any hand in the purges, and millions of people clung to the illusion that if only he knew what was happening, Stalin would himself put an end to the terror.

It was said that Stalin received such long ovations because nobody dared to be the first person to stop clapping. 'What could we do?' asked Nikita

Khrushchev, who was later to emerge as his successor. 'You only had to look at him and the next day you lost your head.' Not until several years after Stalin's death was the cult of his overpowering personality challenged.

The most bizarre aspect of Stalin's rule is that when his propaganda spoke of modernizing an entire economy and transforming a backward country into a great modern industrial and military power, and when his critics spoke of him as an insane tyrant who was guilty of crimes on a scale never matched before, both were telling the truth.

threw on my father. My father gestured to me, but the man said, "He's almost ready, he's almost dead." When my father gestured to me I knew that I had to go and hide. I crawled away on my hands and knees. And that's why I survived.'

One source of strength and comfort to the peasants was the Russian Orthodox Church, but it represented the old regime and was now also relentlessly attacked. The communists declared that there was no God. All over the country, priests were ridiculed and harassed, and forced publicly to renounce their faith. Izrail Chernitsky saw how one village priest was treated. 'The priest came to the meeting. He took off his cassock, and put it on the table. The barber came and cut off his hair. And the priest proclaimed, "There is no God, I have lied to you." Men began to shout, "How could you lie to us? We built a house for you, and now you are saying there's no God!"'

The years of terror

Not even the horrors of the famine and the murder of the kulaks in the early 1930s, however, matched those of the Great Terror later in the decade. Now it was not just the peasants who suffered. It began in the Smolny Institute, where Lenin had inspired the victorious workers' and soldiers' deputies with talk about 'peace, land and bread' in 1917. There, on 1 December 1934, an assassin sent by Stalin murdered Sergei Kirov, head of the Communist Party in Leningrad. This set off a chain reaction of purges – of the party, of the army, and of innocent people caught up in the machinery of terror. Stalin was obsessed with destroying all potential opponents and resorted to brutal methods. The terror was to continue until Stalin had eliminated every scrap of opposition that spying could detect or paranoia imagine.

To root out those he called 'enemies of socialism' among people throughout the country, Stalin controlled and conducted the terror himself. When the purges were over, by the best estimate at the very least twelve million citizens had been arrested

CHEERFUL RAILWAY WORKERS *listen with the eager attention of disciples to the 'Father of the People' in this stylized painting. The engines symbolize the strength of the modern Soviet Union.*

DESTROYING THE CHURCH *All over the Soviet Union churches and monasteries were pulled down, damaged or given over to other uses. The Russian Orthodox Church represented a challenge to the new orthodoxy of communism, and was not to be tolerated. It made no difference that religion could give meaning to the lives of many Russians.*

FORCED LABOUR
(RIGHT) *made up a large part of the Soviet workforce by the late 1930s. Many prisoners died, 'under the complete and utter control of people deprived of any human feelings whatsoever,' as one of the survivors still bitterly remembers.*

LISTING THE VICTIMS
Stalin's purges were carried out from lists of arbitrary quotas for every town and region, guaranteeing fear throughout the country. Stalin himself scribbled additions to the quotas; this one reads: 'Give a supplementary quota of 6000 people in the first category to Krasnodar'. Category 1 meant death; category 2 meant the camps.

and sent either to prison or to the harsh labour camps of the far north and far east of the Soviet Union. At least a million of them were executed; a further two million died of illness, exhaustion or maltreatment. Even those who had been early enthusiasts for communism could become victims. Karl Rianne, who had stormed the Winter Palace twenty years before, was among those arrested and imprisoned. The electrical engineer Ella Shistyer, who had worked so hard for Stalin, was sent to prison in Siberia. During the long winter journey there, with nothing but salt fish to eat, she developed a huge thirst. 'I remember when there was a hard frost how I used to lick the ice off the metal screws and bolts inside the wooden cattle truck, fearing only that my tongue would stick to them. That's how we travelled for nearly a month.'

By the end of 1938 there were about nine million people in captivity, a million of them in prison and the rest in the camps, where at least a tenth, perhaps as many as a fifth of the prisoners died every year. These arrests and executions had come about as a result of a system of spying, informing, torture and trials in which false evidence was used. The whole of society was infected with corruption, and tens of millions of people lived in agonies of fear. 'The most terrible thing was understanding that I was deprived of any rights,' explains Lev Razgon. 'They could do whatever they wanted, and if it were just me that would be one thing, but they could do whatever they wanted with people who were close to me as well.' After his colleagues and close relatives were arrested, he lived in terror until his own arrest. 'When finally the doorbell rang one night there was a feeling of relief. When I was taken into the cell the elder of the cell said to me, "Sit down. Breathe in the freedom. You don't have to fear any more. Your arrest is over." He expressed what we all felt.'

Stalin called himself an 'engineer of human souls'. Fear was not his only tool; loyalty could also corrupt, and so could belief in the party and its ideology. Valentin Astrov, a journalist on the newspaper *Pravda*, gave evidence against Stalin's rival, Nikolai Bukharin, in 1936. He reflects: 'Of course I sacrificed general human values, as well as my conscience, to class and proletarian values. Soviet power demanded this; I did it. If the party asked me to say that I was an English spy, I would agree to it. If the party

THE MAD DOG OF FASCISM (BELOW) *A cartoon drawn by Boris Yefimov to Stalin's order shows a two-headed creature whose heads are Trotsky (despite his having been disgraced and exiled) and Bukharin who had dared to criticize Stalin.*

wanted to take my life away, fine. If it wanted to take my honesty, well, that was fine too.'

Boris Yefimov, whose brother had been shot in the purges, was the official cartoonist at Bukharin's trial. Stalin himself dictated the subject for each cartoon. 'I felt like a fowl that would be glad if it woke up in the morning at home and not in a cage...especially because Stalin's unwritten law said that a wife must answer for a husband, a son for a father, a brother for a brother.' And yet Boris Yefimov's feelings about Stalin, like those of many others who experienced first the revolution and then the dictatorship, were ambivalent. 'We lived in a kind of nightmare. We saw his despotism, his autocracy. And at the same time you just had to lower your head, because Stalin must know best. It was like a terrible god who ruled us. We had to obey. We didn't judge. We didn't argue.'

THE MIDNIGHT KNOCK

THE RUSSIAN TSARS had all relied on secret police and their cruel methods to protect themselves. Lenin recreated this force, the Okhrana, with his own, the Cheka. Its role was to seek out all counter-revolutionaries. Its victims included political opponents, the nobility, the bourgeoisie and the clergy; its methods were murder, torture and the camps.

When Stalin succeeded to supreme power, he immediately set out to protect his dictatorship from his perceived enemies by equally ruthless methods. Under a succession of names – Cheka, GPU, OGPU, NKVD, MVD and KGB – the secret police exercised immense power in Soviet society. Every citizen came to dread the midnight knock.

During the years of collectivization the OGPU carried out the deportation and murder of the kulaks. Its chief, Genrikh Yagoda, staged the early purge trials, but was removed from power by Nikolai Yezhov, and condemned to death. As his successor, Yezhov lent his name to the Great Purge of 1936–38 – it was called the Yezhovshchina – only to disappear in his turn in 1939.

Lavrenti Beria, who took over in 1938, managed to survive for longer than his predecessors. He even survived Stalin, but was tried and executed in 1953. The following year the functions of the MVD were taken over by the KGB (Committee for State Security), which was responsible for border control and foreign intelligence as well as internal security.

SECRET SERVICE BADGE *A memento of the sinister power of the OGPU.*

A new superpower

In the very years when Stalin was terrorizing the people of the Soviet Union, communism's prestige and influence around the world was at its highest. In the 1930s it seemed that only the communists, allied with socialists and liberals, could be an effective force standing between democracy and the threat of fascism. The perception of the Soviet Union as the last protector of pluralism and human rights was reinforced by awe for the sheer strength of the Soviet state. It seemed as though the communist dream had come true. Almost everyone in the Soviet Union could now read; people had opportunities in their work that had never before been possible. By 1939 the Soviet Union had become the world's second industrial power after the United States, and was frantically manufacturing warships, tanks and aircraft in its bid to become the world's foremost military power. In that year, visitors to the New York World Fair were dazzled by a huge map of the Soviet Union, a mosaic made out of precious and semi-precious stones. Few realized that the stones had been mined under atrocious conditions by political prisoners and by the victims of Stalin's purges.

The wonderful promise Lenin had made in 1917 that 'the oppressed masses would themselves form the government' had not been fulfilled. Soviet citizens found themselves not liberated but subordinated, in a country where decisions were still imposed from above by a leadership that had shown its deep distrust of the very people in whose name it ruled. For Lev Razgon this was its fundamental defect. 'The right to choose is the main right, the main distinguishing feature of a human being...communism deprived people of this right.'

As the Soviet Union was brought into the Second World War in 1941 it was still the world's only communist state. After the war more than a hundred million people in eastern Europe would come under communist rule, the great majority of them against their heartfelt wishes, as the Soviet sphere of influence extended westwards. In China in 1949, and elsewhere in Asia, genuinely popular uprisings created new people's republics under the red flag of communism. But they too would eventually be transformed into ruthless party dictatorships on the Russian model, each under its own 'terrible god'.

1918 – 1939

Lost Peace

THE INTER-WAR YEARS

I T WAS THE ELEVENTH HOUR of the eleventh day of the eleventh month of 1918 when the guns on the Western Front fell silent. Dazed men climbed out of the trenches from which, for so many months, they had been trying to kill each other. Now, hardly able to believe what was happening, they staggered towards each other and shook hands. The fighting had ended.

Away from the battlefields, Armistice Day turned into a carnival for the winning side. In towns and cities people poured into the streets to celebrate. In France, which had suffered most in the war, the rejoicing was not just for victory but for survival. Georges Clemenceau had led the French to victory; his grandson Pierre remembers that day well. 'Paris was fantastic, everybody was in the streets, everybody was kissing everybody. My brother had the sense to tell a policeman that we were the grandsons of Clemenceau. So we got into his residence and went upstairs, and my grandfather looked at us – he was surrounded by all sorts of great people, of course – and he said,

"What are you doing here? You should be in school!" And then he took us in his arms and kissed us and said, "All right, it is a special day!"'

In Britain, when the ceasefire was declared, the church bells of London began to peal. Doors banged. Feet clattered down corridors. No more work was done that day as all London ran into the streets to celebrate peace. It was the same in New York. For the gleeful crowds on Broadway the war had been shorter, but no less glorious. The Americans knew that their intervention had been decisive in gaining victory for the Allies, and they celebrated enthusiastically their part in the war whose ending would surely make the world safe for democracy.

Whether celebrating victory or having to come to terms with defeat, everyone was relieved that the war was over. But the atmosphere of idealism and hope that surrounded the armistice was soon to change to one of disappointment and bitterness. The war itself had ended, but the world was not yet at peace.

JUBILANT CROWDS *of Parisians take to the streets to celebrate Armistice Day.*

The trauma of war

The end of the war left Europe in a state of deep shock. The Great War had been more destructive than any other, both in its scale and in its human toll, leaving in its wake an entire generation of people affected by its horrors. About nine million men had been killed and millions more mutilated in body or mind. The whole economic, political and social structure of the continent, which had taken centuries to develop, had been shaken to its foundations. The great empires of Austria-Hungary, Germany, Russia and Turkey had been destroyed, and the focus of economic power in the world had been moved from Britain and France to the United States. The countries on whose soil the war had been fought – France and Belgium in the west, Italy, Serbia, Poland and the Baltic states in the east – had been flayed by high explosives and machine-gun fire. Their peoples had been assailed by hunger and by the diseases that follow armies and the refugees they drive before them.

Soldiers of all the nations that had experienced the terrible reality of war were determined that it should never happen again. Captain Donald Hodge, who had witnessed the deaths of many of his fellow soldiers, was one of them. 'Their mothers didn't have those sons to be blown to pieces. It was a blasphemous waste, throwing back in the Creator's face all the goodness that He has given us.' Donald Hodge's fervent hope that 'all the awful horror and waste we'd endured would never be repeated ...that it was a war to end wars', was shared by millions of people across the world.

Karl Nagerl, who grew up in Germany during the war years, was relieved that they were over and wanted life to return to normal. 'I was happy that my father was home...we expected a manageable peace. A peace that would give the German people a chance to work again, and to lead the kind of life that any normal citizen can expect....We expected

SHOULDER TO SHOULDER, *members of the Allied armed forces celebrate victory. The end of the war meant that those who had survived could at last return to their homes and families.*

THE DESPAIRING CIVILIANS (LEFT) *in this poster highlight Austria's plight after the war. As Germany's ally, Austria was also forced to pay reparations, despite its crippled economy and its people's suffering.*

a just peace.' But many people in the victorious countries wanted recompense for their great loss and suffering. They felt that the Germans had caused most of the damage and now looked to Germany to pay for it. Walter Hare, who had fought with the British army in the First World War, felt no pity for the Germans. 'I felt that they'd brought it upon themselves, so they had a right to suffer.' Others, like Maurice Bourgeois, who had served in the French army throughout the war, felt more pride in victory than horror at its price. 'What was important for us,' he recalls, 'was that we had beaten the Germans. They had wanted to wage war against us, and so they had to be punished.'

DISPIRITED GERMAN TROOPS (ABOVE) *make their way home after the armistice has been signed. For Germany, relief that the war was over was tinged with the bitterness of defeat.*

CLEARING A PATH

through the crowds (BELOW) *for Woodrow Wilson (centre, in top hat) as he leaves the palace of Versailles after signing the peace treaty. The Fourteen Points contained in his 'Program for Peace' made an appeal on behalf of the 'silent masses of mankind'.*

THE SIGNING OF PEACE

(OPPOSITE) *took place in the ornate grandeur of the Hall of Mirrors at Versailles after six months of negotiations. In this painting by Sir William Orpen, the Allied leaders look on while the two German delegates (in the foreground) sign the treaty.*

Program for the Peace of the World

By PRESIDENT WILSON January 8, 1918

I. Open covenants of peace, openly arrived at, after which there shall be no private international understandings of any kind, but diplomacy shall proceed always frankly and in the public view.

II. Absolute freedom of navigation upon the seas, outside territorial waters, alike in peace and in war, except as the seas may be closed in whole or in part by international action for the enforcement of international covenants.

III. The removal, so far as possible, of all economic barriers and the establishment of an equality of trade conditions among all the nations consenting to the peace and associating themselves for its maintenance.

IV. Adequate guarantees given and taken that national armaments will reduce to the lowest point consistent with domestic safety.

V. Free, open-minded, and absolutely impartial adjustment of all colonial claims, based upon a strict observance of the principle that in determining all such questions of sovereignty the interests of the population concerned must have equal weight with the equitable claims of the government whose title is to be determined.

VI. The evacuation of all Russian territory and such a settlement of all questions affecting Russia as will secure the best and freest cooperation of the other nations of the world in obtaining for her an unhampered and unembarrassed opportunity for the independent determination of her own political development and national policy, and assure her of a sincere welcome into the society of free nations under institutions of her own choosing; and, more than a welcome, assistance also of every kind that she may need and may herself desire. The treatment accorded Russia by her sister nations in the months to come will be the acid test of their good will, of their comprehension of her needs as distinguished from their own interests, and of their intelligent and unselfish sympathy.

VII. Belgium, the whole world will agree, must be evacuated and restored, without any attempt to limit the sovereignty which she enjoys in common with all other free nations. No other single act will serve as this will serve to restore confidence among the nations in the law which they have themselves set and determined for the government of their relations with one

another. Without this healing act the whole structure and validity of international law is forever impaired.

VIII. All French territory should be freed and the invaded portions restored, and the wrong done to France by Prussia in 1871 in the matter of Alsace-Lorraine, which has unsettled the peace of the world for nearly fifty years, should be righted, in order that peace may once more be made secure in the interest of all.

IX. A readjustment of the frontiers of Italy should be effected along clearly recognizable lines of nationality.

X. The people of Austria-Hungary, whose place among the nations we wish to see safeguarded and assured, should be accorded the freest opportunity of autonomous development.

XI. Rumania, Serbia and Montenegro should be evacuated; occupied territories restored; Serbia accorded free and secure access to the sea; and the relations of the several Balkan States to one another determined by friendly counsel along historically established lines of allegiance and nationality; and international guarantees of the political and economic independence and territorial integrity of the several Balkan States should be entered into.

XII. The Turkish portions of the present Ottoman Empire should be assured a secure sovereignty, but the other nationalities which are now under Turkish rule should be assured an undoubted security of life and an absolutely unmolested opportunity of autonomous development, and the Dardanelles should be permanently opened as a free passage to the ships and commerce of all nations under international guarantees.

XIII. An independent Polish State should be erected which should include the territories inhabited by indisputably Polish populations, which should be assured a free and secure access to the sea, and whose political and economic independence and territorial integrity should be guaranteed by international covenant.

XIV. A general association of nations must be formed under specific covenants for the purpose of affording mutual guarantees of political independence and territorial integrity to great and small States alike.

Wilson's grand design

The man to whom all looked to build the foundations of a lasting peace was the president of the United States, Thomas Woodrow Wilson. Born in Virginia, he had been a professor of history at Princeton University and was a Democrat who had been elected to the presidency in 1912.

While the world was still at war, in January 1918 Wilson drew up a fourteen-point programme outlining his ideas for a peace settlement. Some were general aspirations, like the proposal for a world organization of nations to prevent future wars and the call for open diplomacy. Others took specific political positions, such as the return of Alsace-Lorraine to France. These Fourteen Points seemed to many to encourage the peoples of the Austro-Hungarian empire to form their own independent nations, and to others to promise the end of old grievances. Wilson's group of young advisers on postwar settlement plans was much influenced by nationalist leaders, such as the Polish virtuoso pianist, Ignace Paderewski, and the Czech, Dr Thomas Masaryk.

By October 1918, with the Eastern Front collapsing, the Germans knew that they must lose the war. Their new chancellor, Prince Max of Baden, asked the United States for an armistice, indicating Germany's willingness to conclude peace on the basis of Wilson's Fourteen Points. This skilful move bypassed Britain and France, who would have demanded harsher peace terms. Negotiations took place for several weeks; the end was hastened when on 3 November Austria signed an armistice with the Allies. Germany now also had to capitulate, signing just eight days later.

Woodrow Wilson, ambitious to bring peace to the world, insisted on crossing the Atlantic to France to lead the peace conference in person. When he landed in Europe on 13 December, power was in his hands. Edward Bernays, one of his advisers, watched from the crowd in the Champs Elysées near the Arc de Triomphe while the audience gave Wilson an ecstatic welcome to Paris, cheering him as a saviour. To Edward Bernays the people's faith was not surprising. 'After all,' he points out, 'if it hadn't been for the United States it's doubtful whether the Allies would have resisted the Germans, and it was Woodrow

PAYING THE PRICE OF DEFEAT

UNDER THE TERMS OF THE ARMISTICE, Germany agreed to pay reparations – compensation for the damage caused by its occupying armies. These included 5000 locomotives, 150 000 railway wagons, 5000 lorries and other goods to help restore ruined land, towns and cities. The principle of reparations had been set by Germany itself in 1871 after the Franco-Prussian war.

The great bitterness among the people of France and Britain for the suffering the war had brought was indirectly acknowledged by a clause in the peace treaty drawn up at Versailles expressly stating – for the first time – that the defeated states alone were responsible for causing all the loss and damage of the war. The resulting demand that Germany should be made to pay for the entire cost of the war led to far heavier penalties being imposed than those already agreed in the armistice. German objections that the terms of the treaty inflicted an unbearably heavy burden were overruled.

Details of the payments were drawn up by a reparations committee in 1921. Germany pleaded that it simply could not comply with the demand that over the next thirty years it should pay the equivalent of 132 billion gold marks in money and goods, and 26 per cent of the proceeds of German exports. The humiliation added to the Germans' despondency in defeat. As Karl Nagerl explains: 'The reparations meant that Germany was destined to be completely ruined. We expected to have to pay something, we had lost the war, but we certainly did not expect that the German population would be enslaved.'

German insistence that it could not meet the schedule of payments was proved right, and during the 1920s a series of conferences was held that gradually reduced them. There were also many practical problems. It would have been possible for Germans to help rebuild the homes and other buildings destroyed in Belgium and France during the war, but local people would not receive them. German industry could

produce more goods than there was transport available to deliver them. France had twice within fifty years been invaded by the Germans; the French wanted to ensure that Germany's capacity to wage war was permanently reduced, and its trading power weakened. Yet if reparations obligations were to be met, German industry had to be rebuilt.

Before the war, Germany and Britain had been each other's best customers; British prosperity after the war was held back by Germany's inability to buy British goods. The widespread sense of betrayal and anger in Germany at the burden of reparations, and at the hardships they inflicted on the nation, were to contribute directly to the economic depression that affected the whole world during the 1930s, to the rise of Hitler, and eventually to the Second World War.

A BEDRAGGLED AND PENNILESS GERMANY (LEFT) stands alone in this cartoon as other countries reveal their empty pockets. The refusal by nations of the world to recognize the hardship that the reparations caused Germany added to the widespread bitterness among its people.

FRENCH SOLDIERS march into Strasbourg (BELOW), provincial capital of Alsace, in November 1918. The two French provinces of Alsace and Lorraine had become part of Germany in 1871 after the Franco-Prussian war. Now their citizens, many of them German-speakers, were once again to find themselves part of France under the terms of the Versailles treaty.

Wilson who made the world safe for democracy.' Winners and losers alike looked to him to impose a just and lasting peace.

From January 1919 the peace conference met in the great Hall of Mirrors in the palace of Versailles. President Wilson tried to take the moral high ground, but he was tenaciously opposed by the leaders of the two powers that had borne the heaviest burdens during the years of war: David Lloyd George of Britain and Georges Clemenceau of France. Clemenceau demanded a peace that would for ever deny Germany the power to invade France again, and was unimpressed by Wilson's idealism. 'God gave us ten commandments,' he observed, 'and we broke them. Wilson has given us his Fourteen Points – and we shall see!'

Wilson failed to gain support for his peace terms. The European leaders insisted that Germany accept full blame for the war. On 28 June the German delegation was summoned to Versailles, and with great reluctance signed the treaty, with its 440 clauses. They had no alternative but to make peace. Nevertheless, they resented the harsh terms of the treaty, which condemned Germany to pay huge sums in compensation to its enemies. As a result of the settlements, Germany lost Alsace and Lorraine to France, more land to Poland, Belgium, Lithuania and Denmark, the port of Danzig and the rich industrial area of the Saar.

For the losers the peace treaty seemed to have been designed to satisfy the vindictiveness of the victors. Paul Quirin was living in Bonn in the 1920s. He remembers how people felt that the reparations were 'like a mortgage which was eventually going to ruin the economy. The amount we had to pay bore no relation to economic prospects. We weren't going to be able to cope with this for long.' In Germany bells tolled in mourning when the treaty was signed, and newspapers appeared with black borders. The German leaders felt bitterly that they had been tricked. They had agreed to an armistice on the basis of the idealism of the Fourteen Points, but the treaty that followed was not in accordance with Wilson's ideals. These had included national self-determination of peoples, yet the treaty expressly forbade the German-speakers of Austria to join the German Reich.

The German leaders had recognized that their only option was to sue for peace, but most of the German people could not believe that the war was fairly and squarely lost. Their armies had still been fighting on foreign territory; they had not been defeated in battle. The *Dolchstosslegende* thus took root – the legend that Germany had not been defeated by its enemies, but had been stabbed in the back by traitors. The hunt for scapegoats began.

An integral part of the Versailles treaty, and of subsequent treaties between the Allies and the other defeated powers, was the establishment of a new kind of international organization, the League of Nations. Its express purpose was to prevent future wars. This was intended to be Woodrow Wilson's master stroke: the league would bring the blessings of New World democracy to the feuding nations of old Europe, and replace their traditionally secret diplomacy with a new and open system of collective security. But Wilson, who had been the principal architect of the peace, now found that he was unable to rally public support for the treaty and the league in his own country.

Many Americans believed that the only way to maintain peace on American soil was to isolate themselves from the conflicts between other nations. Edward Bernays explains how many people felt: 'Most of the American public at that time had either been immigrants or the sons or daughters of immigrants...they had wanted to leave Europe and discover a new home. Any attempt of a president to make America international was not well regarded...there was no great feeling for any internationalism as a basis for peace and prosperity.'

Without United States support, the league was established in January 1920. Membership was limited to the Allied states and their supporters; Germany, like other former enemy nations and neutral states, was not yet included. The league at first had some successful interventions to its credit. It supervised the division of Upper Silesia between Germany and Poland, settled a dispute between Finland and Sweden over the Aaland islands, and for a while held in check the mutual hatred of Germans and Poles in Danzig. Only time would show how illusory was its real power.

DANCING FOR JOY *in the streets was one way for people in the victorious nations to celebrate the signing of the peace treaty. Life was returning to normal as men took up civilian life again, and women left their war work in the factories.*

NEVER AGAIN! *declares this anti-war cartoon* (RIGHT) *depicting soldiers marching into the jaws of death. It appeared in a Tacoma daily newspaper on the same day that President Wilson visited the city on his tour of American states to win support for the League of Nations.*

AMERICANS TURN THEIR BACKS ON EUROPE

WITHIN THREE MONTHS of the Versailles treaty being signed, it was in trouble in the United States. Opposition to it was woven from many strands of opinion. Among them were those of German-Americans who resented the harsh peace imposed on Germany, and Irish-Americans who were hostile to Britain. Many people felt that the United States had been manipulated by France and Britain into fighting the war, and wanted to prevent the possibility of this happening again.

Opposition among the American people was reflected in the attitudes of their political leaders. The Senate was now controlled by the Republicans and was split into three factions: those with minor reservations, those – led by Senator Henry Cabot Lodge – who had strong reservations, and those who would not have the treaty at any price. Lodge believed that the treaty robbed the United States of its sovereignty. He was willing, he said, to ratify the treaty without the League of Nations, and even to accept its covenant provided that Congress had the right to vote before the

United States went to war; without these conditions, he would oppose it.

At each of several stages Woodrow Wilson could have saved his treaty and kept the United States in the league, in which case it might have been strong enough to resist the dictators in the 1930s and keep the peace in Europe. But Wilson insisted that the Senate ratify his treaty as it stood, and made this a party issue between Democrats and Republicans. The exertions of a 13 000-km (8000-mile) speaking tour to seek support for the treaty exhausted him. He was already a sick man, and his health now deteriorated dramatically.

In March 1920 the treaty and the covenant of the League of Nations as proposed by Wilson were defeated in the Senate by fifty-three votes to thirty-eight. Lodge proposed a compromise that also failed to win the two-thirds majority needed under the constitution to ratify a treaty.

For the next twenty years United States foreign policy would reflect the belief that it was best not to intervene in European affairs.

ELATED SOLDIERS *wave goodbye to their military camp on their way back to civilian life. This was the first generation of Americans to have been involved in a war abroad.*

*"**M**y mother was weeping, and of course I asked, 'Why are you weeping? Everybody is so happy!' And she said, 'We have freedom.'"*

ANNA MASARYKA

The springtime of nations

Apart from Austria and Hungary, seven new states came into being as a result of postwar settlements. Poland was re-established from the provinces that had been taken by other states – Austria, Prussia and Russia – in the eighteenth century. The Croatian, Montenegrin, Muslim, Serbian and Slovenian peoples merged their national identities uneasily in the new south Slav kingdom of Yugoslavia. Four new republics emerged in the Baltic: Estonia, Finland, Latvia and Lithuania.

The republic of Czechoslovakia was first proclaimed in the United States on 18 October 1918, before the war had actually ended. Andrew Valucher, from a family of Czech immigrants in the United States, was seven years old at the time and was taken to Philadelphia for the event. 'There was this gentleman with a beard talking and telling the people that Czechoslovakia would be free, so there was tremendous excitement.' A few weeks later, the schoolboy Jiri Stursa heard the republic being proclaimed in Prague. 'My aunt took me down to the main street. There was a big crowd there and we met our neighbour, a police inspector. He asked my aunt, "Madam, have you heard the news? We have no Austrian empire any more, we have our own state."'

The bearded gentleman who proclaimed the republic of Czechoslovakia, first in Philadelphia and then in Prague, was Dr Thomas Masaryk. His granddaughter, Anna Masaryka, remembers that day very clearly. 'There were many, many people, all screaming, cheerful, embracing each other, and my mother was weeping, and of course I asked, "Why are you weeping? Everybody is so happy!" And she said, "We have freedom."'

FINDING A NEW HOME *As national boundaries were re-established after the war, hundreds of thousands of citizens moved to live among their own people. Under the terms of the Versailles treaty, plebiscites were held so that the mixed populations of some disputed regions could vote to choose for themselves which country their region would belong to.*

Plebiscite

New state

NEW BEGINNINGS FOR ARABS AND JEWS

TENS OF MILLIONS OF PEOPLE were affected by the disintegration of the Ottoman empire after the First World War. Before the war, though its European and African possessions were greatly diminished, Ottoman rule had still held sway over a huge Asian territory.

During the war Turkish soldiers fought bravely at Gallipoli and in Mesopotamia. After the war ended old feuds with Italy and Greece continued – both countries sent troops to Turkey in 1919. They were repulsed by the Turks under their new leader, Mustafa Kemal Atatürk, who had led the revolution against such humiliations and established a secular modern republic in Turkey. The substantial Greek minority living there were expelled: more than a million Greeks were forced to 'return' to a homeland their ancestors had left up to two thousand years earlier; in retaliation some 410 000 Turks had to leave Greece.

Already by 1917 much of the Arab world had been in revolt against Turkish rule. In the postwar peace settlement the Allies divided the Arab territories of the Turkish empire among themselves. Some became independent (Saudi Arabia); others were administered under League of Nations auspices as 'mandates' to Britain (Iraq, Palestine and Trans-Jordan) and France (Lebanon and Syria). In 1917 the British government had promised to establish in Palestine a national home for the Jewish people, many of whom cherished a dream of returning to their ancient homeland. Jews had begun to settle in Palestine in the late nineteenth century; by 1925 there were 100 000 settlers living there.

As nationalist fervour grew, the Arab states gradually began to achieve independence from their European governors. Palestinian Arabs became increasingly resentful of British plans to divide their country as Jewish refugees from Nazi persecution in Germany poured into Palestine during the 1930s. As the Second World War began, Britain was trying to maintain its influence in a Middle East that was modernizing rapidly; that was bitterly divided over Jewish immigration; and on which, because of its vast oil resources, Italy was casting covetous eyes.

Ottoman empire 1914

League of Nations mandate

THE PLEASURE PRINCIPLE

THOSE WHO HAD SURVIVED the dark, sad years of war wanted to rebuild their lives, put the pain behind them and make the most of the peace. Among the well-to-do in the 1920s to be modern was the thing. In music, dance, fashion and behaviour the old rules were challenged. Jazz became the rage, and lively dances accompanied it.

The hard-working independence women had found during the war was now expressed in a new way of dressing. Layers of long, smothering garments were abandoned in favour of simple clothes; the more daring even wore trousers. Women challenged the demure, ladylike manners expected of them; drinking and smoking in public became more common, and more women began to wear make-up and go to restaurants without a chaperone. While some celebrated the new freedoms, others complained bitterly of decadence and immorality.

The search for pleasure sometimes seemed frenzied. Contestants collapsed at dance marathons, clubs stayed open all night long. Risky plays were staged, erotic film stars were admired. On gramophone records and radios the latest dance music crazes could be heard in millions of homes, and advertising increasingly reminded people of what they could aspire to. Sports cars brought speed and freedom; travel brought adventure. Newspapers and magazines fed the public's appetite for sensational stories. People worked hard at having fun. There was a spirit far removed from the austerity of the decade before.

DINING OUT IN STYLE (ABOVE) *For those who could afford it, like the fashionable Parisians in this contemporary print, there was gaiety and entertainment on a new scale in the 1920s. Young people in particular wanted to enjoy themselves and forget about the war.*

It was a strange experience to live through, this dismantling of empires and birth of new nation states. Gerhard Stütz, a German-speaker growing up in the little town of Gablonz, once part of Germany and was now in Czechoslovakia, remembers the day the Czechs arrived. 'My mother wanted to go shopping in the market and she came back quite shocked because there were Czech soldiers and they refused to let the people go to the market ...the Czechs had laid down for themselves a preferential status. In Gablonz, for example, which had 85 per cent German population, all the street signs had to be in the Czech language and beneath the Czech name was the German translation in small print. The grotesque situation was that all our streets were named after German writers – Goethe, Schiller – so the street signs read Goethovadice, Schillerovadice, or Eichendorffovadice.' Changes like these took place in towns and villages all over Europe.

No more war

In all the countries that had fought in the war, many people remained preoccupied with their memories of sacrifice and death. In the late 1920s a stream of people visited the war cemeteries, where hundreds of thousands of men lay buried. Great memorials, like the marble Menin Gate outside Ypres, in the Flanders battle-fields, were dedicated to the simple proposition: no more war. Films, poems and books about the war reinforced this theme. In Britain a play set in a dugout at the front, *Journey's End*, became a huge popular success.

Young people, too, were aware of what war was about, and the need to avoid it. Growing up in the United States, George Watt and a friend were deeply affected by reading a German book, later made by a Hollywood studio into one of the first sound films: Erich Maria Remarque's *All Quiet on the Western Front*. 'It was the most realistic presentation of war, it was filled with humour, it was filled with gruesome brutalities of war, and also sadness...we both swore that we would never go to war.' Later, at Columbia University, he took a peace pledge.

George Watt and his friend were part of a new, international peace movement that was beginning to influence the politicians. The financial collapse that began with the Wall Street crash in New York, and triggered the economic depression of the 1930s, threw millions of people out of work across the world. In poorer countries, social conflicts also sharpened and demagogues profited. Governments in industrial countries were troubled by mounting unemployment, and turned to economic protection in the vain hope of escaping disaster – and so embittered relations with their own best customers. There was renewed anger at the resources wasted on armaments.

To reduce the threat of war, it was necessary to reduce the weapons used to fight war. Germany had been almost completely disarmed; in the early 1920s wartime stockpiles of munitions were reduced; Britain, Japan and the United States had agreed to limit their fleets. Not until 1932 did the League of Nations organize the first disarmament conference, in Geneva. By that time peace was already threatened by the rise of extremism in Germany and of militarism in Japan. Ramsay MacDonald, Britain's Labour prime

THE HORRORS OF WAR *were portrayed in films such as* All Quiet on the Western Front. *A new generation learned through entertainment that war was not glamorous and heroic but tragic and brutal. When the film was shown in Germany there were demonstrations against it, and the film was eventually banned there.*

PETITIONING FOR PEACE *at the Geneva disarmament conference. Millions of signatures were collected from people all over the world, putting pressure on governments to respond to popular demands for arms reduction and the end of war. Women were particularly active in the peace movement, gaining a new voice in world affairs.*

minister, said he would go to Geneva to reduce what he called 'this enormous, disgraceful burden of armaments'.

Jenifer Hart, a British peace campaigner, was present at the opening session of the Geneva conference. 'People came from all over the world,' she remembers, 'petitioning for disarmament.' One of the conference organizers put the nub of the question before the delegates: 'No one doubts that disarmament is possible, but the common man wants to know whether the governments with great military, naval and air forces are really in earnest in their desire for peace.' If they were, the whole international atmosphere would change 'as if by magic'. Although it was not a member of the league, the United States (where over a million signatures had been collected for the petition) sent a delegation to Geneva, and hopes rose even higher.

They were to be disappointed. It was one thing to announce a high-minded desire for peace, quite another to take the political risks associated with reducing a country's defence. As Ignace Paderewski, now Poland's prime minister, explained: 'It's a very good intention, a very fine idea, but a very difficult task. Everyone expects the other fellow to disarm, but he's not ready to disarm himself.' And by the 1930s there were leaders in power who made it quite plain that they saw the other fellow's disarmament as mere weakness, to be exploited without mercy.

Fading hopes for peace

The League of Nations had no power to impose peace. When Japan – a member of the league council – was formally criticized for invading Manchuria in 1931, it left the organization. Adolf Hitler came to power in Germany at the beginning of 1933, and one of his first actions was also to take Germany out of the league, which it had joined in 1926. In Italy, the fascist leader Benito Mussolini promised not peace but a sword. Italy's invasion in 1935 of Ethiopia, a fellow member nation of the league, dealt a serious blow to international peace.

The league's failure to deal with the dictators in Africa, the Far East and Europe weakened people's confidence in its potential as a keeper of international peace. Of the great powers, Germany, Japan, and Italy had left, and the United States had never joined.

IMMOBILIZED BY THE SNAKE'S GAZE, *the rabbit is rendered powerless in this political cartoon illustrating the weakness of the League of Nations. The league had been set up to provide a voice for weak as well as strong nations, but was increasingly unable to fulfil its potential peacekeeping role in the face of growing international aggression in the 1930s.*

ITALIAN TROOPS *being reviewed by their leaders. Mussolini sought to solve Italy's economic problems by seizing Ethiopia. The Ethiopian emperor, Haile Selassie, made a dignified appeal for help to the League of Nations. 'I must fight on until my tardy allies appear,' he said, warning that 'if they never come, I say to you without bitterness, the West will perish.'*

THE JAPANESE IN MANCHURIA

ON THE NIGHT OF 18 SEPTEMBER 1931 Japanese troops guarding the South Manchurian Railway to the north of the town of Mukden set off explosives along the track, and accused the Chinese of the sabotage they had themselves inflicted. The Mukden incident provided the pretext for the Japanese army to take over Manchuria, a strategically important region of China bordering the Soviet Union, with major mineral and industrial resources.

The powerful military elite of Japan had watched with mounting anger as the Chinese government worked with other leading world states to establish peace – to Japan's military disadvantage. When the Depression affected world trade at the end of the 1920s, Japan's economy was badly hit, as it had been dependent on the United States market for rice, silk and silk products. The impoverished farmers of Japan, and increasing numbers of unemployed urban workers, had little faith in the new democratic style of government that brought them so much hardship. The time was ripe for nationalist extremists to influence public opinion.

Secret associations were set up to work towards establishing military government. By 1931, as unrest grew, ambitious young officers turned to Manchuria as an opportunity for action. The government learned of their intentions and felt compelled to warn the emperor, who forbade any operations against China to be undertaken. It was too late. The Japanese army stationed in Manchuria went ahead with its plans. While most members of the government were shocked by the news, it was welcomed with patriotic delight by many Japanese people, who were aware that to have the assured market and the resources of the region at their disposal would ease their problems.

The unprovoked aggression that the invasion represented in the eyes of the world was just the kind of incident that the League of Nations had been established to contain. A commission was sent to investigate. The report of its findings so offended the Japanese that in March 1933 they withdrew from the league in protest. A puppet regime under Japanese control was set up in Manchuria (renamed Manchukuo). This was an important step in Japan's long campaign to change power relationships in the Far East in its favour. It was also the first public evidence that the league could do nothing to prevent international aggression – a failure that the German and Italian leaders observed with particular interest.

VICTORIOUS JAPANESE OFFICERS *toast the success of the Manchurian invasion with cups of saki. The invasion was used as a springboard for Japanese expansion into the Chinese mainland during the 1930s.*

Collective security began to seem a naive illusion. As governments once again feared war, they prepared to rearm. Ignoring the restrictions of the Versailles treaty, in 1935 Germany also began to rearm. There was much disappointment, confusion and anger. Some people still clung to the ideal of peace, and continued to look to the league to enforce it.

There seemed to be no answer to this question, so others turned to a more radical position: pacifism. They wanted each country to renounce war altogether. In Britain, pacifism reached its height in 1936. The Peace Pledge Union persuaded 130 000 concerned men and women to sign a declaration that they would renounce war. A Methodist preacher, Donald Soper, was one of the leaders of the campaign. 'It was comparatively easy,' he recalls sixty years later, 'to persuade an audience of the rightness of what you were asking them to believe, and also dangerously easy to ask them at that point to sign on the dotted line. We had a great deal of immediate conversion. The problem was to maintain the ardour and spirit of it when workaday problems became more difficult and more complicated.'

In the United States there had also been a strong movement for peace since the 1920s. A number of 'no more war' marches took place in New York. Robert Burgess was sixteen years old when he joined the Green International march. He enjoyed taking part in it. 'I remember my pleasure when I signed up for this and received in the mail my green shirt...like any parade the people line up on the kerb, some of them sympathetic, encouraging you, some of them opposed, throwing words at you...it was a mixture. My feeling at the time was that if a few people were impressed, it justified the parade.'

DONALD SOPER (BELOW) *addresses the crowd to rally support for the Peace Pledge Union. Pacifist values were based on a belief that peace and love could triumph over violence and hatred. As the threat of war became more real, the popularity of pacifism grew.*

Robert Burgess recalls wryly that a lot of students were interested in peace issues in the 1930s partly because they themselves would have to fight. 'They recognized that if the war system continued, they after all would be the ones that would be primarily involved, and I think there was a profound disappointment, on the part of students particularly, that the ambitions and objectives of the First World

MASS DEMONSTRATIONS *taking place* (LEFT) *in the same square in which British crowds had celebrated Armistice Day in 1918. In 1935 they gathered in support of peace after eleven million people had voted in the National Peace Ballot. In New York* (BELOW) *in the same year 75 000 people took part in a peace parade in Central Park. By now it had become clear to most people that the hopes of 1918 – that war could be prevented from ever happening again – were going to be in vain.*

War, which after all was billed as a war to end all war, the war to make the world safe for democracy, had done quite the opposite.'

For a large number of Americans, isolationism was a more attractive response to the new rumblings of war from Europe. The press took a strong line, influencing many people. In Chicago, the Bone family read the intensely anti-interventionist *Tribune*. Hugh Bone was no more than nine years old when his brother had come back from France with bitter memories of the war. 'The family of course…wanted to know about what he did in the war, his exploits. He literally refused to answer. He had told us time and time again, "I don't want to talk about the war." That influenced my thinking that never again, never again are we going to send our boys overseas.'

KARL NAGERL *rode into Austria on horseback. He was among the German troops welcomed by some 300 000 civilians when Austria was united with Germany in 1938. He remembers clearly how 'the barrier was lifted, our regiment's musicians marched ahead playing away, behind the border the Austrians were standing in crowds with swastika flags and they cheered out to us loudly: "One people, one empire, one leader". Finally the brother nation was reunited again with the brother nation.'*

The threat of war

When civil war erupted in Spain in July 1936 it increasingly became clear that nationalism and dictatorships were more than just threats to peace. For some, like the American George Watt who volunteered to fight in Spain, it meant an end to pacifism. 'We began to realize that an oath not to fight no longer had much validity with the rise of Hitlerism....When I came back from Spain I felt that the United States had to get involved in what was going on in Europe...we couldn't stick our heads in the sand.'

In March 1936, five years after the Allies had withdrawn their troops from the Rhineland, it was reoccupied in breach of the treaty by the Germans, who illegally 'remilitarized' it. Two years later Hitler reunited his native Austria with Germany, ignoring the explicit terms of the Versailles treaty. The people of Austria welcomed the union (*Anschluss*) and gave the Germans a rapturous welcome. Britain and France did nothing. Hitler now turned his attention to Czechoslovakia, claiming that the Versailles treaty had given two million Germans to the new Czechoslovak republic.

Strong feelings were aroused by the new national borders and minorities. Gertrud Pietsch was one of the Germans who lived in the Sudetenland, the area of Czechoslovakia lying on the border with Germany. 'A new Czech school had been built in Marienbad....It was a very nice modern school, but because the Czechs didn't have enough children they needed more pupils and approached my father, asking him to send his two daughters to the Czech school. He refused to do this because he thought we should learn German first and then Czech. Half a year later my father was dismissed, they told him they were cutting down on his job. Later on my father found out that a young Czech with two or three children got his job.' Relations between the Pietsch family and their Czech neighbours were strained. 'There was a strong feeling of resentment in our family towards the Czechs in general – and we children were aware of this.'

The Czechs, who had made a success of their young and independent republic, knew they were threatened by a strong Germany under Hitler. To support their large, well-equipped army they built a line of fortifications along the German border, and looked to Britain and France to come to their aid. At last the

REBELS AND CAUSES IN SPAIN

THE SPANISH CIVIL WAR symbolizes the conflicting political affiliations of the 1930s. Throughout Europe, people were nervous about the rise of fascism and the growing threat of war. For many politically aware young people the civil war had an intense emotional impact. Some 35 000 foreigners from fifty-four countries chose to fight for the republican side in the . International Brigades, so called because their members volunteered from many different countries; smaller numbers supported the nationalist cause. Their principles led them to regard the war as, from one point of view, a fascist conspiracy to destroy democracy; from the other, a communist plot to overthrow law, order and religion in Spain.

The war was a bitter fight between the democratic government of the republicans, supported by the political left and trade unionists in Spain and the communist government of the Soviet Union, against Spanish conservatives, military rebels and the Falange party, backed by the Roman Catholic Church, monarchists, and the fascist leaders of Germany and Italy.

There had been military coups in Spain before. This one, led by General Franco in 1936, failed to overthrow the government; it took three years, the devastation of the country and the deaths of half a million people before fascism triumphed in Spain.

In a war characterized by massacres and bloody reprisals, civilians were badly affected. In April 1937 the small market town of Guernica was bombed by aircraft of the German Condor Legion. There was widespread horror at the devastation caused, which was to prove a grim portent of the war to come.

FLEEING FROM WAR *Spanish civilians leave their homes to seek refuge in France from the fighting.*

REDEFINING GERMANY *by reclaiming the Sudetenland had been as easy as moving a border post. The German people living there had been denied a plebiscite after the war, but now they had what they wanted. Karl Nagerl, who took this photograph, remembers how the Sudeten Germans hurried to the border with tears in their eyes to welcome the German soldiers as 'liberators from the suffering they had had to bear under the Czechs'.*

ANGRY CROWDS (OPPOSITE) *express their fear and dismay as German troops drive through Prague. Having gained possession of the Sudetenland, it was easy for Hitler to invade the rest of Czechoslovakia. But here, as Karl Nagerl recalls, the people 'threatened us, they waved their fists in the air... they made it quite clear that they didn't want us there.'*

impotence of the League of Nations was recognized, and Britain and France took matters into their own hands. In September 1938 Neville Chamberlain, the British prime minister, and Edouard Daladier, the French premier, went to Munich to discuss the Czechoslovakian crisis with Hitler. The three leaders agreed that the Sudetenland would immediately be transferred to Germany. When Chamberlain flew back to Britain and announced that he had brought 'peace in our time' the crowds rejoiced, believing that peace really had been secured by giving Hitler the Sudetenland. Chamberlain had brought back a paper with Hitler's signature on it, and declared that settlement of the Czechoslovak problem was only the prelude to a wider peace.

Daladier was greeted with a similar response by the French public. Etienne Cruchanel, who flew with him, saw a huge crowd waiting; he thought people had come to hiss and boo, but instead there was a wave of applause and enthusiasm. Daladier had none of Chamberlain's illusions. 'These people are mad,' he said.

The Czechs understood all too well that their country had been sold to Hitler. For Josef Beldar this was 'a terrible betrayal, a horrible treachery of our country by the Western powers, and especially France and England. We thought that this should never have happened, and even then we somehow felt that it was to be the beginning of some horrible world conflict.' On 3 October German troops crossed the Czech border, and the Sudetenland became part of the German Reich.

Czechs living in the Sudetenland had to choose between remaining in Germany under Hitler or leaving their homes as refugees. The British journalist Iverach McDonald was in Prague, and witnessed the Czechs' reactions to the Munich pact. 'The people were out demonstrating...but they were not speaking, they were just utterly crushed and were weeping with grief, despair and utter sorrow.' One of them came up to him and said, 'Every night I pray that God may forgive France for her infidelity and Britain for her blindness.' The Czechs celebrated their country's twentieth anniversary that autumn with deep foreboding.

The Sudeten Germans were the only people with cause to rejoice. In Gablonz on the river Neisse, Gerhard Stütz remembers, 'the whole village went spontaneously to the biggest square in town and just cheered and cheered "*Heil!*" We were immensely relieved that it had not led to any war. We were very glad that the oppression of the Czechs had ended and we had achieved self-determination for our people.' Gertrud Pietsch and her family were overjoyed that they could remain German, and that her father was reinstated in his job. 'We cried,' she remembers. 'We were so happy that we cried, we scattered flowers on the streets.'

The Munich agreement bought only six months of peace. In March 1939 German troops marched across Czechoslovakia into its capital city, Prague. Jiri Stursa, who had seen the Austrians leave in 1918, now watched the Germans arrive. 'My uncle came to us that morning and said, "Those bastards have marched into Prague". We went into town and saw that the German armoured vehicles and troops were there. What could we do? Nothing. We couldn't fight them with our bare hands. The fact is, though, that people shook their fists at them. The Germans seem to have felt that they were hated, they must have seen it.'

Back to war

At last the veil was lifted from the eyes of the people in Britain and France. Neville Chamberlain posed the now unavoidable question: 'Is this the last attack upon a small state, or is it to be followed by others?' Hitler's answer was to embark within months on the next phase in his plans for conquest by invading Poland.

For another two years, Americans were to cling to the belief that, unlike the people of the European democracies, they could stand apart. The issue, Franklin D. Roosevelt said, 'is whether our civilization is to be dragged into the tragic vortex of unending militarism punctuated by periodic wars, or whether we shall be able to maintain the ideal of peace'. While President Roosevelt argued with the isolationists in the United States, all over Europe young men were opening the brown envelopes that contained their call-up papers.

The Frenchman Marcel Batreau had managed to survive the First World War, though twenty-five of his thirty classmates had been killed. He explains: 'It was hard to believe it could all happen again. To have peace, you have to be well-protected and always in a state of readiness. We needed to be armed, and we needed the Germans to be scared of us. The Germans took advantage of our sleepy state. I am not a military man, but I am a patriot.' He was prepared to fight again. Another First World War veteran, the Englishman Walter Hare, felt disillusioned as war loomed once more. 'I felt that what I'd done had been a waste of time. I was concerned because my son would soon be of military age, and I didn't want him to go through what I had gone through.'

In Geneva, the great white palace of the League of Nations stood empty. It had represented the belief that international cooperation and open discussion could put an end to war. The chance of lasting peace had seemed to be in humanity's grasp, but for the present it had been lost. Six years later, this ideal would be tried again, but by then some fifty million people would have died in another world war.

AT THE CROSSROADS *of war and peace, German troops prepare to invade Poland in August 1939. As Poland's allies, Britain and France were then obliged to declare war on Germany. As the war began, Karl Nagerl remembers, 'We thought back to the end of the First World War and hoped that it would not be repeated again, that this incident in Poland would be a short-lived tension and that the war would not become more widespread.'*

ENLIST, RE-ENLIST *urges this French war ministry recruitment poster (ABOVE) in 1938. Soldiers stand at the ready on the Maginot Line, a permanent defensive fortification. It had been built in the 1930s to prevent the Germans from advancing into France as they had done in the First World War. French soldiers who had fought in that war were now being asked to re-enlist, together with the young men of the new generation.*

WAR WAS DECLARED *(RIGHT) on 3 September 1939. At the final meeting of the League of Nations, its president warned: 'We do not know what the future will bring. We cannot even foretell tomorrow. We leave this assembly in grave anxiety for every nation.'*

On the Line

The effects of mass production

ONE HOT DAY IN AUGUST 1913, at the Ford Motor Company in Detroit, a young worker picked up a rope and slowly pulled a car chassis past the mechanics who fitted the various parts onto it. Instead of workers moving to the job, the work was moved past the workers. The following year, Henry Ford applied to car manufacture the technique he had first seen in the slaughterhouses of Chicago: he hooked the chassis onto a continuously moving chain.

As the car chassis moved down the assembly line, the workers had to perform their set tasks before it had passed by. The most important skill now was speed, as anyone could learn the simple, repetitive tasks in a matter of hours. Ford could produce more cars in less time and at less cost.

Other factories followed Ford's example. The moving assembly line dramatically increased production. Arthur Herbaux, who worked on the Renault line near Paris in the 1930s, found the new rhythm of work almost unbearable. 'You had to assemble so many parts per hour....No sooner had you finished one part than the next arrived. No stopping allowed. The workman was just part of the machine. At the flick of the switch the machine went into action and the workman had to keep pace with it. It was worse than hard labour...it was no better than being a galley-slave.'

This new way of making things transformed the lives of those who made them and those who used them. It brought within many people's reach products once luxuries only for the rich, from cars to fountain pens and electric stoves to vacuum cleaners. Ever higher production targets were set for the new mass markets as living standards rose with better wages. But the pressure of work also increased. Huge industrial complexes sprang up that employed tens of thousands of workers who were expected to become just as standardized and interchangeable as the parts that they bolted and welded together. As the discontent spread, more of them joined trade unions, and took part in the sit-ins and strikes that would eventually set new work standards for many of the world's workers.

MOVING WITH THE TIMES *Changing methods of assembly will transform the lives of industrial workers throughout the world.*

Early mass production

Many of the principal features of mass production already existed well before the assembly line was introduced. Firearms were assembled from standardized parts; sewing machines and railway engines were made in large factories. As mass production spread to other industries – shoes, clothing, clocks, typewriters, bicycles, and agricultural machinery were made in large quantities – the new processes increasingly reduced the role of those who worked in manufacturing. Semi-skilled and unskilled workers were not eligible for membership of the craft unions, and were refused the right to join new trade unions by their employers. They had no voice, no way to make their feelings clear.

It was in car manufacturing, one of the newest industries, that the greatest innovations took place, leading the way for the transformation of industrial production throughout the world. When cars were first made in France and Germany at the turn of the century they were individually built, costly works of craftsmanship. The early car industry in the United States began to use new techniques: the Olds factory made its cars using a trolley system, Cadillac used interchangeable parts, and the new General Motors Corporation brought out several new models. By 1908 the Ford Motor Company in Detroit was producing a hundred cars a day at its Highland Park factory.

Henry Ford wanted to go further. He spent six years planning a light, cheap car for a mass market; when he launched the Model T it was an instant success, not only in the United States but also in Britain. The Trafford Park plant in Manchester began making cars for Ford in 1911, and became the largest single car producer in Britain. When most British cars cost more than £300, a Model T was only £135. As orders for the 'Tin Lizzie' continued to flood in, Ford was unable to produce enough cars cheaply to satisfy the growing demand, and sought new ways of speeding up their manufacture.

ILLUMINATING INVENTIONS *The increasing use of electricity brought with it a growing demand for light bulbs. New technologies created new possibilities, boosting the market for many mass-produced goods and bringing new jobs for women – here working in a German light-bulb factory in 1910 – as well as for men. Electricity also powered the machines of mass production.*

LINKS IN THE INDUSTRIAL CHAIN (ABOVE) *Skilled workers in a metal plant in the United States producing parts needed in other manufacturing industries. With the use of new machine tools and standardized parts there was a gradual shift to semi-skilled and unskilled labour. The craftsman's pride in making something using his skill and training was no longer part of working experience.*

THE FLOW OF MASS PRODUCTION

IT WAS NOT THE MOVING ASSEMBLY LINE alone that revolutionized the way goods were produced. In factories of every kind, systems of organization such as the division of labour and the use of specialized machinery and equipment were all central to mass production. Improved transport networks meant that both raw materials and finished products could be taken over greater distances. Stronger, faster machine tools with greater precision and the use of lighter, more reliable metals made it easier to make standardized parts. Instead of skilled workers fitting metal parts that had to be cut to the right dimensions and then individually fitted with a hammer and file, unskilled workers could now simply assemble ready-made, interchangeable parts. The skill and long training of craftsmen became superfluous: now the skill was in the machine rather than in the coordinated eye and hand of human beings.

The workers and the way they worked came under scrutiny, and were also standardized. Believing that rationalization was the key to efficiency, F.W. Taylor developed a system he called Scientific Management in which the way people worked was analysed and reorganized. Complex tasks were broken down into simple, repetitive, timed jobs. This was designed to let man and machine work together to maximum capacity.

Instead of grouping general-purpose machines in separate buildings, under the new system the specialist machines were grouped around the point where they would be needed on the assembly line. Sub-assembly lines, like tributaries that flow into a river, fed the main assembly line with parts. The logic of flow production and the assembly line created factories on a scale the world had never seen before. Massive new industries were born – processing rubber to make tyres and glass for the windows. Everything possible was done to speed up and cut the cost of the manufacturing process.

WAR WORK *in a British munitions factory during the First World War. New manufacturing techniques were important in mass-producing weaponry. The war also brought thousands of women into factories for the first time to undertake jobs previously done by men. When peace returned many European factories adapted the techniques to make new consumer products along American lines.*

> "*If you had to build that car by hand, each piece, you couldn't afford to pay for it. But mass production, that's where the profit was, and that's where our jobs were.*"
>
> TOM JELLEY

BEFORE AND AFTER *Large, hand-built touring cars like the six-cylinder Ford model of 1906 (*ABOVE*) were costly: this model was priced at $2500. It was mass production combined with simpler design and finish that dramatically reduced the price; the new Ford Model T (*BELOW*) was a more rugged car which came only in standard black. By 1913 nearly every American town had a Ford dealer, and by 1915 there were over a million Model T cars in the United States, where a huge, widespread rural population boosted the market.*

Time and money

It was the assembly line that proved to be the real breakthrough in cheap, efficient mass production. In 1913, when the Ford Motor Company already employed 25 000 men making 500 cars a day, cars were still assembled on wooden 'horses', and the men moved from car to car. It took them twelve-and-a-half hours to finish each one. When the moving assembly line was installed, that time was reduced to an hour and a half. The Highland Park factory was transformed. Few of the assembly line workers took the time to think about the changes; they were too busy worrying about how to keep pace with the moving line.

One Ford worker, Jim Sullivan, sums up the changes. For the economy, he says, the assembly line was good. 'But if you were on that line and you had a certain job to do and the cars came by as fast as they did, and you didn't get your part on there, you were in trouble.' The new pace of work was relentless, monotonous and fast. The workers were expected to make more cars in the same time, and for the same wages. After a very short time no one wanted to work on the moving line; the men complained that they had become little more than servants of the machines. Only a few weeks after the assembly line first creaked into motion, ten workers were leaving for every one who stayed.

Henry Ford then came up with an idea as revolutionary in its way as the assembly line that had made it necessary. The new way of making cars was proving so profitable that he could afford to double the workers' pay by including them in a profit-sharing scheme. Further changes soon followed. On 5 January 1914 Ford reduced the working day to eight hours and added a third shift, instantly creating thousands of new jobs. And for those eight hours of work Ford paid an unheard-of $5 a day. It was more money for less time than anyone had ever paid factory workers.

Tens of thousands of new immigrants arrived in search of a job at Ford. 'They were coming here from all over the world,' remembers Tom Jelley, who worked at the Ford factory as a tool and die maker. 'All the different nationalities...they were piling

in here for the five or six dollars.' Detroit rapidly became a boom town. Archie Acciacca's family left Italy to seek a new life in the United States at that time. With some reluctance, his father got a job at Ford, where the high wages made even the unrelenting, back-breaking work of the assembly line worth it, at least for a while. 'At that time, five dollars a day was very big money....We were able to have a respectable, decent living. They put food on the table, had a rented place...with five dollars a day they were able to raise seven children.'

Ford had realized that his well-paid workers would in due course be able to buy his cars themselves. By paying more for a stable work force, he also guaranteed a new market among people who had never before dreamed of owning a car. Erv Dasher, who was twenty years old when he got his job at Ford, was delighted with his new pay packet. 'You were in the bucks – you could afford this, you could afford that and you could afford a new car.' Etta Warren became the first black woman to be employed by the Ford Motor Company. 'People here, they made money and they put it to good use. They all bought homes and bought cars and educated their children.'

PEER PRESSURE was intensified as each worker had to keep up with the production line in order to safeguard the job of the worker next to him. As the assembly line, built at waist-height for maximum efficiency, brings these flywheels to the workers it regulates their pace.

LINING UP for work (RIGHT). Many immigrants who settled in the United States found work in the new industries. But Archie Acciacca (ABOVE) remembers that his father soon left his job at Ford. 'The monotony of working that production line, day in day out, was too much for the man.'

AROUND THE CLOCK
*that regulates their working
lives, Italian auto workers at
the Fiat Corso Dante plant
in 1916 punch their time
cards as they begin and end
shifts. This rational
organization of the workplace
was adapted from the
American model.*

**FACTORY OF THE
FUTURE** (OPPOSITE) *A
poster illustrating plans for
the new Fiat works on the
outskirts of Turin in 1917.
Its test track for new cars was
on the roof. Giovanni Gobbi
remembers how highly people
spoke of it. 'A factory like
this one, with a track that
was so high up, was a bit
of a marvel in those days.'*

Life on the line

In 1924 Ford made its ten millionth Model T; by 1925 half the cars in the world were Model Ts. In the late 1920s the Ford Motor Company had established its assembly plants in parts of Asia, Australia, Canada, Europe, South Africa and South America. This was also a time when many other new goods – radios, irons, refrigerators, vacuum cleaners – were also being mass produced in factories where assembly lines had been introduced.

The European automobile industry, which had been slower to develop, also began to adapt to the new production methods. The heads of major European companies – André Citroën, Louis Renault, Giovanni Agnelli of Fiat, William Morris and Herbert Austin – all visited the United States to learn about the American methods. After adopting them, the French firm Citroën was able to make 400 cars a day. The largest French car factory of all, at Billancourt, belonged to Renault, which also set up plants in Britain and Germany.

In Italy Giovanni Agnelli also modelled his new factory in the Lingotto district of Turin on the American pattern of mass production, realizing that success in the market depended on it. 'Senator Agnelli and also the plant managers...were often in America, and they were on good terms with Ford. So what would happen there, we would try, if it was progress, to bring it over here,' remembers Giovanni Gobbi, who worked for Fiat.

In Europe, as in the United States, for the workers on the production line 'progress' meant working to rigorous new rules under strict controls, changes that were resented by workers at the Fiat Lingotto factory. When they decided to go on strike in 1922, the management responded by bringing in the army. Felice Gentile, posted to Turin, was one of the soldiers involved. Four machine guns were positioned around the plant, though they were not loaded. 'It was just to frighten the workers,' he says.

When Fiat installed new assembly lines in 1926 conditions in the plant became even more difficult. Felice Gentile, now out of the army, found himself on the other side when he himself took a job at Fiat. 'The atmosphere, the control, everything would go according to plans,' he remembers. 'The moulds, the timings, the pay – everything was programmed, and so we just had to submit

WORKERS' LEISURE

HAPPY WORKERS WERE PROFITABLE WORKERS. While conditions in the factories were sometimes stressful, the management of large companies in most industrialized countries did attempt to encourage their workers' leisure-time pursuits – football pitches, gyms, swimming pools and halls for leisure activities were often provided. Les Gurl was very impressed by the 'wonderful sports facilities' that Morris provided in Oxford. 'Every sport that a man or woman could take part in was supplied by the company.'

In the intensely political atmosphere of the 1930s governments also became involved in the efforts to give people something enjoyable to do after work, especially in Germany and Italy. In Nazi Germany a new movement called Kraft durch Freude, 'Strength through Joy', was launched with slogans such as 'Happiness on the bench means higher productivity'. German workers were offered cheap excursions to the Bavarian Alps and Italy, and sea cruises to the Norwegian fjords. In 1936 six million people took advantage of these facilities.

By that year two and three-quarter million workers in Italy were enrolled in the Opera Nazionale Dopolavoro (National Afterwork Agency), which held that 'greater well-being of personnel would have favourable effects on output'. What began as a social welfare agency had become a national movement to support the economy.

At Fiat Dopolavoro provision was extended after 1932 to reduce the level of discontent among workers. The aim was to transform a class-conscious workforce into an elite, isolated by its privileges from other groups of working people. Fiat workers' sense of being a close-knit, privileged community was bolstered by sports facilities and cultural events, including opera performances, symphony and band concerts, choirs and drama, and a 10 000-volume library. Fiat also published its own newspaper, *Bianco e Rosso* (white and red); it took its name from the colours of the leading professional football club, Juventus, which had emerged at Fiat.

When he worked there Giovanni Gobbi enjoyed the activities, though the uniformity required of factory workers was never far away. 'When we were in the Dopolavoro building the uniform was shorts or long white pants, and then a red jersey with Fiat written on it.' He remembers how the Fiat complex housed a film theatre, and rooms for 'reading, language lessons, music lessons, table games, chess and billiards'. In 1933 it became compulsory for all Fiat workers to join the Dopolavoro. The advantages of these facilities were genuine, even if they were provided as much in the interests of the factory as in the interests of the workers.

YOUNG EXPLORERS (LEFT) *on an outing in 1925, organized by the Fiat employees' association for their children before the Dopolavoro was introduced.*

to these norms. There were never any discussions. If someone did not follow the rules they would be punished, or moved away or given a different position.' Felice Gentile understood the pressures that had driven the workers to act. 'On the job, we would work and you couldn't smoke and even when you went to the toilet they would check to make sure the worker was sincere or if he was going for a chat. But if he stopped for a chat and a guard were to come by, or the foreman, or even a director and find him there in the toilets he would fire him.'

American time and motion study was used in the European factories too. Fifteen-year-old Giovanni Gobbi was told to time the men at work. 'My boss put a stopwatch into my hand and said, "Go and measure how long it takes to do that job".' He felt awkward. 'One of the first people I had to time was a man who could have been my grandfather....The poor man was working away and I was the young kid having to time him. It was awful.'

In Britain, the Morris car plant at Cowley, outside Oxford, introduced many of the techniques of mass production during the 1920s, though like other British factories at the time it did not yet use a moving assembly line. Instead of pacing production by speeding up the line, the Morris factory increased its output by continuing to pay workers on a piece rate system: in addition to an hourly wage they earned a bonus for getting ahead on production; falling behind the given quotas meant lower earnings.

Unlike their American counterparts, British workers were sometimes still able to use their initiative. As a teenage boy Les Gurl worked out a new way of supplying hinges so that the men could fit more of them in a given time. They were so grateful that one of the workers came up to him and said, 'Put your hands together.' And he poured nearly a week's wages into Les Gurl's hands, saying, 'If you can keep this up, we'll have a whip round for you every week.' Les Gurl was delighted. 'It allowed me to give my pay packet to my mother and still have a load of money. I could live like a lord.' The benefits of higher wages were set against the drawbacks the workers had to contend with: strict working conditions and management that assumed total control. They had no voice in the way the factory was run or the speed at which the line operated.

PIECE WORK *at the Morris car factory in Britain opened the door to prosperity for workers whose mastery of a particular task earned them higher wages. After the moving assembly line was introduced in 1934 the pace of work was transformed, as Les Gurl (*ABOVE RIGHT*) remembers. 'Say you have got twenty cars going up the line; you have only got a minute and a half, two minutes to do your job. If you are hanging a door, you have got to put three hinges on with nine screws in two minutes. You don't find any time to leave the job. You don't even get time to take a sandwich into work and eat it.'*

"If you had a job at Ford, you were made for life...they would say you have got the best job that is going in the country, no matter what you did. "

LEN SMITH

INDUSTRIAL GIANT *The ambitious Ford River Rouge plant became the hub of a national and international economic empire. By 1927 it had 145 km (90 miles) of railway track to link its ninety-three structures housing 53 000 machine tools and a huge workforce.*

Symbol of affluence

The Ford emblem represented not only the achievements of the tycoon whose name it bore; it also acted as a badge of identity for the thousands of factory workers who wore it on their overalls. It gave the Briton Les Holder, who worked at Ford, a measure of respect in the community. 'It was one of the main sources of employment in the area, and once you got the Ford badge,' he remembers, 'you were treated very highly by the shopkeepers in the area because the rate of pay was superior to any other at the time.'

For workers in the United States, discipline in the factories grew even tighter as competition among major car manufacturers increased the need to step up production even further. 'They were dictatorial, slave-drivers,' remembers Warren Hart, who started working at Ford in 1919. 'You had a set figure to produce...and if you didn't do that, then you were criticized or maybe moved to another location.' John DeAngelo was sixteen years old when he and his father went to work at Highland Park. He stayed at Ford for the rest of his working life, but his father lasted less than a day. 'Look,' he told his son, 'if you want to stay here, you stay here. I think these people are crazy. I wouldn't work here.' He found it so bad that he did not even go back to collect his pay for the three hours he had worked.

In 1927 work was finally completed on a new Ford factory on the River Rouge in Dearborn, Michigan, and in December of that year Ford introduced a new car, the Model A, to replace the now outmoded Model T. The River Rouge plant was the biggest factory complex in the world, employing some 80 000 people. It included a foundry to make steel for the car bodies, an electricity generating plant, a glass works, a railway and a port – all the manufactured and raw materials needed to make the cars were owned by the company. Iron ore, coal, sand and rubber went in at one end, and Model As drove out the other.

THE COMPANY TOWN

LOW-COST COMPANY HOMES were provided for workers in the mill towns and villages of industrial Britain and the United States long before the days of mass production. Pioneered for textile workers in Scotland and in the United States, the company town continued to flourish until the 1930s.

Some companies experimented with model communities. In addition to housing set in attractive landscapes and green parks, workers and their families were offered education, recreational and sometimes cultural facilities. In the town of Bourneville, built by the British firm of Cadbury, employees were offered gardening classes as an antidote to the tedium of the factory; medical care and social reforms were also introduced. At Port Sunlight in Britain, a model industrial village built for the workers of the Lever Brothers soap and detergent company, residents had access to clubs, a theatre, a church and an art gallery; houses were built there until 1934. N.O. Nelson, a manufacturer of plumbing equipment, went even further, providing residents of Leclaire, Illinois with a library, dance pavilion and cooperative stores. The town's population grew from 400 workers in 1890 to 2000 in 1934.

Company towns were not always appreciated by those who lived in them. The paternalistic policies of employers were often reinforced; they took responsibility not just for people's jobs but for the homes and personal lives of their workers. Workers could not own their homes, and had little say in local affairs. In some towns there were even rules governing behaviour. Residents of some of the mill villages redesigned for the growing textile industries of the southern United States from 1917 were not allowed to smoke or drink; their children, who left school at an early age to work in the factory, received instructions in industrial discipline. Strict guidelines for cleanliness and hygiene in the home issued by Johnson & Johnson in its factory town in Chicopee, Georgia were enforced by company nurses.

Some company towns were isolated from the outside world, and the constant presence of the factory and its pollution could shadow domestic life. Irene Keyser, who worked for Westinghouse Electric in the United States in the 1920s and grew up in its factory town, remembers how 'people worked very hard on their homes to keep them clean...the porches we had to clean every day because the smoke, little black cinders, would come right up to the porch.'

From about 1925, while mill villages declined as a result of changing social conditions, several companies in the American West – Climax in Colorado, DuPont in Washington and Trona in California – continued to build new towns around their factories. From the 1930s, however, workers increasingly resented the dependence the company town imposed, and changing industrial relations brought a revision of company responsibility.

WORKING COMMUNITIES *Not all families benefited from the improved housing companies could provide. Attracted by employment prospects in local industries, families such as this one in Pennsylvania in 1938 often put up with poor living conditions because of the need to live close to where the work was to be found.*

MAN AND MACHINE *are the focus of* Modern Times, *a phenomenally successful Charlie Chaplin film made in 1936 about the manic nature of factory work. It brought the message of the overpowering character of modern industry to many people who had never experienced the inside of a factory for themselves.*

Following in his father's footsteps, Archie Acciacca got a job at the River Rouge where he was put in the stamping plant. He had been raised on a farm in the countryside and this was his first experience of factory work. 'When I first went in there,' he describes, 'I saw people working rather fast and I was wondering if I could do that.' Like most people, he got accustomed to it. 'Once you start that production going…you have just got to think, I have got to keep up with this line, because if you didn't keep up with the line, you're in trouble.' As John DeAngelo remembers, 'You have got to make that production for them. If you weren't feeling good you couldn't say, I don't feel good so let me rest a couple of minutes, that was out of the question.'

In Britain plans were progressing for a scaled-down version of the River Rouge plant to replace the Manchester-based Ford factory, now unable to keep up with demand. The chosen site was at Dagenham, east of London. It was to be three times the size of Trafford Park, and like the Rouge, fully integrated, with access to the river Thames and a railway to bring in materials.

NEW CAR MODELS (RIGHT) *like the highly successful 1928 Chevrolet, which outsold its Ford rivals, were a sign of the increasingly competitive nature of the motor industry. General Motors came to include not only Chevrolet but also – in ascending order of cost –Pontiac, Oldsmobile, Buick and Cadillac, establishing it as one of the United States' leading car manufacturers. By 1930 the United States dominated the world car market.*

Work at any price

As the world economic depression of 1929 began to have an impact on the car industry, profits fell. The Model A Ford, outsold by rival cars, was discontinued. As sales plunged the River Rouge factory no longer needed to take on more workers. 'Thousands and thousands of people had been invited to come to this area, to work here,' as Paul Boatin remembers. 'They were being lied to.' Those lucky enough still to have a job needed to keep it at all costs. Mass unemployment in other industries meant that there were always new workers ready to fill the place of anyone who was dissatisfied, failed to keep up with the pace of production, or complained when wages were reduced.

Paul Boatin and his father joined the large crowd waiting for a job outside the Ford gates, across Miller Road. 'The majority of people just stood and stood, and waited and waited. You had a bunch of strangers, expressionless, looking down at the ground. They looked like they were half dead, hopeless. And when you looked into their eyes you thought maybe that is what you looked like too.' Espedito Valli, whose father already worked at Ford, remembers how cold it was waiting there. 'We stood out there in the yards, in a parking lot, like cattle out in the yard....We had to put newspaper under our coats, under our jackets, under our shirts, in order to stay warm....We stood in the severe cold for three, four hours at a time.'

There were similar queues outside the new Ford plant at Dagenham. When it opened in 1931, Britain too was in the depths of the Depression. The new factory brought much-needed work. Fred Ferguson grew up in Dagenham, and had seen the factory being built. Now he watched the influx of people in search of work. 'Two thousand workers with their families, which amounted to 7000 people, descended on Dagenham,' he recalls. Les Holder got a job there, and had to adjust to the new rhythm of work on the line. 'Start at half past seven. Finish at 12 noon. Half an hour lunch. Back on the job until 4 pm. These operations were very quick. So it was pick up, put it in the machine, clamp, press the button, drill the holes, retract, unclamp, and that is how it went on the whole time.' He made a hundred parts an hour.

HIRING AND FIRING
employees at short notice was one direct effect of the Depression. Espedito Valli (ABOVE) remembers how his father 'was laid off about three times from 1929 to 1932' by Ford, which wrote him this letter confirming his fluctuating employment for tax purposes. When Espedito Valli finally got a job at Ford he wanted to leave. 'It was work, work, work – like a slave. You couldn't even move away from the assembly line where I worked without getting reprehended for it.'

VEHICLE OF CHANGE

MASS PRODUCTION on the land as well as in industry was made possible with the development of a new source of mobile power for the farm – the tractor. For hundreds of years farmers had depended on their own muscles and on horse power to plough their land and harvest their crops. It was at the turn of the century that tractors first began to replace horse and human power, and gradually took agricultural production to new heights.

The first tractor was made in Illinois in 1889; soon manufacturers in Canada and the United States began to design mobile machines, some with wheels and some with tracks, for ploughing. More farms adapted to new machinery, while many farm workers and their families were leaving the land to find new jobs in factories and cities. Tractors enabled the farmer both to save labour costs and to cultivate land that had once been needed to grow fodder for the horses.

The first large market for tractors was in North America. In 1907 there were some six hundred tractors in the United States; by 1950 there were 3.4 million. The Fordson tractor, first made in 1917, was a huge success, and Ford quickly monopolized the home market. The Canadian manufacturers Massey Harris were eventually to become the world's largest tractor manufacturer.

In the 1920s, as agricultural production in Europe was picking up after the First World War, tractor sales to prosperous farmers increased there too. Adapting to the new tractors was not always easy. Len Sharman, who worked on a farm in Britain, can remember how the Fordsons were 'real demons to start in the cold mornings.... There was no cab. I've had two overcoats on, two pairs of gloves, a pair of leggings, and still been so frozen I could howl with cold.'

As the rest of the world faced economic depression in the 1930s, the economy of the Soviet Union was expanding. Tractors began to play an important part in the attempt to meet the demanding new agricultural production targets. Thousands of tractor machine stations were set up to hire out tractors to collective farms. As well as importing thousands of machines from the United States, and the spare parts and expert advice needed to operate them, the Soviet Union began to produce its own tractors: the Stalingrad works alone were making 50 000 tractors a year by 1930, and within ten years there were more than half a million tractors at work. In just one generation, the tractor had transformed the age-old patterns of farming and brought mass production to agriculture.

TIME FOR TRACTORS
It was in Germany that stationary gasoline engines were first adapted for use in agriculture. Lanz was one of several companies that began to manufacture tractors at an early stage. By the late 1930s there were 60 000 tractors in Germany, which was also beginning to mass produce its highly successful version of the people's car – the Volkswagen.

The workers were under constant pressure to keep up, and men from the security lodge would walk along the overhead catwalk to ensure they did. 'If you were eating a sandwich or an apple, or not paying attention, or talking, that would be put down as a misdemeanour,' Les Holder recalls. 'There was always a queue of people outside the gate waiting to come in. You were paid by the hour, but you were dismissed by the minute.' It was the same at the Morris factory, as Les Gurl remembers. 'The foreman had absolute power over everybody who was in his shop, to hire and fire....You knew that those men were waiting outside the gates, so you never gave them a chance to get your job.'

In the United States the effects of the Depression were at their worst by 1932 in most manufacturing industries. David Moore, still waiting for a job at Ford, noticed a change in the atmosphere. 'The momentum was gaining every day. People were taking action. The people were in motion and it was all because of hunger, denial, disease, unemployment.' Discontent in Detroit

grew as, with no prior warning, the assembly lines came to a halt and the mighty Rouge plant was shut down. Anger erupted in Miller Road. Ford had promised work, but there was none. The men felt betrayed. Paul Boatin remembers, 'Ford said, "Anybody that wants to work, unless he's lazy, let him come," so we marched down towards Gate 3, the heart of the Ford Motor Company.'

As the workers in their thousands marched down Miller Road, they encountered a cordon of armed police. David Moore describes what happened. 'None of us were armed, we didn't come there to confront anyone. But you can imagine 80 000 people marching down a road, and for no reason at all on a cold day in March, six below zero, the water hoses are turned on you. And to see your friend being shot, blood running on Miller Road. All hell broke loose and that made people more determined than ever to do something. Out of that came a bond of brotherhood.' As Paul Boatin says, 'Instead of getting jobs, we got lead, we got bullets and blood. The workers had made their point, even though they didn't get any jobs.' Four men were killed at Miller Road that day. It marked a turning point for the men and women who worked on the American assembly lines.

STRIKING WORKERS

scuffle with police outside a Cadillac plant in Detroit. One of them struggles to hold aloft a placard bearing the slogan: 'This line is rough on rats'.

PAUL BOATIN (ABOVE) *and his fellow workers were featured in a mural based on the River Rouge plant by the Mexican artist Diego Rivera, commissioned by the Detroit Institute of Art. Paul Boatin describes its impact. 'The muscles, the brows, the strength that was shown in the faces was intimidating to some people because if they ever came off the wall they might prove dangerous.'*

Industrial action

The United Auto Workers (UAW) now began to recruit members among the workers of Detroit's car plants. The union offered hope of change to workers who had few means of bargaining with their employers over conditions, pay and hours of work, and who were under constant threat of dismissal. 'It was born out of desperation,' says Charlie White, who worked at the Fisher Body plant, part of the General Motors group. 'We'd just as soon there wasn't a need for a union. If they would give us what they rightfully should give us, there would be no need for it. But they couldn't see it.' Jim Sullivan, who worked at the Rouge, remembers how in the 1930s unions were associated with the radical element, and at first were treated with suspicion. But as they became more dissatisfied, the workers began to pay more attention to the union movement.

At first people often joined secretly, and did not necessarily tell even members of their own family. Jim Sullivan discovered that his father was a union member only during a discussion at the Sunday dinner table. 'I said to him, "Dad, if I stay at Ford's it's going to be a miracle. I don't like the way they are treating the people." So he said, "Well, Jim, you've got two things you can do. You can either quit or join the union." And I said, "Well, Dad, I belong to the union." And he said, "Thank God," and with that he flipped his collar and there was his union button.'

It could be dangerous to join the union. Ford's Protection Department employed strong-armed security men who watched union organizers carefully, intimidating and even assaulting them. Workers were scared of losing their jobs, and scared of the power of the Protection Department. Tom Jelley remembers how the department's boss, Harry Bennett, 'had the whole say of running the plant. And his goons, they would go into the toilets and you were sitting down there, and they would say, "Out!" – just like that. No dignity at all. So far as I'm concerned, that was one thing that brought the union in here.'

At the Morris factory in Cowley working conditions also deteriorated after four assembly lines were installed there in 1934. Some of the Morris workers decided to protest; in 1935 there was a stoppage in the B block trim shop. Lord Nuffield, as William Morris was now called, was as hostile to the unions as Henry Ford

A UNION MEMBERSHIP CARD *Joining the union was an important step for Steven Richvalsky, who worked at General Motors from 1935. But he remembers that the management's refusal to recognize or tolerate the unions made it necessary to be secretive. 'We were organizing clandestinely… no one was aware of it because if you got caught talking unionism at that time, you were automatically fired. You were finished. No questions asked, nothing.'*

TAKING A STAND
A crowd of strikers' families gathers outside New Bedford Mill in the United States in 1928 to listen to the president of Workers' International Relief. Powerful craft unions had long been established in the textile, engineering and coal mining industries. Public meetings helped to inform workers about their rights.

WORKERS FIND A VOICE

THE NEW INDUSTRIES of the early twentieth century created a great mass of unskilled workers. Trade unions had originally been established to protect the wages and working conditions of skilled artisans and craftsmen; in the changing industrial climate a new 'industrial' unionism came into existence, not just to protect workers but to demand industrial power and also protection from the state.

Britain's old craft unions were supplemented by the rising number of unions recruiting unskilled or semi-skilled labourers, and transformed by their adoption of socialism. The union movement was represented by the Trades Union Congress (TUC).

During the First World War unions supported the war effort and accepted wartime controls. Shop stewards were elected to represent their fellow-workers' interests in discussions with management. After the war industrial relations deteriorated, coming to a head in the General Strike of 1926 when workers went on a sympathy strike in May after miners were threatened with pay cuts and longer working hours. During the 1930s more people joined the unions, which adapted in response to the changes in working conditions as mass production methods became more widespread. By 1935 there were four million union members in Britain.

In France, Germany and Italy the growth of unions was disrupted and concealed by wars, revolution and foreign occupation. Only after 1945 did powerful industrial unions, in some countries organized in communist, socialist or Roman Catholic federations, transform industrial relations. In the Soviet Union the communists succeeded in doing what the Italian fascists and German Nazis had also tried to do – making the trade unions subject to the ruling party and the machinery of the state.

In the United States the craft unions that formed the American Federation of Labor (AFL) had two million members by 1914, but here too the majority of unskilled workers, especially immigrants, women and black men, remained unaffiliated to unions in the booming industries of the 1920s – automobiles, steel, glass, electrical manufacturing. In 1935 John L Lewis led the way for unionization of these industries by forming the Committee for Industrial Organization (CIO). Soon workers in many mass production industries began to join CIO unions in large numbers, donning union badges and carrying membership cards.

Auto and steel workers strengthened their voice through the United Auto Workers (UAW) and the Steel Workers' Organizing Committee. By 1945 union membership reached an all-time high of almost fifteen million, more than 35 per cent of the non-agricultural workforce. Four million people were members of the CIO, which was eager to recruit black workers, and the rest belonged to the AFL. Many workers, especially new immigrants and black migrants from the South, were helped to join the mainstream of American economic and social life through their unions.

in Detroit and Giovanni Agnelli in Turin. 'Lord Nuffield reacted very quickly,' Les Gurl remembers. 'He put up large notices saying that he would not tolerate the union in his plant, and if the feeling in the plant among the people working there became strong enough to form a union, then he would shut the plant down.' Despite this threat, union leaders in Britain also recruited widely.

In the mid-1930s, as the Depression lifted, business at Ford was booming again. In 1935 alone Ford produced a million cars. Paul Boatin, David Moore and Espedito Valli finally managed to get jobs at the Rouge and a chance to earn a living, but at a price. 'We had to become complete strangers. You were being turned into a dead weight...worse than being a cog,' says Paul Boatin. 'Forget all the people that you had met out there. Forget all the bonds that you had established, forget all the new understandings, the little things we had told to one another. You felt complete frustration and isolation.' As they became angrier, workers began to talk in whispers about joining the union. David Moore, who was working in the foundry, met someone who said, ' "We're going to get a union in this place". He gave me some literature, and said, "Don't let anybody see you. Just put it in your pocket and read it when you get home." ' In mass production industries throughout the nation workers began to respond to greater drives for unionization made by the American Federation of Labour. Factory workers in their thousands began to join the newly formed Committee for Industrial Organization.

It was in France that the alienation and frustration of life on the line first boiled over into organized protest. Against a background of political turmoil a series of strikes erupted in 1936. They began in the aircraft and car factories, and then spread all over the country to different kinds of industries – to workers in department stores, hotels, restaurants and on farms. In May 35 000 auto workers in the Renault factory decided to stop working, incensed by speed-ups on the assembly line caused by higher production targets. 'We went from assembling 100 parts an hour to 110 and from there to 120,' remembers Arthur Herbaux. One day something snapped. 'We'd had enough. We weren't machines.'

The Renault workers downed their tools and occupied the factory. Their families brought them food. Management called in

"**Y**ou couldn't tell a white man from a black man in the foundry – dust, smoke, the iron, sweat, the toilets....No consideration for an individual's health....The conditions in the plant at that time were almost unbearable. "

DAVID MOORE

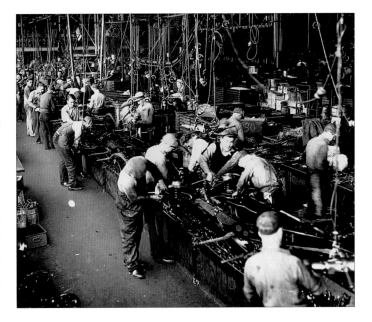

HARD AT WORK *Factory workers were often surrounded by loud and sometimes dangerous machinery. As Archie Acciacca remembers, 'When that press would come down and hit that die and there's thousands of machines operating at one time, it was very, very noisy.'*

DWARFED BY THE MIGHTY MACHINE (OPPOSITE)
A worker at the Fiat factory in Turin in 1934 poses beside the huge press from which he is pulling a red-hot steel crankshaft. During the 1930s the Fiat press office released a number of publicity photographs that glorified the power and beauty of machinery. Under fascism people were servants of the state as they were servants of the enterprises for which they worked.

"*You have no idea what a tremendous joy it was for everybody to get paid holidays. The whole of Paris, all the workshops, all the factories, everywhere people went crazy.*"

RACHEL LALLEMENT

ZENAIDE PROVINS (ABOVE AND LEFT), *who worked at a plastics factory in France, took part in the workers' strikes in 1936. 'The men occupied the factories and the women would go there every day,' she remembers. 'We were pretty organized really. We played cards, we danced – we managed to have some fun too, it wasn't all bad.'*

the police. The workers locked the doors to keep them out. 'That's how the fight started,' Arthur Herbaux remembers. 'People hurled bolts, bits of wood, chairs...at the police to stop them from getting into the factories....I'm not saying it was right to occupy the factory,' he reflects, 'but it was necessary. The way we lived, the money we earned, it wasn't right. It had to change. We had to strike to get it, we had to get angry.' And it did bring changes. Social reform bills were passed through parliament. As well as a statutory forty-hour week they won holidays with pay. One factory worker, Zenaide Provins, took her very first holiday at the seaside. 'Although I was a Breton and I'd grown up just thirty kilometres away, I'd never seen it.'

The Renault workers had successfully demonstrated the vulnerability of the assembly line in the face of collective action. At the Rouge, union organizers also grew bolder. Jim Sullivan began secretly recruiting union members in his welding booth away from the watchful eye of the security men. David Moore was arrested for passing out union literature. In 1937 John DeAngelo also joined the UAW; many others were doing the same. But Ford retaliated. 'They started to fire people because they were active in the union, so then at Ford's it died out,' John DeAngelo recalls.

In 1937 another confrontation over recognition of the union erupted. This time it was between workers and management at the General Motors plant in Flint, Michigan. Howard Washburn remembers how it began. When he went to his workstation, 'The foreman said, "Let's go to work". We said, "No, we are not working, we are on strike".' For several weeks workers controlled the Fisher Body Plant No. 2 in a sit-down strike, resisting the police and soldiers of the National Guard until the company finally agreed to recognize the union.

For Howard Washburn the success of the strike meant that the workers now had a new voice. 'If you had a grievance you could have somebody to take it up for you...and they set up a seniority system, which they never had before.' He realized that the workers at General Motors in Flint were lucky compared with their Ford counterparts. 'Ford was terrible. He was the biggest anti-union person in the world....They had some terrible times.' The victory of workers at General Motors inspired others to act.

In 1941 union organizers at the Ford factory tried again. Paul Boatin saw one union official assaulted by company service men for speaking publicly to the workers. 'They pulled his coat over his head and they broke his ribs. They were trying to teach the union a lesson.' The assault had the opposite effect. The spark that set off the final explosion was a fight between a foreman and a worker; at this, the workers decided to strike. 'Force was going to get us what we wanted,' says John DeAngelo.

The Rouge was shut down again, but this time the workers were in control. When David Moore pushed a red button to stop the assembly line, his foreman immediately rushed over to him.

'"What the hell do you think you're doing?" I said, "Strike! Strike!" Everybody went out hollering, "Strike! Strike!"' All they had to do, Jim Sullivan remembers, was shout, '"We're on strike!" I felt real good. I was jigging and dancing. I made history, I shut down the Ford Motor Company!' Archie Acciacca was working the afternoon shift when he heard what was happening, and he shut down his press. 'Masses of people got together. Some of them went over there with crowbars and what have you, and busted the windows....The whole plant shut down that afternoon.' John DeAngelo recalls how 'a big march went to Gate 4 and all around. And we picketed there, until seven days later Henry Ford said, "Get these people in here and give them what they want".'

Working together

Ford signed its first contract with the UAW in July 1941. The contract guaranteed the assembly line workers a seniority system, health insurance and a pension. It also gave them something more than that. Jim Sullivan sums up what he felt that was. 'You got a little bit of human dignity,' he says. 'You had someone standing with you. Before, you had nothing to say about anything. In order to make progress you have got to learn to walk. In order to walk, you have to get off your knees. And that is what we did in 1941. We got off our knees, and we took some giant steps.' For Archie Acciacca things went from one extreme to the other, 'From almost being a slave to being the guy that is running the plant.'

After the conflicts between mass production workers and management, which had been centred on the car industry, both sides came to realize that it was in their interest for factories to run smoothly. The workers gained greater recognition and were able to participate in decisions about what they did and how they did it, even if management stayed in control; the workers recognized that ultimately their pay depended on efficient production. Trade unions continued to grow as the United States entered the Second World War, and its factories concentrated on war production as those in Europe had already done. The war became more than a military conflict; the speed and efficiency of industrial production became part of the international struggle, and an essential element in the effort to defend democracy and freedom.

'Strike is settled' *announces the newspaper headline to the delight and relief of the workers at the Fisher body plant who had put their jobs at risk in the struggle for better working conditions. Now these men, many of whom had remained in the factory throughout the weeks of the occupation, could return home to their families.*

Industrial mobilization (opposite) *became top priority as the United States prepared for war in 1941. As civilian car production was set aside for war production, women filled the places of the workers who had gone to war. Britain's factories had begun making weapons in 1935; after 1939 factories in France, Germany, Italy and the Soviet Union were relocated to remote sites to avoid air attacks. By 1945 a fifth of the United States' military output had come from its automobile factories.*

Sporting Fever

THE GROWING APPEAL OF SPORT

THE CENTENARIO STADIUM in Montevideo, Uruguay's capital, was so new at the start of the 1930 World Cup that the concrete was still soft. The Uruguayans were proud to be hosting this new event, and to be welcoming European teams to their country.

In the final the Uruguayan team met their neighbours and arch-rivals, the Argentinians, who had beaten them just once a few years before. When its team crossed the River Plate to Uruguay a popular Argentinian newspaper boasted, 'The World Champions Return to Montevideo'. A Uruguayan football coach, Ondino Viera, recalls the reaction this provoked. 'This was a declaration of war, and the championship developed into a great war between Uruguay and Argentina.'

On the day of the final supporters began to fill the stadium in the early hours of the morning. Some 90 000 fans managed to get in; a multitude had to stay outside. At half-time the Argentinians led by two goals to one. Gradually they gave way before the storm of sound from the stands and the sheer will to win of the Uruguayan team. Two-all.

Three-two. Four-two to Uruguay.

All through the night church bells rang, car horns blared, and ships' sirens wailed down at the waterfront, and the following day was declared a national holiday. Ondino Viera joined in the celebrations in Montevideo with some friends. 'The scene was almost indescribable...the celebrations began at the stadium and extended through all the streets of Montevideo. The enthusiasm included everyone: men, women and children....The parties lasted all week.' In Buenos Aires the defeated Argentinians raged; mobs took to the streets, even stoning the Uruguayan consulate, and diplomatic relations between the two countries were broken off.

Football was one of the many sports that both brought people together and divided them during the twentieth century. Sport could bring new opportunities, becoming a road to fame for poor children; it developed into an enormous industry, and reflected the competitiveness and pride of nations. It attracted millions of people, both as players and as spectators, as sporting fever spread across the world.

EMBRACING VICTORY *Triumphant Uruguayan players rejoice in their success in the first World Cup.*

123

CROWDS LINE THE STREETS *to watch the cyclists flash by. Local and national press follow the progress of the great Tour de France all over the country. Launched at the beginning of the century as a publicity venture to improve sales of a new sporting newspaper, the race quickly became popular. Initially covering more than 2000 km (1250 miles), its route soon extended over 5745 km (3570 miles).*

Amateurs and professionals

By the time the 1930 World Cup took place in Uruguay, English football had already become firmly established as a professional sport played for mass audiences. At the turn of the century it was played in many countries throughout the world – from Austria, Belgium, France, Germany, the Netherlands, Russia, Sweden, Switzerland and Turkey to South America. It was introduced by the British, whose children played football, rugby and cricket in the private schools and who as adults continued to play for personal enjoyment rather than for financial gain. Similarly, in Canada and the United States baseball, boxing and American football, which developed out of college rugby, were played at an amateur level. By 1900 there were also professional footballers and cricketers in Britain, and professional baseball players and boxers in the United States. Separate organizations catered for professionals, who needed to play for money, and for amateurs, who could afford to play for pleasure.

The amateur ideal of playing for enjoyment of the game and the desire to win, rather than for money, inspired the revival of the ancient Greek Olympic Games by a Frenchman, Baron Pierre de Coubertin. The first modern Games, held in 1896, also took place in Greece. The amateur ethic was at first rigidly enforced. At the 1912 Olympics in Stockholm, an American athlete forfeited his medals after it had been revealed that he once accepted payment for playing baseball in a minor league. At this stage the talent and skill of individuals was regarded as more important than national pride and prestige, though from the 1908 Games competitors entered as members of national teams rather than as individuals.

National pride became all too real during the First World War. When it ended and the troops returned, people could begin to settle back into peacetime life and interest in sport revived. In the 1920s the number of hours in the average working week was reduced, and at the same time wages were increased. There was a hunger for excitement among those who had more leisure time to enjoy and more money to spend, and by the 1920s sport began to attract larger and larger audiences. Sports journalism ensured that people could read about their favourite game in the new sporting magazines and newspapers, while sport itself offered exciting

LEADING MARATHON RUNNER *Dorando Pietri in the 1908 Olympics. In a gesture characteristic of the times, when he collapsed at the finishing line officials helped him across it.*

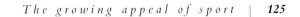

TURNING TO TENNIS

THE YOUNG FRENCH TENNIS STAR Suzanne Lenglen caused a sensation when she appeared at Wimbledon in the 1919 British championships. She was a formidable player who, wearing a simple, calf-length, sleeveless dress that attracted as much comment as her sporting prowess, successfully challenged not only her opponents but also existing attitudes to women in sport. She fuelled women's sporting aspirations by winning six championships in Britain, six in France, and two gold medals at the 1920 Olympic Games. The press, devoting more space to sport as its popularity grew, needed players who could be fashioned into sporting personalities, and Suzanne Lenglen gained worldwide fame.

At the turn of the century tennis was one of the limited number of sports that were regarded as suitable activities for women. It was possible to play badminton, croquet and golf, to dance, ride and skate in the long, heavy clothes and restricting corsets that women were accustomed to wearing; but it was difficult to be more active until new freedoms were expressed in new fashions.

At a time when women were struggling for political recognition and for better opportunities in education, their participation in many sports was also deliberately obstructed. The arguments against higher education – that too much study would damage women's health in general and their ability to have children in particular – were also given as reasons for discouraging women from playing any but the most genteel sports. Field sports and team games were both deemed unsuitable, and only non-competitive gymnastics were acceptable. At the 1908 Olympic Games there were only three events in which women could compete. Both gymnastics and track and field events were excluded from the 1920 and 1924 Games. In defiance of this policy, separate Women's Olympics were held at four-yearly intervals between 1922 and 1934; they attracted competitors from many parts of the world, and drew many spectators too. Gradually, women's place in sport began to be accepted as it was in other fields.

entertainment to people looking for ways to enjoy themselves. John Cracknell, a cricket and football enthusiast, remembers how important sport was when he was growing up in London. 'There weren't the activities in those days that there are now....Sport was the great thing in your life.' As public interest grew, commercial interest in sport also gained momentum.

LEAPING TO VICTORY

Suzanne Lenglen competing at Wimbledon, where she dominated the Centre Court for six years.

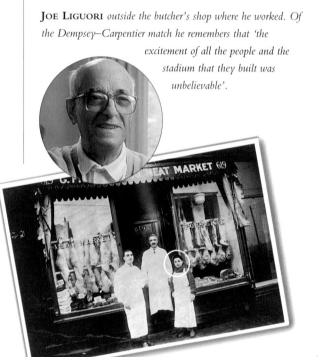

JOE LIGUORI *outside the butcher's shop where he worked. Of the Dempsey–Carpentier match he remembers that 'the excitement of all the people and the stadium that they built was unbelievable'.*

THE HUGE ARENA (RIGHT) *that Tex Rickard had ambitiously conceived to stage the 1921 world heavyweight boxing championship was built within weeks. By filling it to capacity he demonstrated sport's great potential for entertaining huge audiences.*

A growing audience

Professional boxing showed the direction in which sport was now heading, by demonstrating how much money could be made. It had always attracted money; betting on the outcome of a prize-fight had been popular ever since boxing rose above the level of street brawls. An American boxing promoter, Tex Rickard, was one of the first to capitalize on its great money-making potential. In 1921 he staged a match in New Jersey between the American fighter Jack Dempsey and a French war hero, Georges Carpentier. Dempsey had been a professional boxer since 1914, and became world champion at his first attempt in 1919. To accommodate the huge crowd he intended to draw, Rickard built a temporary wooden stadium in an empty plot in Jersey City. Joe Liguori, who was twelve years old at the time, lived just down the street. 'I used to come and watch them build the stadium,' he remembers. 'It was a very exciting thing to see. And they built it in such a short time. Within a matter of weeks they had it up.'

Before long the novelty and scale of Rickard's plans and the unprecedented media promotion he obtained promised to justify his claim that this would be the fight of the century. Fans came from as far away as California and even Europe. Joe Liguori was

taken to the match by his boss. 'I was all excited about it – at that age I had never been to a fight. On the night of the fight you couldn't walk the street there were so many people around. The whole downtown area of Jersey City was just cluttered with cars. It was one of the biggest events I remember....It put Jersey City right on the map.'

Hundreds of reporters and telegraph operators arrived to relay the news to the world on live radio. More than 90 000 people poured into the stadium, the largest crowd ever assembled for a sporting event. Admission prices rose to as much as fifty dollars, the highest ever charged. The audience included celebrities whose presence gave a new stamp of social approval to this once renegade sport. The fight of the century was a short one. It was all over by the fourth round: Jack Dempsey won, and rose to superstardom overnight. Tex Rickard became a rich man; altogether Dempsey made him over $10 million. Boxing was now mainstream popular entertainment for thousands of people. The purpose-built stadium was dismantled shortly afterwards, but the big business of mass sport was here to stay.

THE LUXURY LIMOUSINE *beloved of Jack Dempsey – he owned six of them – symbolizes the affluent lifestyle his boxing success brought him. Winning the world heavyweight championship against French boxer Georges Carpentier (*TOP*, featured on the cover of a monthly magazine) established Dempsey as a popular hero who had risen from obscurity to fame and fortune.*

STREET FOOTBALL, *unlike many other sports, required no special equipment or location. Wherever adults had established football, children too could be found playing the game, reflecting football's fast-growing popularity.*

Spectator's passions

The Dempsey–Carpentier fight proved such a successful business venture for Rickard because it provided wonderful entertainment. People were prepared to pay to watch the spectacle. The 1920s were not as prosperous in Europe as they were in the United States, and people had less money to spare than their American counterparts, but in Britain too people now worked fewer hours a week and sport played an important part in their lives. Billy O'Donnell grew up in Liverpool; he remembers the times as 'bad days – squalor, disease, vermin…it was terrible.' In the summer he played football barefoot in the street. 'We'd make a ball out of rags, old clothing or paper, with string, and we'd be playing till eleven or twelve at night.' For him and many like him, sport, and football in particular, provided a welcome escape from the poverty and hardship of the postwar years. For Sidney Garner, a loyal supporter of the London team West Ham, football provided 'relief from work, from war…it was a way out. In the late 1920s the times were very hard.'

The enthusiasm that drew large crowds to watch boxing, and the even more popular baseball, in the United States, had also taken root in Britain. Football had become a passion, especially among people in the industrial north of England and in Scotland. Before 1900 a handful of professional teams had attracted huge crowds in Liverpool, Manchester, Newcastle and Glasgow, and public support for the game grew rapidly throughout the country. By the 1920s there were more than eighty professional football clubs. When he was a little older and could earn some money, Billy O'Donnell went to watch his local team play every Saturday. 'It was always football in Liverpool. Nothing else. That was the only recreation at the weekend. There was very little on at the cinemas. Football was the main thing for most lads my age. You looked forward to Saturday coming. There was an old-time fruit market where I lived, and I'd go there at six o'clock in the morning to earn a few coppers. If I earned a sixpence I'd give half to my mother and

I'd put the other threepence away so I could go to the match on a Saturday. Everything, as far as I was concerned, was football on a Saturday. I sold papers as well to boost it up. Things were really bad in those days.' He could not afford a seat in the covered stand, so with his friends he would stand on the open terraces, following the game in all weathers, one week from the Kop, the cheap end at Liverpool football club's ground at Anfield, the next week at Goodison Park, home of Liverpool's great rivals, Everton.

The football industry was growing quickly and becoming increasingly commercial, but the ritual gathering of fans and their passionate team loyalties remained. Sidney Garner would turn up at matches to support West Ham wearing a hat and scarf in the team colours, brandishing his rattle. Football became a focal point for whole communities, with friends meeting regularly at the weekly match to enjoy themselves together. 'I would go with most of my footballing pals....Saturday or Sunday we'd all go together,' Sidney Garner recalls.

As more and more fans flocked into the spectator stands, new and larger stadiums were needed to accommodate them. In 1923 a new stadium complex opened at Wembley, in the London

Football cards

COLLECTING CIGARETTE CARDS *was a popular pastime for football fans. As Billy O'Donnell explains, 'If you got ten cigarettes you got a picture....That's if you could afford to buy the ciggies. They went in sets of about fifty. If you didn't have one or two, you could swap them with your friend – maybe he'd have what you didn't have.'*

SIDNEY GARNER (BELOW, *in the top hat) and his friends followed their team around the country, jubilant when it won and broken-hearted when it lost. Thousands of supporters turned up for every match, following the game and enjoying the shared excitement.*

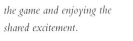

FILLING IN THE COUPON
(BELOW) *The Littlewoods
pools were started in 1923.
After an initial distribution
thirty-five coupons were
returned, and the winning
dividend was £2.60; by the
1930s about ten million
people participated, with
winnings of up to £30 000.*

suburbs. It catered not only for football matches but for other
events including tennis, boxing, ice hockey and greyhound racing.

That year a huge crowd flocked to Wembley to watch the
Football Association Cup Final. 'All everybody wanted to see was
the big game. It was the first cup final played at Wembley,' recalls
Sidney Garner, who went to the match with his friends. So many
people were trying to get in that the crowds overflowed onto the
pitch. 'We made our way towards the main gates, and there were
literally thousands of people. We couldn't go where we wanted to
go. We had to go where the crowd pushed us....All of a sudden
there was a great surge at the back, fences went down...a lot of
people fell, got trampled on.' Mounted police, led by just one
policeman on a white horse, managed to push the crowds back off
the pitch so the match could begin. Nothing like this had ever
happened before, and it confirmed the enormous popularity that
professional football had now acquired.

**CROWDS FLOOD THE
PITCH** *at the first cup final
to be held at Wembley
Stadium. As Sidney Garner
explains, 'It was made to
hold a hundred thousand.
Well, that day there must
have been two hundred
thousand.' It took three-
quarters of an hour to clear
the pitch before the game
could begin.*

The fever spreads

As interest in football spread it had a similar effect on other European nations, arousing in many people around the world more passion than any other sport. By 1929 there were more than 3500 football clubs in France, while in Austria a wealthy Austrian businessman and an English coach had produced a *Wunderteam*. Publishing and broadcasting helped the sporting fever to spread: in France *Le Vélo* kept sports fans informed; Italians could follow their favourite team in the daily *Gazetta dello Sport*; thousands of enthusiasts bought the German weekly *Der Kicker*. International governing bodies were established to regulate the game in different countries, and to set uniform rules as professional leagues were introduced.

Popular passion, national fervour and commercial investment were also extending beyond Europe, to South America and later to Africa and Asia. Football had been introduced to South America by the families of British administrators of the mines, railroad, waterworks and telephone companies in Uruguay. Diego Lucero, who played for Uruguay in the 1920s, describes how the game developed: 'It was a novelty...they called it the game of the crazy English, because they wore short pants....It was a strange game, and very difficult to understand, but the local kids watched them play, and they imitated the players, and began to think they were better than them.' United by the game, locals began to play in the English teams, and eventually formed their own. 'In 1915 we founded our football club,' Diego Lucero recalls. 'In 1916 we joined the league to play championships, and we were born. We were big, we were strong, we were proud. So, there the journey of football had begun.' The local style of play evolved differently. The English, in heavy boots, played a hard, physical game, with long, high passes, while the South Americans played the ball along the ground, a subtle, athletic game; in their soft, flexible shoes they soon outplayed the big boots.

Organized championships were held in Uruguay, and soon extended to neighbouring countries. Diego Lucero remembers how the great rivalry that soon developed between Uruguay and Argentina made matches particularly important. 'The international games between Argentina and Uruguay were, at first, great social

FOR DIEGO LUCERO *in Uruguay football was an opportunity to establish a sense of community, increasing people's pride in themselves and their country. 'Football was a great benefit...from the social and economic point of view, it held extraordinary importance. Without a doubt it was a great thing football players did for the country.'*

The World Cup

THE MOST COVETED TROPHY *in football was named after the Frenchman Jules Rimet, who proposed the tournament. Held every four years, it was the first official international competition and provided a showcase for the world's best players.*

NATIONAL HEROES *in international sport. The players of Uruguay and Argentina's rival football teams became famous names and faces at home, and ambassadors for their countries – little known outside South America – when they competed overseas.*

gatherings. The ladies came all adorned, the president of the Republic, all the ministers....The times were changing, and the upper class was losing its affection for football. The popular flood was taking its place, and converting it into a more rugged, rustic, people's spectacle.'

Football in South America not only provided a new spectacle for the people, it also brought new opportunities for wealth and fame to players, strengthened national identity and enabled poorer countries to compete on equal terms with rich industrial nations. In the international arena the Uruguayan team dazzled the Europeans at the 1924 and 1928 Olympics, winning two gold medals. When the team arrived in Paris for the 1924 Olympics, they found that their opponents had never even heard of Montevideo. In Diego Lucero's view, football completely changed the Europeans' attitude to his country. 'The people of the world began to look at their maps to see where Uruguay was. They became interested in its population of 1 800 000 inhabitants; interested in the products of its land, especially in the meat.' When Uruguay hosted the first ever World Cup in 1930, and went on to win it, the country gained even greater renown.

PRESENTING THE ITALIAN AND HUNGARIAN TEAMS
By the time the World Cup was held in Paris in 1938 the rites and ceremonies of football were well established. Playing the national anthem of the competing teams before a match began reminded both players and spectators that national pride was at stake.

Sporting heroes, sporting fans

While sport brought new status to the nations of South America, in North America it elevated individuals to the status of heroes. People's passion for the sport meant that players could now make a living from it. In no sport was this more true than in baseball, the national pastime of the United States. Like football in Britain, baseball had long been an important part of American life, growing in popularity since the first professional teams emerged in the 1870s. It was cheap to play, it was fun at any skill level, and it required no elaborate playing field or equipment. In the new sporting environment of the 1920s baseball thrived, its audiences grew, and national heroes soon emerged.

William Werber, who went on to play with the New York Yankees team after graduating from college, grew up playing baseball in the Washington DC area. It was *the* game for him and his friends, who played on unused ground. 'Our cities didn't have as much concrete on them as they've got today,' he explains. 'They had vacant areas where people would scrape off the grass....Every spring a whole mess of kids at agreed upon times would come there with lawn mowers and hand scythes and hoes, and we'd scrape out the infield and get it in shape and then cut out the outfield....And that's where we played, all summer long.'

Close to the newly built Yankee stadium in the Bronx area of New York, an immigrant family from Germany ran a steak restaurant. Anna Daube Freund and her sisters grew up with the game. 'Baseball and everything that had to do with getting you out of the whole Depression feeling was important, so sports were still a good outlet....We would go to ball games rather than the movies. And my worst punishment was to be told, "You cannot go to the ball game".' Anna Freund got to know all the Yankee players, including William Werber. They were all well-known stars, but the biggest star of all was Babe Ruth. She remembers walking home to the restaurant from her grandmother's house and finding the street full of people. 'They were all saying, "Babe Ruth's in there!" When we went in actually the whole 1927 team was there, but Babe was the calling card.'

Babe Ruth, a self-styled 'bad kid' who had been brought up in a home for 'incorrigibles' in Baltimore, joined the Yankees in

> *The baseball cap*
>
> THE PEAKED CAP *worn by baseball players to shield their eyes from the sun was soon adopted by fans of the game. Designed in team colours and carrying team emblems, it became a badge of loyalty, and eventually a popular piece of headgear among fashion-conscious youngsters even in countries where baseball was not played.*

PLAYING BASEBALL IN THE STREET *was almost a national pastime for American children. All that was required was a ball, a bat and possibly a mitt. For William Werber, 'It was not organized ball. It was not sponsored by anybody.' In the United States baseball crossed social barriers as football did in other parts of the world – anyone could play.*

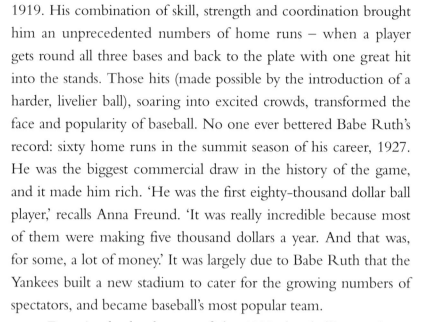

1919. His combination of skill, strength and coordination brought him an unprecedented numbers of home runs – when a player gets round all three bases and back to the plate with one great hit into the stands. Those hits (made possible by the introduction of a harder, livelier ball), soaring into excited crowds, transformed the face and popularity of baseball. No one ever bettered Babe Ruth's record: sixty home runs in the summit season of his career, 1927. He was the biggest commercial draw in the history of the game, and it made him rich. 'He was the first eighty-thousand dollar ball player,' recalls Anna Freund. 'It was really incredible because most of them were making five thousand dollars a year. And that was, for some, a lot of money.' It was largely due to Babe Ruth that the Yankees built a new stadium to cater for the growing numbers of spectators, and became baseball's most popular team.

Even in the hard years of the 1930s baseball's popularity continued to grow, and players could still earn a fortune. The Freund family was just one of the many immigrant families for whom baseball was part of the business of becoming an American. It crossed national boundaries too. Organized baseball had been played in Mexico and Cuba since the nineteenth century, and in Japan it was elevated to the status of a national sport.

Britain's bat and ball game was cricket. It too produced popular heroes; it too was a spectator sport with a mass following, and one that everyone could play. From the age of eight John Cracknell would join the older boys on Saturday afternoons at their local ground, the Oval in south London, specially to watch the outstanding batsman Jack Hobbs. 'I lived about a mile away from the Oval. And once it came through that Hobbs was batting

TIP TOP WEEKLY

"An ideal publication for the American Youth"

Issued weekly. By Subscription, $2.50 per year. Entered as Second Class Matter at the N. Y. Post Office by STREET & SMITH

No. 170.

Price, Five Cents.

FRANK MERRIWELL'S BALL TEAM
OR WINNING THE FIRST GAME

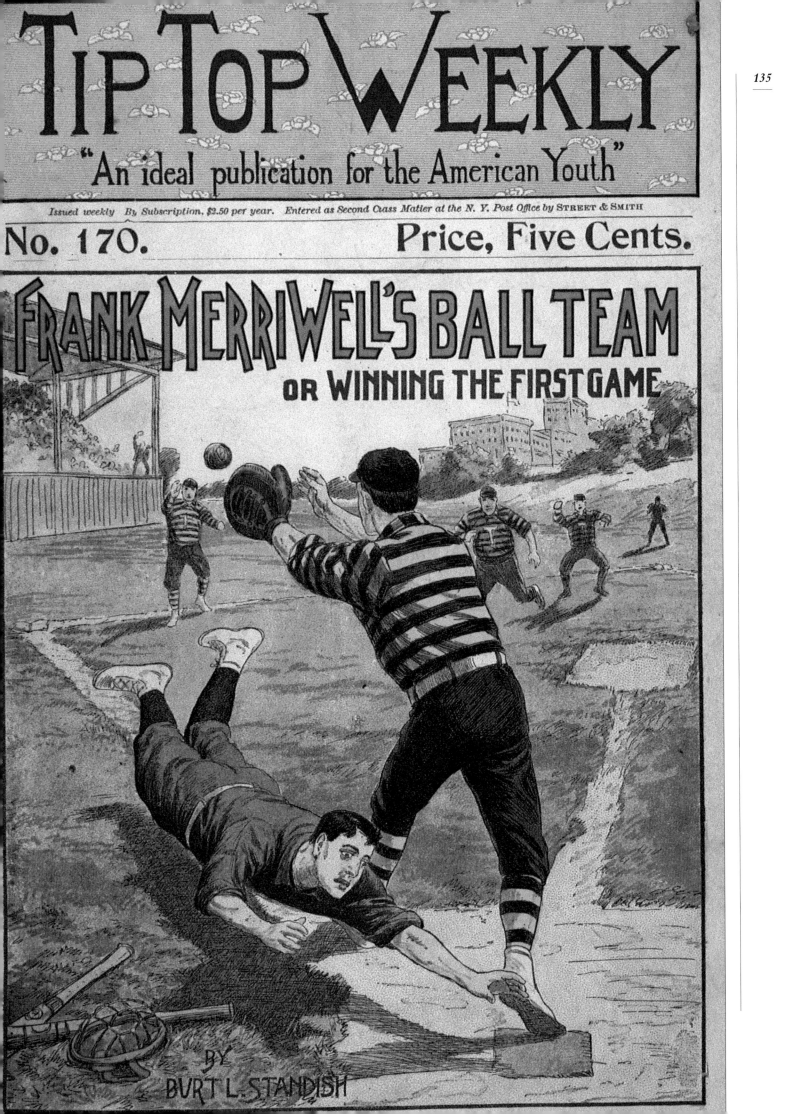

BY
BURT L. STANDISH

we would go indoors, get some money from our parents and run all the way up to the Oval, just to see Jack Hobbs bat. He certainly drew you there.'

Jack Hobbs was England's greatest cricketer, scoring 197 centuries in his long professional career. He played for England in sixty-one test matches and scored a record 61 237 runs. Like Babe Ruth, Hobbs drew the crowds. 'I thought he was tremendous,' John Cracknell remembers, 'his technique was so good and he was always very composed...an absolute hero. People would go to see Jack Hobbs bat, that's what they went for.' Another fan, Bert Culver, also remembers the crowds at the Oval. 'It was amazing, the enthusiasm in those days....We were really squashed...and it was most uncomfortable really, but we didn't notice that because we were so enthralled.'

In cricket it was the international games, the test matches, that drew the largest crowds of all. John Cracknell was not allowed to watch the matches himself, but he does remember the queues. 'Crowds used to line up all night long outside the Oval for the test matches, the place was packed....They queued up from, say, seven or eight o'clock in the evening till the following morning.' As Bert Culver, who did go to watch, explains, 'It was a different game in those days. It's not the same today, the cricket...test matches were very important.'

A test series in the 1932–33 season between Australia and England proved just how important cricket had become. The Australian team had a particularly brilliant young batsman from New South Wales, Don Bradman. The English had noticed his one weakness: he did not like really fast bowling. The English captain, Douglas Jardine, planned to exploit the speed of his fast bowlers, especially Harold Larwood, by adapting an old tactic – bodyline. Bowled with great accuracy, the balls would reach the batsman fast, high and in line with his body. As the ball reared up off the pitch the batsman would try to defend himself, and be caught out by the ring of close catchers surrounding him.

Among the Australian crowd at the third test, held at the Adelaide Oval, was eighteen-year-old Cec Starr. 'People were anticipating something would happen, and they didn't have very long to wait. Woodfall was hit just below the heart by a sharply

AN IMPROMPTU GAME OF CRICKET *In the 'playstreets' children could practise their favourite sport in peace. John Cracknell and his friends did little else in the streets where he grew up in the 1920s. 'We played cricket all day long. We would play in the street with a chalk wicket against the wall or we would go round to the local park....From my point of view, it was my life. It was the one thing we had in those days.'*

IT'S JUST NOT CRICKET *Douglas Jardine's bodyline bowling strategy, also known as leg theory, provoked unprecedented outrage during the 1932–33 tour and even threatened trading relations between Australia and England. It was seen as the end of cricket's gentlemanly tradition. As Bert Culver recalls, at that time test matches were 'always a life or death struggle, particularly with Australia'.*

IN REGRETFUL MEMORY OF CRICKETING IDEALS

PAS

LEG THEORY

rising ball and fell to the ground, dropping his bat, and some of the players went to his aid....The air became volatile, electric...the crowd really got terribly upset.' Two Australian players were hit that day, and the Australian press and public were vociferously hostile. The Australian Board of Control sent a telegram to the cricketing authorities in London, claiming that the England team's tactics were 'unsportsmanlike' and warning that friendly relations between the two countries were in danger. 'England were not very responsive,' Cec Starr explains. 'It was probably the first time in the history of the game that politicians had been requested to do something about the conduct of the game.'

The power of sport to stir the feelings of an entire nation affected other countries, too. Cricket, which had become popular all over the British empire – in India and the Caribbean as well as in Australia and New Zealand – gave whole communities a new sense of their collective worth, and would not be dominated by the privileged white world for much longer.

HEROES ON THE ROAD

IN 1900, ONLY TWELVE YEARS after the very first automobile was bought in Paris, thousands of people lined the route from Paris to Lyons to watch cars race by, excited by the rumour that there was one car capable of speeds as high as 80 km per hour (50 mph). A glamorous new sport had been born.

From the outset motor racing was a sport in which few could afford to participate but that attracted many spectators. It was also dangerous. On the first day of the 1903 Paris–Madrid race more than two million people stood to watch, some witnessing the accidents that caused the death of two drivers, two mechanics and several spectators. In Europe races were at first held on public highways over long

distances. On roads built for horse-drawn vehicles, all except the leading driver were enveloped in a cloud of dust, and accidents were very common. To reduce risks, roads were closed to traffic while the race was held. Road racing dominated for about fifty years – races such as Le Mans, the Mille Miglia and Targa Florio.

In Britain road racing was banned, but special circuits were built instead: Brooklands opened in 1907. In the United States the Indianapolis Motor Speedway circuit opened the following year. These provided grandstands with a clear view of the circuit for the growing number of spectators. Motor racing soon became a commercial enterprise rather than an adventure for the rich. Early road races were not profitable, but

the purpose-built racetracks, and in particular the circuits built in the 1920s and 1930s that combined the convenience of the racetrack with the demands of road racing, drew large crowds. Prize money attracted professionals who drove cars designed specially for racing. The skill of the driver was as important as the speed of the car; these masters of machines were much admired by the people who flocked to see them race.

LAP OF HONOUR (ABOVE) *Crowds applaud the Fiat team, winners of the Italian Grand Prix at Monza in 1923.*

The colour of sport

White supremacy was also being challenged in the boxing ring. In the United States boxing offered new opportunities for wealth and fame to successive waves of poor immigrants, who literally fought their way out of the slums of New York, Chicago and other big cities. First Irish-Americans dominated the ring, then they were challenged by Jewish, Polish and Italian-American boxers. But black boxers were often treated with hostility.

In 1910 the powerful middleweight Stanley Ketchel was knocked out by the black boxer Jack Johnson. In that year Johnson fought the retired champion, Jim Jeffries, and beat him as well. The publicity surrounding the fight was unprecedented, and so was the money paid to the fighters: $117 000 to the white loser; only slightly more, $120 000, to the black winner.

White America bitterly resented Jack Johnson's seven-year reign as heavyweight champion, and thereafter blacks were banned from championships until 1937. When one black champion did emerge who was capable of regaining the heavyweight crown, his backer warned him never to have his picture taken with a white woman, never to go into a nightclub alone – and to 'keep a solemn expression in front of the cameras'.

His name was Joe Louis Barrow, the son of poor Alabama farmers who had moved to Detroit. As a young man Eddie Futch, who had given up amateur boxing to become a trainer, belonged to the same boxing club as Joe Louis. 'Now imagine me...feeling that after Jack Johnson I would never see another black heavy-weight champion. I was standing shoulder to shoulder with Joe Louis, with this thought in mind, that I would never see one, that I'd never live that long.'

Eddie Futch remembers that Joe Louis 'had so much ability, and by the boxing writers coming up with their opinions on this great-looking prospect, the promoters in New York began to get the idea, "Why not use this talent? It's sensational". And so it was.' He was happy to have been proved wrong when Louis did eventually become the world heavyweight boxing champion.

CHALLENGING PREJUDICE *Jack Johnson (centre) became the first black world heavyweight champion. Despite the appearance of racial harmony, the white sporting community was intent on maintaining its supremacy and produced numerous 'Great White Hopes' to challenge him. But it was seven years before Johnson conceded the title.*

MONTREAL ROYALS (RIGHT) *meet the Dodgers in Daytona, Florida. Jackie Robinson (seen here with another black sportsman, Johnny Weight) was the first black player to be signed up for a major International League club, heralding the end of segregated baseball.*

RAISING THE FIST
Flanked by his trainer and manager, and surrounded by officials and well-wishers, Joe Louis celebrates his victory over James Braddock in the eighth round of the world heavyweight championship in Chicago in June 1937.

IN A LEAGUE OF THEIR OWN

BASEBALL WAS PROMOTED as a sport open to all, but black players were excluded from the big league teams. The stage for black talent was the Negro National League.

The NNL was a big success. The teams toured the nation, playing to huge mixed-race crowds in big league stadiums at big league prices. The high point of the season was the East–West All-Star Game in Chicago, which drew crowds of more than 30 000 people.

Although players earned half the wages paid to their white counterparts, the Negro leagues were among the largest black-owned businesses in the United States. They also helped sell thousands of copies of black newspapers to a white as well as black readership. The all-star teams were chosen by readers voting through the two largest black newspapers.

Professional black baseball stars were symbols of achievement for black people: they had excitement, glamour, and more money than most blacks could ever hope to earn. Yet life was still hard. They played every day of the year, and up to three matches a day. In the winter players went south to Florida, Cuba or Mexico, where they could enjoy the warm weather and mix with white people both on and off the baseball diamond. One player, Willie Wells, told a reporter in Mexico, 'Not only do I get more money playing here, but I am not faced with the racial problem. In the United States everything I did was regulated by colour. Here in Mexico I am a man.'

The NNL implicitly recognized segregation, but its founders hoped their teams would make it to the major leagues. Although that did not happen, their huge popularity paved the way for individuals to win acceptance. As white sports columnist Dan Parker wrote, 'There is no good reason why, in a country that calls itself a democracy, intolerance should exist on the sports field, that most democratic of all meeting places.' When Jackie Robinson signed with the Montreal Royals in 1946 it was just the beginning; within a few years, a high proportion of all major league players would be black, as their skill became more significant than the colour of their skin.

Joe Louis had fought his first professional match in 1934; within a year he defeated the Italian heavyweight champion Primo Carnera, who had recently killed an American boxer in the ring. Another twelve months later Louis suffered one of his rare defeats: he was knocked out in the twelfth round of a fight against the German heavyweight Max Schmeling. These fights began to take on a new political significance as in both Italy and Germany fascist governments began to issue their challenge to democracy.

A SEA OF SPECTATORS *surrounds the ring at Madison Square Garden. This enormous sports arena was built on the site of a railway station principally to provide a venue for boxing contests in New York.*

The political arena

By the 1930s people's passion for sport – whether baseball, boxing, football, cricket or athletics – had firmly established it as an activity to be exploited for commercial gain and national prestige. As national identity became increasingly linked with sporting success, winning or losing could unite or divide not just communities but entire nations. The desire to win international sporting events at any cost intensified as political tensions across the world were heightened. In the turbulent atmosphere of the late 1930s politital leaders took advantage of people's sporting passions, manipulating their feelings to build up nationalistic fervour and increase hostility towards regimes and peoples in other countries.

Football was adopted both by the communist government in the Soviet Union and by the fascists in Italy, whose national team dominated international competition in the 1930s. In the Soviet Union sport became an important instrument in creating the new Soviet man and woman. In Italy it was included as a weapon of foreign policy with the intention of arousing both fear and respect, and added to the determination that resulted in two successive victories in the World Cup, in 1934 and 1938. The Nazi ideal of populating Germany with a new Aryan super-race was also promoted through athleticism and sporting achievement.

It was against this background that 70 000 people entered the Yankee Stadium in New York in June 1936 to watch Joe Louis fight Max Schmeling. Protesters denounced Schmeling as a Nazi, while the Nazis criticized him for demeaning the white race by fighting a black man. Despite his colour, Louis won the support of the American public; for black people he had become a symbol of their faith in democracy and their hopes for fair treatment within the American democratic system.

Sam Lacy, who worked as a journalist for more than fifty years and paid close attention to sports involving black athletes in the 1920s and 1930s, recalls that when Jack Johnson fought for the heavyweight title the press was against him, but when Joe Louis, 'with his squeaky-clean self, proved he could fight, the whole nation embraced him.' In his judgement, 'Joe Louis and Jackie Robinson had a greater impact on social life in America than any other individual, including Dr Martin Luther King'.

POLITICS IN THE RING

Despite what the match between Joe Louis and Max Schmeling in 1936 came to stand for – political hostility between Germany and the United States – the souvenir issue of the boxing magazine The Ring offered the public genuine sporting statistics on the two contestants.

"The climate was right for Louis...after he proved he could fight the entire nation embraced him."

SAM LACY

Max Schmeling's victory was seen as a significant political triumph for Germany as well as a sporting one, and the Nazis who had criticized him now honoured him with a hero's welcome. For American fans and followers, as Eddie Futch recalls, 'It was like a great president had died. That's how mournful people were...this was a very sad day.'

After Joe Louis lost, support for him was strengthened rather than diminished. 'When Max Schmeling defeated him,' Sam Lacy remembers, 'that galvanized the whole American public behind Louis. "We can't have this. We'd much rather have you, despite your complexion, than have this German."' Sam Lacy's mother, a fervent Joe Louis fan, used to follow the fights by listening to them on her crystal radio set. 'When he got beat, she never listened to another fight...he was held in such high regard that it was a blow to all of us, including myself, and I'm supposed to be objective because I'm a newspaper man. But I, like everyone else, had felt that he was indestructible, that he was the best, absolutely the best.'

A political Olympiad

No one exploited the political power of sport better than Adolf Hitler. Despite protests, the International Olympic Committee declared Berlin the setting for the 1936 Olympic Games. The ideal of the amateur spirit, on which the modern Olympics had been founded, was far removed from this Olympiad. The size of the audience had changed dramatically, as had the nature of the competition itself, which was transformed by Hitler into a mass propaganda event. The games were the first to be televised – to more than 160 000 people in and around Berlin.

The Olympic village had been designed on an enormous scale and for maximum effect. Thousands of athletes and 100 000 spectators from around the world converged on Berlin in August. The athlete Helen Stephens from Missouri was eighteen years old when she was selected to represent the United States. 'It was a sort of shock to go from peacetime America and a depression time, and to go over there to Germany and find that they were seemingly living pretty good.' The Uruguayan Diego Lucero, who attended as a journalist, was equally impressed by the spectacle. 'They organized a festival that was truly luxurious.' But he also

OLYMPIC POSTER

(OPPOSITE) *The setting of the 1936 Olympic Games in Berlin provided Adolf Hitler with the perfect opportunity to promote Germany and the Nazi Third Reich, and to prove the superiority of Aryan athletes in front of an international audience.*

HELEN STEPHENS *set a new world record when she won the 100 metres for the United States. She was received by Hitler in his glass box overlooking the stadium.*

SPRINTING TO VICTORY *The son of sharecroppers and the grandson of slaves, the American Jesse Owens distinguished himself and his country by winning four gold medals at the 1936 Olympics. Unlike Helen Stephens, he was not invited to meet Hitler privately, an omission that was widely interpreted as a deliberate gesture intended to snub Jesse Owens because he was black.*

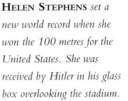

understood very clearly just what Hitler and the Nazis were hoping to achieve. 'Everything was organized towards a political end...to show a brilliant Germany....Their effort was a triumph for them because people left enchanted with the country and the treatment they had received. This Olympiad deserved the title of a political Olympiad.'

The German athletes did not fail their leader, winning most gold medals throughout the games. But to Hitler's dismay, black athletes in the American team dominated events on the field and track. The success of Jesse Owens, who won four gold medals for the United States – the 100 metres, the 200 metres, the last leg of the 4 x 100 metres relay and the long jump – spoiled Hitler's careful plans for turning the games into propaganda for his ideas about Aryan superiority.

End of an era

All the forces that were beginning to define sport – promotion and money, nationalism and propaganda – now came together in a single event. In June 1938 a second fight between Joe Louis and Max Schmeling took place at the Yankee Stadium. The world heavyweight title was at stake, but sport played little part: this was racial and political confrontation. Beyond the ring, the stakes were even higher, as Hitler had started on the road to war. Eddie Futch believed that now 'Louis wasn't just a black American...he was the representative of all America'. And Joe Louis did not his let his country down. He demolished Max Schmeling in the first two minutes. The symbolism was not lost on the watching world.

When the real war began both boxers still had their part to play. Louis was drafted into the United States cavalry, and the government made the most of his huge following to boost the war effort. The Germans used Schmeling, serving as a paratrooper, in the same way. They were just two among many sporting stars and heroes who fought alongside their fellow countrymen.

In the years after the war sport was taken up again with even greater enthusiasm. Millions of people played, and millions more thrilled at the exploits of their heroes. Commercial interests and politicians continued to use sport's power to move and motivate, and television brought live action to those who stayed at home.

GOING FOR GOLD
Winning an Olympic medal in 1936 was as much a symbol of political supremacy as it was a reward for sporting achievement.

JUBILANT AMERICANS
(RIGHT) *in Harlem, New York, celebrate Joe Louis' victory over Max Schmeling in 1938. The fight had epitomized the links between sport and politics, involving participants and spectators in the struggle for power.*

Breadline

THE YEARS OF DEPRESSION

ON THE MORNING OF Thursday 24 October 1929 at the New York Stock Exchange on Wall Street the unthinkable actually happened. Wall Street was the financial heart of the modern world – and on that day the heart missed a beat. The market had been nervous for days, but on the Thursday, as chaos turned to panic, it collapsed. On that day nearly thirteen million shares changed hands, at prices that transformed dreams of wealth into a nightmare reality of poverty.

Thomas Larkin was a trader on Wall Street. He remembers the crazy days of the boom, and then the suddenness of the crash. 'Before 1929 everybody would be calling me up buying stocks, and they never asked what price they were going to pay...you just bought them, and you couldn't believe it but the market still kept going up and up. Then one day I couldn't sell the stocks any more...the ticker tape didn't stop all night...I couldn't understand the amount of selling that was being done. It was almost like somebody opened an enormous faucet and let everything through it. I worked three straight days without taking my clothes off. Everything was just down, down, down, there didn't seem to be any bottom at all....We saw all kinds of people walking around as though they were zombies. They thought they were rich one minute, and the next minute they weren't rich any more – if they had anything left at all.'

The stock market had become the focus of the prosperous, eager years of the 1920s. About a million people in the United States had caught the fever of investment and speculation, which reached its height in the first six months of 1929. But the boom could not last; instead, the impact of the crash of 24 October would be felt for years. It triggered a period of unemployment, homelessness and hunger not only in the United States but throughout the world. The crash was the beginning of an economic disaster on such a large scale that governments were shaken and millions of people's lives were shattered.

BEWILDERED NEW YORKERS *throng the streets in the chaotic days after the Wall Street crash.*

From riches to rags

The Great Depression was so traumatic partly because it came so suddenly. During the previous few years there had been a period of unprecedented prosperity, a mood of optimism and confidence, particularly in the United States. The American economy was, however, more vulnerable than it seemed, because its banking structure was weak and the organization of business unstable.

Few investors realized that the boom could last only for as long as new speculators or new money from established investors were entering the market. As soon as the pace of demand to buy shares slowed down, confidence began to wane, and the whole unsteady edifice tottered and collapsed. It was not just ordinary investors who were deluded in thinking that the boom years would last for ever; businessmen, politicians and economists all continued to proclaim their confidence in the capitalist system and also appeared to be taken by surprise when disaster struck.

One of New York's telegraph boys, Bill Bailey, had the unenviable job of delivering telegrams bringing news of their ruin to many stock market investors. 'Most of the telegrams said the same: "Things are bad…give us more money to haul up your interests or else you are kaput." It was sad, because eventually not only did we deliver to the same door three or four times a day, but the people wouldn't even answer the door. They were so afraid of what was taking shape, and so bewildered. It was shortly after that we found out that people were jumping out of windows, going bananas…and figuring that was the best way to go, head first.'

Bill Bailey shared the bewilderment of the people who responded so dramatically to the news he brought. 'Nobody had any idea what was going on, that was the funny part of it. Why would the stock market have such a bearing on everybody else around us? We couldn't understand why it was the stock market played a role in us losing jobs, warehouses left full of stuff, people thrown out of factories.' Only later did he understand the way everything was affected. 'We had no idea because we didn't understand the system…until we found out that the stock market was the main aorta of the system, and that how the blood flows through it has a big bearing on everything else.'

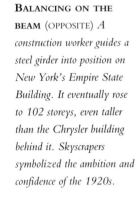

BALANCING ON THE BEAM (OPPOSITE) *A construction worker guides a steel girder into position on New York's Empire State Building. It eventually rose to 102 storeys, even taller than the Chrysler building behind it. Skyscrapers symbolized the ambition and confidence of the 1920s.*

THE DREAM OF WEALTH (BELOW) *turns to a nightmare of debt for the speculator who once proudly drove the car he is now so desperate to sell. As the stock market crash brought havoc to the lives of thousands of investors, it became harder to find buyers for once valuable possessions, however attractive the price.*

TRADING ACROSS THE WORLD

PEOPLE EVERYWHERE were becoming part of a global manufacturing machine during the 1920s, a time of rapid economic growth. Plantation workers in the British and French colonies in Southeast Asia tapped rubber for the tyres for automobiles that were made with steel from works in Britain, Germany and the United States. In the mountains of northern Chile, men mined copper ore that was shipped to the Renault factory in France, where the workers wore overalls woven from cotton picked by Egyptian workers or American sharecroppers. These workers all came to depend on each other for their living.

The first steps towards a global economy had been taken a long time before; the pace had accelerated during the nineteenth century. Britain was the first nation widely to export manufactured goods and coal, importing raw materials and cheap food from its colonies and from the United States. From about 1870 American, German and later Japanese manufacturers began to export to the British markets in Africa, Asia and South America.

After the First World War the United States had more spare capital than the exhausted European states, and not only invested in the railways and factories of developing countries but also poured money into Europe. Gradually the centre of gravity of the world's financial system shifted from London to New York.

In the thriving economic climate of the 1920s many people's expectations rose, and the idea became widespread that almost everyone could make money. But all those who benefited from the prosperity of the 1920s – the individuals, the companies they worked for, and the countries in which they lived – were now dependent on the state of the world economy.

BESIEGED BY THE UNEMPLOYED *Desperate Americans try to attract the attention of the overworked officials in an employment office. As the Depression bit harder, the chances of finding work became increasingly remote.*

Playing the game

AT A TIME WHEN REAL MONEY *had become almost worthless, Monopoly money helped players learn how to stay financially sound themselves while buying and selling property and forcing their opponents into bankruptcy. Originating in the United States, Monopoly became the world's best-selling privately patented board game.*

Shock waves

When the stock market collapsed other disasters soon followed. Many investors had bought stock 'on margin' – with borrowed money. As the value of their shares fell, they could not pay back their loans. But it was not only investors who were affected. Panic-stricken depositors hurried to remove their savings, and banks were forced to close. As investment dried up and demand collapsed, the crash soon turned into a slump. The consequences were devastating: prices rapidly fell, trade withered, goods were stacked up unsold, factories closed, wages were cut, millions of people lost their jobs. Both individuals and nations faced similar problems – they could not pay their debts, and were unable to borrow to see them through the hard times.

For many, life now became a grey, discouraging struggle for mere survival. Millions of people found themselves in absolute want. With no public welfare provision such as unemployment benefit to help them, hundreds of thousands of Americans found they had no alternative but to line up for the free soup that churches and private charities began to provide. Many survivors

ONE DOLLAR A WEEK is all the payment being asked by these labourers and firemen. Both skilled and unskilled men endured the humiliation of having to beg for work in a country that had recently been proud of its growing prosperity.

A GOOD TIME FOR BEER

URING THE DEPRESSION, at a time when many Americans might have wanted to drown their sorrows in drink, alcohol was banned in the United States. Prohibition was hailed as a great experiment at the time, but it was in fact a disaster. Millions of Americans became criminals simply because they continued to buy beer, wine or whisky.

The National Prohibition Act, known after its congressional sponsor as the Volstead Act, had become law in January 1920. It banned the manufacture, transportation, sale and consumption of alcohol. Its unintended consequence was the temporary creation of a vast illegal network of liquor smuggling, serving thousands of 'speakeasies' – illegal drinking places.

The drive for prohibition had been coordinated nationally by the Anti-Saloon League. It originated not only in the religious and ethical beliefs of the Protestant churches but also in the prejudices of 'old stock' Americans of the Middle West and the South against the cities and their German, Irish and Italian inhabitants. These newer immigrants were seen by the Anglo-Saxon Protestants as drinkers prone to immorality and crime.

It was in fact prohibition itself that triggered a national crime wave. By 1927 drunken driving offences had risen by 467 per cent, and deaths from alcoholism by 600 per cent. Attempts to legislate morality offer new opportunities to criminals in the evasion of the law; what is forbidden may become more desirable. And so it proved.

There were twice as many illegal bars in New York as there had been legal ones before the Volstead Act. Bootleggers (named after seventeenth-century smugglers who had concealed bottles of liquor in their boots) smuggled liquor into the United States across the Canadian and Mexican borders, from the Bahamas and from ships anchored outside territorial waters.

In most major cities rival criminal gangs fought over the huge profits being made from the illegal drink trade and from the prostitution and gambling associated with it. The income bought cars and machine guns, increasingly used in self-defence and to eliminate rivals. And it also bought people: police forces were corrupted, and political influence brought the gangsters immunity from the law. In Chicago between 1927 and 1931 there were 227 gang murders – and not one conviction.

Chicago was called by one of its aldermen 'the only completely corrupt city in America'. One of the first gang bosses was murdered; his successor was shot by his bodyguard and his empire of illegal breweries, distilleries, truck fleets and speakeasies was eventually taken over by the most notorious gang leader of all, Al Capone. He drove around Chicago in an armoured Cadillac; both feared and admired, he was said to have ordered some 400 murders.

A commission reported in 1931 that prohibition was unenforceable. Although organized crime continued to flourish, the stream of money that had flowed into the coffers of the criminals slowed to a trickle as the Depression advanced. Prohibition was repealed in December 1933 as part of Roosevelt's New Deal. He himself observed: 'I think this would be a good time for beer.'

A WAISTCOAT OF WHISKY *finds ready customers in a speakeasy during the years of prohibition.*

remember the helplessness, the shock of sudden poverty, the acute sense of loss and failure being almost worse than the experience of hunger and the new physical hardships they had to endure.

When the pink slip came to tell them they were out of work, many people at first felt ashamed. Bill Bailey remembers the humiliating effort to find another job. 'I would get out and maybe hustle fifteen places a day, banging on warehouse doors, trying to find a job – but it was impossible. I ended up selling apples on Wall Street.' Others tackled the helplessness they felt by finding quite different kinds of work, sometimes in circumstances for which their upbringing had not prepared them. For a few of those who would compromise, it was still possible to earn large sums in unexpected ways, such as performing in the new nightclubs, while most people were queueing for hours each day in the soup lines.

'There was nothing that struck the imagination more than seeing a soup line of five hundred people,' explains Bill Bailey, 'and two days later a thousand people in the same line. It kept on growing until they went all around the block....To stand in line at any place like soup kitchens where you are trying to get some-thing free is very humiliating. Of course later on it becomes a way of life, you don't care any more because everybody else is there.'

A young economics student, Robert Nathan, wanted to understand the processes that had led first to speculation and then to depression. He already knew that the difficulties of the 1930s lay in what had taken place in the 1920s. One of his professors explained away the crisis. 'He said, "Business cycles are part of the capitalistic system", and I remember he took a rubber band and pulled it way out and said "Boom"; then he let go and it collapsed back and he said "Bust". Capitalism is bound to have booms, which are prosperity, and also have busts, which are recessions and depressions.'

Robert Nathan was taught that this cycle of boom and bust was inevitable and that nothing could be done about it. This was what most economists believed at the time. But he thought it was wrong, that inertia was unacceptable and that something should be done, because the economic theories did not take into account the effect the cycle had

THE AVERAGE CITIZEN
(LEFT) *often struggled to understand the forces that could make him rich or reduce him to poverty, and became bewildered by the complexities of economics and the jargon of financial affairs.*

A Chicago soup line *set up and supported by the gangster Al Capone. Without any federal social security system, American citizens were dependent on charity to alleviate hardship during the Depression.*

on people's lives. 'The hardship was something you couldn't escape from. The lectures and the writing it off as an inherent element in the free enterprise system made less and less sense to me, because I saw that here were the plants closed down, here were the people wanting to work, here were the people who couldn't afford to buy anything, so you had a kind of vicious circle operating and nobody was prepared or willing to undertake major measures.' This sense of helplessness was a reality very different from the

THE DUST BOWL

THE CATASTROPHE of the American Dust Bowl was the result of some fifty years of inappropriate farming. The Great Plains, which had been opened up towards the end of the nineteenth century by the railroads, could be cultivated with the new steel ploughs, which were strong and sharp enough to break up their tough grasses. They were ploughed up to grow wheat, though the topsoil was thin and the climate semi-arid, with recurrent droughts.

The 'sodbusters', small farmers who bought a 'quarter section' of 65 hectares (160 acres) for about $200, and larger commercial farming enterprises ignored the difficult conditions. They set out to tame the land. They learned to survive prairie fires and plagues of grasshoppers, and to produce crops despite a continental climate of heatwaves and blizzards, drought, hail and flash floods. During the First World War the grain and cotton of the Great Plains fed and clothed the Allies, and production was further increased after the war, when Russian grain exports were no longer available to the European cities.

Farming methods that had been successful in the rich farmlands back east were eventually to prove unworkable in the Plains, with their thin, fragile soils from which the protective grass cover had been stripped. Single-crop farming and increasing mechanization worsened the problems, exhausting the soil. During periods of drought the bare earth turned to dust that was whipped by the prairie winds into huge dust storms.

In April 1933 there were 179 dust storms. These were black, brown, yellow, grey or even red according to which county's soil was being blown away. In one storm in May 1934, 350 million tonnes of dust from the southern Plains blew over Boston, New York and Washington. City dwellers woke up to find dust covering their floors. Dust was blown out to sea onto the decks of ships almost 500 km (300 miles) offshore. The storms caused breathing problems, derailed trains, and destroyed half the wheat in Kansas and a quarter of the Oklahoma crop.

Loye Stoops was a young woman on her family's farm in Oklahoma, and she remembers the storms well. 'We planted crops but those storms would come...and the sand would just cut them off at the ground....The dust was everywhere, you would have to sweep it out, shovel it out. The dust storm would come every few days. You couldn't see – it was like smoke, only it was red. We held out and kept trying to farm until the water level dropped and there was no water in the wells. I think it had been about three years that it had not rained.'

Loye Stoops and her family were among the half million 'Okies' (as they were called whether they came from Oklahoma or not) who decided to leave. Most had little left to lose. Long lines of cars filled with dispirited, exhausted families travelled slowly west in search of work. Some 300 000 people journeyed to California, where life in the fruit-picking camps was almost as tough as it had been in the Dust Bowl.

FAMILY LIFE *for many American farmers was reduced to pitiful levels of deprivation. In the grip of economic forces beyond their control or understanding, millions of families had to choose whether to stay at home and risk starvation, or abandon their homes and seek a better way of life.*

WAVES OF SAND *cover the land around an isolated Texan farmhouse during a dust storm.*

public image of the United States.

During the early years of the century millions of Europeans had emigrated to the United States, full of confidence about their prospects there. John Takman reached Chicago from Sweden only weeks before the Wall Street crash. 'I saw the misery all around me, tens of thousands of people evicted from their apartments, whole families and old people sitting in rocking chairs on the sidewalk, nowhere to go, no food, nothing except the small things they had with them, and I couldn't stand it.'

John Takman decided to go west, as he had heard that 5000 jobs were available picking apples in Washington state. Seasonal farm work paid little, but drew many. When he arrived he found 25 000 people also hoping to get a job. 'I saw families with haunted eyes, men probably starved for a long time in order to give the children something. We knew that when people didn't have the money to buy bread, the wheat was burned; if they didn't have money to buy meat, the mounds of meat were destroyed with kerosene. There was huge destruction of food in the United States at the same time that millions were starving.' Farm prices had dropped so low that it was not worth the farmers' while to pick their crops. In Idaho wheat was even priced at minus three cents a bushel. So while hunger threatened the unemployed and homeless in the cities, good food rotted in the fields or was used as fuel.

Bill Bailey travelled around the country in search of work by rail, by boxcar. 'You have to pick the car up when it is doing five or ten miles an hour. After that you are taking a chance of losing a leg. Some of the cars were full of dirt, filth and slime – it was almost impossible to lie down and get any rest. We are talking about thousands of people on the rail every single day.' But there were hardly any jobs, however far afield they travelled. 'So they found themselves drifting around aimlessly, cursing at themselves, becoming more demoralized and wondering where the hell they are going to go from here. It was sad to see humanity in this state.'

KEEPING A LOOKOUT
Riding for free on trains was a risky way to travel, but was often the only option for those who had no money and no possessions.

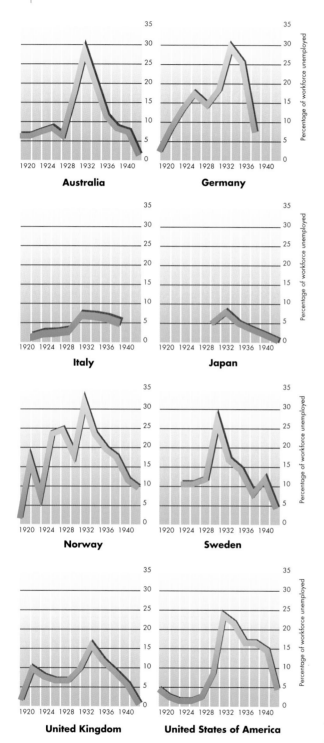

Percentage of workforce unemployed

Australia

Germany

Italy

Japan

Norway

Sweden

United Kingdom

United States of America

PEAKS OF UNEMPLOYMENT *followed similiar patterns in all the world's industrial nations as the Depression took hold in the early 1930s. Detailed statistical evidence is lacking for the countries that supplied raw materials – such as Chile and other Latin American states – but their working people were equally badly affected.*

Collapsing trade

The shock waves of the Depression began to be felt throughout the world. Measures taken in Europe and the United States to protect their economies brought the volume of international trade down even further, and in 1931 it virtually collapsed. Disastrous as this was for the industrial countries, it was even more catastrophic for the nations that depended on supplying their raw materials – copper, cotton, rubber and wool.

In independent countries such as Australia, New Zealand and the South American republics, prices, output and trade all declined steeply. The powerless peoples of the British, Dutch and French empires were even worse hit. In January 1933 the gold price of sugar, for example, was half what it had been in January 1929; the price of cotton fell by two-thirds over the same period, and that of rubber by 87 per cent. Manufacturers, processors and even consumers complained vociferously; the sufferings of those most badly affected, the plantation workers, went unheard.

In Chile prosperity was new and fragile. It largely depended on just one product, copper, and for that copper largely on one source – the American-owned opencast mine at Chuquicamata in the Atacama desert. The price of copper dropped by 29 per cent in only four years. For tens of thousands of miners, like Fernando Liborio Suazo, 'The crisis took us by surprise. It was as if you were walking in the street and something hits you and you are simply stunned. New York was far away, but when your own patron tells you that you no longer have a job, that the work's over, well that's the moment you go into shock. As he was a humane person, he gave us one year more, working there. He didn't sell that copper, he just stored it there. He didn't have a buyer.'

As an engineer, Eugenio Lanas understood the importance of the copper: without it, the city dies. He explains: 'The bakeries work for those hundreds of miners who come on donkeys or in light trucks to buy bread, the workshops work for the miners who need an engine fixed. The whole activity of the city is for the benefit of these people. The moment these rocks disappear, the cities themselves start to disappear.' That is just what happened.

The Chilean economy also depended on its 'white gold' – nitrates that were exported to North American farmers. Claudina

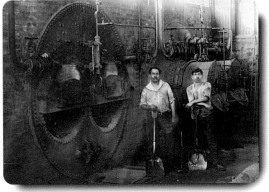

MAKESHIFT HOMES
(LEFT) *in Valparaiso, Chile.*
In the 1920s expanding
industries attracted people
from the countryside to the
towns in search of a better
way of life, but often the
only shelter available was
in shantytowns.

TWO STOKERS (ABOVE)
standing by nitrate boilers at
San Enrique, Chile. The
nitrate workers depended for
their livelihood on the
ability of American farmers
to buy the fertilizer. The
cartoon (TOP) *highlights*
their suffering.

Montaño Diaz lived in Humberstone, one of the many nitrate towns in the Atacama desert. It employed more than 150 000 miners and their families. 'It was our bread, our bread was the nitrate. That was our security and that was our life. We didn't have anything else. One day in December we knew that they were closing the works. They did not come to talk to the people. They just gave the orders. We didn't have anyone to complain to, though we had suffered this abuse, we had suffered a lot. It was very sad. The men of course were angry, because the workers were exploited and we were left with nothing. What could we do? Beautiful towns were abandoned. That was the crisis of the 1930s, that crisis was outrageous.'

Nearly 13 000 km (8000 miles) away in the northeast of England the crisis affected a town that depended on another once thriving industry: shipbuilding. With the collapse of world trade the shipbuilding, steel and coal industries all suffered: orders for new ships ceased, so the shipyards stopped buying steel plates, and the steel works stopped buying coal and iron ore.

Con Shiels's father worked at Palmer's shipyard in Jarrow on the river Tyne. In 1930, when he was four-teen years old, Con Shiels himself started to work there. 'Of course it was only natural for the sons to follow their fathers, which I did. He was working as a riveter and so naturally I started with him as a rivet catcher. You had to heat up your rivets, and carry them along the deck in a box of ash – and that was me with a job.' He started work hoping that he would be there for life, to learn a skilled trade and later to marry on the wages. 'But it didn't happen because one afternoon the foreman came round and said, "Con, you're finished tonight" – just like that. So that was me finished. Out. Got my books and money and away I went.'

He was just one among hundreds. Palmer's was closed as part of a scheme to reduce capacity in order to protect the more modern yards. When the Palmer's yard was demolished, many of the people who lived in Jarrow turned out to watch its twin cranes come down. They had been the town's principal landmark. Con Shiels speaks for many when he explains how he felt. 'They were just part of your life...honestly there were tears in our eyes seeing them go down, because we knew that if they came down the yard was finished. They were a symbol. Once the symbol had gone, that was it. A terrible day.' Almost overnight, in a town of skilled, hardworking men, the level of unemployment rose to 75 per cent. People called Jarrow 'the town that died', but Con Shiels would put it more strongly than that. 'It was murdered. A good town, just cut off like that, like a hangman dropping a noose. Once the yard was closed it was as though a blanket had dropped over the town...it was really very depressing for the future and for our children.'

IDLE SHIPS AND IDLE WORKERS (LEFT) *dramatically portrayed by the photographer Humphrey Spender. 'What I found on Tyneside was rather frightening,' he recalls. 'On the quayside I found despondent and idle men.' On his repeated visits to the hard-hit northeast of England his photographs became harsher as he depicted conditions with increasingly unsparing honesty.*

CON SHIELS *photographed with fellow trainees on a government scheme in 1936. His years of unemployment came to an end when he joined the navy.*

'WE MARCH AGAINST STARVATION' *declares one of the banners carried by the unemployed men of Jarrow, who walked to London in protest in 1936. Con Shiels's father was among the marchers.*

I KNOW 3 TRADES
I SPEAK 3 LANGUAGES
FOUGHT FOR 3 YEARS
HAVE 3 CHILDREN
AND NO WORK FOR
3 MONTHS
BUT I ONLY WANT
ONE JOB

Years of deprivation

Between 1929 and 1936 deprivation spread across the world like a disease. The coal industry was one of the worst affected. Miners in Belgium, Britain, France and Germany were all caught up in the cycle. It was coal that provided essential power for industry, but with industrial production dramatically reduced, the demand for coal fell too. In the Borinage coal basin in Belgium there were 100 000 miners and their families living in appalling conditions. In the summer of 1932 the miners had gone on strike to protest against a 5 per cent cut in their wages. They were dismissed from their jobs, blacklisted from future work, and evicted from their company-owned homes. Two young film-makers, Henri Storck and Joris Ivens, found out what had happened and decided to publicize the miners' plight. 'We wanted to do a revolutionary film,' Henri Storck explains. 'We became totally indignant. Joris and I were sons of tradesmen, we didn't know much about work-men. We thought this was really impossible. These people were abandoned, they were treated cruelly by the colliery directors. It was something we couldn't tolerate, this incredible poverty – they didn't have any money at all.'

The Mouffe family were among those who were filmed to draw attention to the miners' hardships. The hunger and poverty they had to endure is vividly described by Yvonne Mouffe, who was a young child at the time. 'I can remember there being only one room. We used to cuddle up to each other to keep warm, it is much warmer that way if you are on the ground. There were nine children, and we slept on the floor. To get some coal they used to go to the slag heaps in the evening – otherwise we couldn't have any, we weren't authorized to have any. Father worked in the mines but during the strike they received nothing at all, so we had nothing but potatoes to eat and from time to time some bread, but apart from that nothing.'

There was worse to come. Yvonne Mouffe's father, who was a communist, was accused of being one of the strike leaders, lost his job and could not find another one. The children were taken from their parents and put in children's homes; Yvonne Mouffe was five years old when this happened, and did not see her parents again until she was forty-two.

THE SAFETY NET

BEFORE THE DEPRESSION, the age-old assumption still held in most countries that families would look after their children, their invalids and the elderly. State provision, where it existed at all, was limited.

The first state system of social security for old age had been introduced in Germany towards the end of the nineteenth century. In 1911 Britain became the first country to provide state insurance for the unemployed; by 1927 twelve million British workers were protected by a contributory state insurance scheme that they had to join. But relief hardly lifted recipients out of poverty, and many turned for help to the poor law, still administered by parishes, and to charities.

Private insurance through companies was confined to higher paid workers, and often failed in times of hardship. Hundreds of thousands of people sought security by setting up their own insurance schemes through 'friendly societies' or trade unions.

Sweden was the first country to replace the poor law concept. By 1914 it had set up a national unemployment commission to provide jobs on public works projects. From 1925 it provided a nutritious daily meal to all schoolchildren. Sweden offered the best protection to its citizens during the 1930s, with unemployment benefit, pension provisions, subsidized sickness funds and medical care, and family allowances.

In the United States, where there had been no state-organized welfare, people could rely only on their families and on the support of community groups. It had been assumed that poverty was caused by personal inadequacy, until a quarter of the working population faced long-term unemployment. Only then, during Roosevelt's presidency, was there the political will to try to solve the problem by introducing the first social security provisions.

Fighting for change

Deprivation and despair led to rage, and rage sometimes led to rebellion. The cause was often simple necessity and desperation. But many people interpreted their own particular experience in terms of an abstract idea. They believed that the world economic system, the capitalist system, was at fault. Some thought it was fundamentally wrong, others that it had just gone horribly wrong. Millions of people concluded that radical change was inevitable. Few countries escaped bitter battles – between capital and labour, between the police, enforcing the existing law, and trade unions and other groups who were equally determined that the old rules should be changed.

In northern Sweden the wood pulp industry, a major source of wealth, was depressed by the collapse of world trade. The pulp and paper companies cut wages. Like the Borinage miners, the workers in the port of Lunde, near the town of Adalen, responded by going on strike. Strike-breaking labour was hired to keep the port functioning. As tension rose, the army was called in.

On 14 May 1931 the Swedish trade unions called their members to a big protest rally in Adalen. Tore Alespong was one of the trumpeters who led the union band on the march. The musicians were playing when soldiers opened fire. 'There was one fellow, who held the scores for one of the clarinettists, who had two shots through his hat. He found the bullets still in the crown. It was a miracle they didn't strike lower down. Some of the shots hit the ground, but most went high and hit people. A girl within touching distance from me began bleeding...she had certainly been shot. That's when I had the impulse to sound the ceasefire on the trumpet....They thought that it was their own bugler who had sounded.' By the time the shooting stopped, five people had been killed. Tore Alespong played the trumpet at their funeral.

People all over the country were shocked at what had taken place in Adalen. In Stockholm there was a mass protest against it. Göta Rosén, a young social worker, was 'devastated that something like that could happen. I went to the town square to attend the demonstration. It was frightening that this could happen to people in distress.' Swedes, like people in many other countries,

'THE SWEDISH PEOPLE'S PATH' *promises this election poster for the Social Democrats, 'is the path of people's freedom and democracy.' Their energy and vision helped to bring the Social Democrats to power.*

TORE ALESPONG (BELOW) *was among the bandsmen who led the march in Adalen that resulted in bloodshed. The tragedy 'did emphasize how people in power behave, people in government', he explains.*

HJALMAR
BRANTING

HANS
HJÄRTA

NSKA
ETS

ÄR

FOLK-
FRIHETENS

OCH

MOKRATINS

VÄG

ÖSTA
ED

TIET SOCIAL-
RATERNA

"I believed in the Social Democrats' programme. I am convinced that they defend the young, the old, the downtrodden."

GÖTA ROSÉN

GÖTA ROSÉN *with a group of orphans. 'My aim was to get away from the communal care of children. I tried to find people to take care of them under the slogan, "The right child in the right family",' she explains. She found the Social Democrats sympathetic to her ideas.*

became increasingly alienated from the ruling party. In the wake of Adalen, and the Depression that had triggered the incident, a new political movement emerged that regarded unemployment not as inevitable but as an outrage. Göta Rosén describes why it appealed to her. 'I saw unemployment as a terrible scourge. I understood that one must do one's utmost to remove that scourge from the people of Sweden, and I joined the Social Democratic party partly because I realized that they were getting things done.'

The Social Democrats were swept to power in the 1931 election. They saw their main priority as restoring confidence and getting the country moving again, rather than balancing its budget at all costs as governments elsewhere were doing at that time. It intervened by creating jobs and restimulating wealth, spending money both to invigorate the economy and to protect the needy.

Roosevelt's New Deal

Restoring confidence also became the key to challenging the Depression in the United States. In 1933 Franklin D. Roosevelt was inaugurated as president. Although he is credited with ending the Depression there, he did not at first have a clear strategy for recovery. He did, however, understand one very important thing: that part of the problem stemmed from lack of confidence. In his inauguration speech he gave new inspiration to the American people. 'Let me assert my firm belief that the only thing we have to fear is fear itself,' he assured them.

In the first hundred days of Roosevelt's presidency, thirteen major measures were passed by Congress to provide structure and support for recovery in banking, industry and agriculture, and to establish federal relief for the needy. Government projects were set up. Some of these, such as the Tennessee Valley Authority and the Civilian Conservation Corps, gave employment to millions of homeless unemployed men, while others were small self-help schemes. By 1936 a system of unemployment insurance and old age pensions had been instituted; in 1938 a new law established a minimum wage and maximum weekly working hours. Measures were also taken to protect union activities: collective bargaining, the right of labour to its own organizations. Employers often resisted these gains, and it took a series of bitter strikes for the changes to be accepted.

Roosevelt's action did not solve all the difficulties of the Depression. The economy did not really recover until war had broken out again in Europe in 1939 and the United States joined in the rearmament boom. But his greatest achievement was to raise people's hopes again, to convince them that something was at last being done to help – itself a major political turnaround.

The economist Robert Nathan describes the effect of the government's activities. 'A lot of the increased spending under the Roosevelt administration had to do with public works...when you put people to work building a dam, you have a lot of cement guys, pipefitters, a lot of guys running, cutting the big hole in the ground to put the dam up – you give a lot of people employment. What does that mean? It means there is more buying power. People have been unemployed and living on $10 a week, say, and

GREETING THE PRESIDENT *American farmers gained confidence as a result of Roosevelt's policy to support farm prices. Many of them would have agreed with Loye Stoops, who remembers: 'I thought he was smart and I thought he cared and I thought he had people at heart because he was helping when nobody else could do anything.'*

DAIRY WORKERS ON STRIKE (OPPOSITE) *give vent to their frustration by overturning a milk truck in Toledo, Ohio, in 1935.*

BILL BAILEY'S INTEREST *in politics began when he saw his mother standing in a soup line. The communists 'were the ones doing the driving, so you became influenced by what they were talking about, that the system wasn't working and nobody gave a damn.'*

ALTERNATIVES TO DEMOCRACY

WHEN THE ECONOMIES of democratic countries seemed to be failing them, many people were attracted by the certainties and apparent successes of communism and fascism. Democratic governments had always regarded economic depression as an inevitable feature of capitalism that could not be remedied. As the Depression fastened its grip, the slump in trade and the rise in unemployment brought desperation that led to tension and violence. Authoritarian regimes of both the left and the right seemed to offer solutions to the chaos and poverty so many people were suffering.

There was one country where there was no unemployment: the Soviet Union. Here the communist approach seemed able to defy the Depression; few people knew of the violence and coercion involved in the adoption of communist methods. At the opposite political extreme, in Germany from 1933 the fascist government also exercised tight controls over the economy to provide work for the six million people – about half the workforce – who were unemployed. And they were successful: by 1936 the figure had dropped to 1.6 million, and continued to fall.

In Italy, fascism was adopted in 1926; fascists came to power in Spain and Portugal too during the 1930s. In Britain and France both fascism and communism made some political gains in the 1930s. In the late 1920s and early 1930s thousands of American citizens applied for visas to emigrate to the Soviet Union, while others stayed in the United States but supported communist ideas. The Communist Party of the United States never became more than a tiny political minority, but in the desperate times of the Depression it had great influence.

After the First World War the expansion of self-determination in Europe and elsewhere was translated into genuine democracy only in a very few countries, such as Ireland and Czechoslovakia. In 1926 there was a military coup in Poland; in 1929 the Serbian king of the new Yugoslavia proclaimed himself dictator. In Hungary, after a brief communist revolution in 1919, the great landowners and smaller squires regained power and diverted attention from the poverty of the agricultural workers, among the most wretched in Europe.

Outside Europe, Kemal Atatürk modernized Turkish society, but granted only limited civil liberties. In India and other colonial territories mass movements for self-government had not yet shaken imperial rule, though the violence both of protest and repression was increasing. In China the nationalist Kuomintang movement was given an authoritarian structure. In alliance with the Chinese Communist Party, founded in 1921, the Kuomintang established its government in Nanking, and moved north to attack the warlords who controlled much of the country.

In Japan there was also restlessness. The Depression badly affected people both in the textile industries and in the countryside. This strengthened the hand of the militarists, who promised to tackle the problem, though their methods threatened Japan's young democracy. Political gangs collaborated with the security police to silence socialist and trade unionist activists, and there were many political assassinations.

In many other countries, too, even before the Depression had taken hold, political stability was threatened and a new culture of political violence was on the increase.

then suddenly they have $25 or $30…you had people that were at least ready and able to spend more, and anybody who suddenly had doubled their income, doubled their purchases.'

Robert Nathan most admires Roosevelt's ability to think of new solutions. 'When it got tough, he was willing to experiment with a whole lot of things that had never been done before. Masses of people really had a lot of confidence in this man because he talked about things that made them feel, "He is worried about me, he is concerned about me, he is going to do things for me". The result was that he was elected president four times.'

The confidence people had in their president was reflected in the growing confidence they had in themselves. The Reverend George Stith had become part of the changing times when he joined the Southern Tenant Farmers' Union as a young man. He can still remember the hardships of his early life. His family had slept three to a bed, and his grandmother had kept them alive on watermelons, wild onions, tomatoes and peas. 'You were in a land that grew cotton to make the best clothes in the world, clothes that we couldn't wear because we couldn't afford to buy them.'

George Stith was a sharecropper, working on a big cotton plantation in the South. The plantation owner decided how much he was going to pay them. 'You never got money. You got a coupon book, you could go to any of the plantation stores and spend them, but there was no money.'

Roosevelt's policies first affected the Stiths when the owner told them, 'We've got to plough up every third row of this cotton because the government says we're planting too much'. What he did not tell the workers was that the government had paid him to plough up the third row, and he had no intention of passing that money on to the people who actually did the ploughing. Joining the union was a dangerous thing to do, because agricultural labour had been excluded from the legislation passed under the New Deal to protect union activities. 'Everyone else had the right to organize, to bargain, but agriculture didn't have the right…they wanted it that if you organized you couldn't get a hearing because you had no right to organize, so we had to do it as best we could.'

In the South every plantation owner virtually made his own laws, and many were hostile to union activities. Meetings were

WAITING ON THE CABIN PORCH *surrounded by possessions, this family in the state of Mississippi in June 1938 is about to be taken to a new home, resettled with the help of the Farm Security Administration.*

raided by local law officers and plantation owners; union members were even whipped and beaten. Despite the harassment, the union continued to grow.

'I sometimes wonder why we did not give up,' George Stith says. 'But I guess we figured it this way: if you have nothing, you can lose nothing. The risk, for a lot of time, was death if they caught you. We had some organizers that did disappear, and we didn't know what became of them. I was very young at that time. They thought a union organizer had to be an older man, and I think that was an advantage to me, being a boy.'

Despite the danger, George Stith continued to believe that the fight for a better life was worthwhile. The Southern Tenant Farmers' Union provided both a fighting platform and a step to freedom for some of those whose lives were not affected by the vision of a prosperous future held out by Roosevelt's policies.

Someone else for whom the changing times brought new beginnings was Mancil Milligan, though his experiences were very different from those of George Stith. He and his wife had been teachers before the Depression and had put aside a little money in a bank, but when the bank failed they lost their savings. For several

Man of steel

SUPERMAN, THE GREAT HERO *of comic strips, reflected the thirst for social justice. He was both incredibly clever and extraordinarily strong. His superhuman powers were at first modest – he could leap hundreds of metres and only a bursting shell could harm him – but were later extended to include X-ray vision and the power to fly to the end of the universe. The strip appeared in four newspapers in 1939; by 1941 it was being syndicated to some three hundred newspapers reaching an audience of twenty million people.*

MANCIL MILLIGAN (ABOVE) *in his uniform as a safety officer at the Pickwick Dam, which employed up to 2500 people. As he explains, 'Everybody got a piece of the pie. When I got a job there I worked six days a week and I hired somebody to haul and chop wood for me, I hired somebody to paint the house' – tasks he had undertaken himself when he had been out of work. The dam brought electricity to the region; Mancil Milligan was proud of his refrigerator, his electric fan and his new radio.*

GETTING BACK TO WORK (OPPOSITE) *Men on their way to work at the Robins Dry Dock Company. As rearmament boosted the American economy, there were better employment prospects for people in many industries.*

years neither the state nor the county could afford to pay teachers. At one point he even had to take half a dollar out of their young daughter's piggy bank to buy a sack of flour. When Roosevelt's new measures began to take effect, Mancil Milligan finally got another job – as a carpenter working in a New Deal conservation corps camp for just $2 a day, 'from sunup to sundown'. Then the Tennessee Valley Authority started a huge project nearby to build the Pickwick Dam, and he applied for a job there. He has never forgotten the telegram that was brought round to his house. 'It read about like this: "Mancil A. Milligan, We are offering you employment at Pickwick Dam as a public safety officer for $1440 a year. Wire back immediately if you accept." ' And he did.

Rearmament

Mancil Milligan was one those directly helped by the New Deal. But there were many others who still continued to suffer, until rearmament put money back into people's pockets. After 1939, when Europe was once again at war, the United States was to become the 'arsenal of democracy'. Roosevelt described the new situation succinctly. 'Dr New Deal is off the case,' he said. 'Now it's Dr Win-the-War.'

By this time Robert Nathan was working for the Defense Advisory Committee. Part of his job was to find the raw materials needed for military production. Chilean copper for the jackets of bullets was one of these. Suddenly, he recalls, 'We started buying copper like mad from Chile'. Badly damaged by the recession in the United States, Chile now benefited from renewed industrial activity there, and prosperity began to come back into the Chilean economy too. The Americans were not their only customers. The Germans and Japanese, and later the British and the French, also came back into the market.

The middle way, the way of Swedish social democracy and of the American New Deal, would by different means both bring full employment to end mass poverty, and a standard of living that, even in the boomtime of the 1920s, only a few people in a few countries could have aspired to. But first, millions of steel bullets would leave their copper jackets, and many of them would tear their way into human bodies.

Great Escape

THE WORLD OF CINEMA

'WAIT A MINUTE! WAIT a minute! You ain't heard nothing yet!' declared Al Jolson to an enthralled cinema audience, but almost nothing could be heard above the cheering and the clapping. The audience were delighted. They had just heard the first words ever spoken in a feature fiction film.

It was 1927 and the opening night of *The Jazz Singer* in New York. Al Jolson's words were to prove prophetic. Once the technology had been developed to synchronize sound to film, the era of silent movies was over. Audiences around the world were thrilled by the introduction of sound, which brought a new realism to the movies. 'We felt we were really there when we could hear it,' says Kathleen Green, who saw *The Jazz Singer* when it was first screened in Britain. The idea of talking movies was so revolutionary that some people just could not believe they existed. 'We told my grandmother about the film when we came back,' Kathleen Green remembers, 'and she would not have it. Absolutely not...she would not believe you could hear them talking.'

The first sound systems were primitive yet highly effective, giving films a completely new dimension that could be used in many ways. Lisetta Salis, who went with her friends to see the film when it came to her home town in Italy, remembers the effect it had on them all. 'We were breathless,' she recalls. 'We kept saying to one another, "Let's watch it again".' And they did.

The introduction of sound was just one of several landmarks in people's experience of the cinema in the twentieth century. As they became increasingly widespread and sophisticated, movies made huge profits and created great industries and international stars. The power of film was so great that it was exploited for political ends. It fuelled people's aspirations, changing the way thousands of people thought about the world, and bringing new experiences, desires and ambitions to men and women whose horizons had previously been limited to their local communities. The cinema created a new, shared human consciousness. It not only showed people what the world was like but also offered them an escape into another one.

THE NEW MAGIC *of sound and screen attracts huge crowds to Warner's cinema.*

Silent beginnings

It was at a café in Paris in 1895 that the Lumière brothers first presented their moving pictures to a paying public audience. The programme of ten short films lasted twenty minutes, and the impact on the audience was immense. Sophie Monneret, whose grandfather was there that night, describes how he returned home 'absolutely marvelling', and exclaiming, 'It's extraordinary! The world has changed!'

At the start of the twentieth century people in countries all over the world paid to watch films of many kinds – comedies, fantasies, information ('actuality') and drama. These early 'movies' found their largest audiences among the poor. Mario Coarelli was growing up in Italy, and describes the first cinema he went to, in a poor suburb, as 'a place for the common people'. He remembers how the movies appealed to whole families. 'There were children, young and old men, women with babies in their laps, and all eating roasted pumpkin seeds.' Sometimes people did not pay much attention to the film itself, but 'when a dramatic film was shown, you saw people crying,' and if it was exciting they 'watched the film and they all started saying, "You swine. Look at that scum!" You started thinking, "Is he really dead? No, they're just faking it." The older people who were there, they were totally fascinated by the cinema.'

When he was only eight years old Luigi Cavaliere was the projectionist at his church theatre in Rome where local children attended catechism classes. 'They were more toys than projectors,' he remembers. 'There was a small crank that had to be turned to project the silent film. We had four or five films in storage, and we showed them over and over again.'

In India early films were shown in tents. When Rajam Ramanathan was seven years old her mother took her to see her first film. 'There would be sand poured on the ground where people could sit, and there were benches, and chairs without armrests, and finally chairs with armrests that were the most expensive seats in the house....There was a person standing in the front of the theatre who would say what the actors were supposed to be saying.'

MOBILE THEATRES *like this early Electric Theatre offering 'moral and refined' film spectacles to the American public were a growing feature of both town and country at the turn of the century. Travelling projectionists could easily set up their tents, bringing the new medium to fairgrounds and marketplaces. By 1905 these makeshift theatres were being replaced by permanent movie houses.*

FILM PREMIERE
With their newly invented Cinématographe, the Lumière brothers showed their films to audiences as excited as the one in this early film poster. Other pioneers of film techniques in Europe and the United States were quick to follow their lead. In 1905, after making thousands of films, the Lumière brothers decided to abandon film production.

INVENTION AND ENTERPRISE

I**T TOOK A FLASH** of inspiration for one man to jump the final hurdle in the race to develop moving pictures. Louis Lumière was that man. His brainwave was to install a mechanism to drive film through a camera, stopping it at intervals when a frame of film was in the 'gate'. The mechanism was based on a device called the presser foot, which shifts cloth through a sewing machine. This idea enabled Louis and his brother Auguste to develop the Cinématographe, with which they could both shoot and project films.

Although it was the Lumière brothers who found the key to projecting moving images onto a big screen, most of the technology needed for cinema, including colour and sound, was already available. Eadweard Muybridge, an English photographer employed by the Californian millionaire Leland Stanford, had broken new ground in the 1870s when he recorded a sequence of photographs showing a galloping horse. He succeeded in breaking down complex movements into a series of images taken at intervals of just a fraction of a second.

Another major breakthrough came in 1888 with the development of light-sensitive paper that could be placed on a roll – a film. The paper was soon replaced by celluloid and marketed by its American inventor, George Eastman, under its trade name Kodak. In the same year Thomas Edison, another American inventor and entrepreneur, also began to take an interest in the development of moving pictures. By 1891 one of his British employees, William Dickson, had built both a film camera, the Kinetograph, and a viewer, the Kinetoscope. By 1894 there were commercial viewing 'parlours' for the Kinetoscope in the United States, but the spectator had to peer into a little wooden box, and it was only possible to produce films of about a minute long.

Edison concentrated on selling the Kinetoscope to wealthy families for individual viewing, and paid little attention to the possibility of projecting the images onto a large screen. It was the Lumière brothers who were the first to recognize the enormous public appeal films would have. In the months that followed their first public showings in Paris in 1895 their representatives travelled the world showing films to excited new audiences.

The silent movies soon became one of the most popular forms of entertainment, eclipsing even the music hall and vaudeville. Many people went to the new movie theatres several times a week. Barry Johnson, who grew up in the country in southern England, remembers going to the cinema from the age of five. It was wonderful to be able to find something new and different to do. 'It was a great relief to be able to walk to the cinema at least once a week to get some amusement. We looked forward to it very much. It was a very small cinema, and had a solid floor with bench seats, and we as kiddies used to call it the "flea pit".'

It was the same in the United States, where the first cinemas were called 'nickelodeons' because the admission fee was just five cents, a nickel. They were usually concentrated in the poorer neighbourhoods, and became a central feature of many immigrant districts. Many of the theatre owners were themselves immigrants from eastern Europe, and some went on to play a major part in the great Hollywood film industry.

Although the films themselves were silent, music was often played to accompany them. Danny Patt grew up in Maine in the United States, and when he was just twelve years old he began to play the piano in his local movie theatre. He describes how he had to match the music to the films. 'A cue sheet was a very important part of the show because it told you what to play and when, and for how long.' No music was given to the pianists, so they had to build up their own collection. 'You had to have a good repertoire of mood music such as hurries, chase music, battle music, fight music, Indians and cowboys, marches and all that sort of thing.'

Part of the success of the early silent movies was due to their universal appeal. Without language, films could be understood throughout the world, and their stars shot to international fame. The first and greatest star was a comedian whose trademarks were a smudge of a moustache, a bowler hat and a cane. Millions of people came to love the exploits of the little tramp. He did not only appeal to adults, as Barry Johnson explains. 'Charlie Chaplin portrayed on screen the simplicity of funniness which the children easily understood, both in his actions and his pathos, the twirl of his stick, his little trip and mannerisms.'

MUSICAL ACCOMPANIMENT *to silent films provided by pianos (ABOVE), organs and even orchestras, together with the cheering and hissing of the audience, meant that the theatre was rarely quiet while a film was being shown. Danny Patt (BELOW) used cue sheets and imagination to play the piano at his local movie theatre. Some cinema organs (ABOVE RIGHT) came equipped with special sound effects: drums, bells and coconut shells mimicked thunderstorms, sirens and a trotting horse.*

"We were growing up in an era when movies were probably the main entertainment medium....Movies made quite an impression on our lives. They really meant something to us."

HARRY HULTS

Audiences all over the world understood and loved Chaplin's films. As a young girl in India, Nimmal Vellani watched every Chaplin film she could. She loved all of them, and 'especially *The Gold Rush*, because it's really beautiful that scene where he eats those boots of his – opens the laces and thinks it's spaghetti or something. It's really lovely.' *The Gold Rush* was the favourite film of Monique Guédant in France, too, who first saw it at a church film show in Normandy. 'When you are young and you see a movie by Charlie Chaplin, it is really enchanting. I remember especially that cabin at the top of the mountain, and the bear circling around the cabin with Charlie Chaplin. We didn't know if we wanted the bear to eat Charlie Chaplin or Charlie Chaplin to eat the bear!' she laughs.

CHARLIE CHAPLIN
(ABOVE LEFT) *or Charlot as he was known in Europe, captivated audiences with his sympathetic and comic portrayals of hardship and poverty. The British-born former vaudeville artist began his film career in the United States in 1913, and later wrote, directed and starred in his own films like* The Gold Rush *(1925), about the adventures of a prospector.*

ROOM FOR COMEDY
(ABOVE) *Some movie theatres showed only comedies, the most popular films of all. People went to the cinema above all to be entertained, and they could choose from a growing number of different types of comic films – from slapstick to chase films – at movie theatres devoted principally to comedy, like this one in the United States in 1915.*

"These theatres had ceilings that were painted blue and special projectors that would project clouds and stars and sunrises on the roof....When the film started the curtain would part...the lights would go down and you would literally be drawn into this thing by your surroundings. **"**

CY LOCKE

THE TOOTING GRANADA (OPPOSITE), *one of the opulent new cinemas in London, accommodated more than 3000 people at each performance. Len Smith remembers those picture palaces. 'They called them a palace and it was a palace...the hangings, the draperies and everything inside the cinema was absolutely wonderful...the cinema was the only place where I had seen this luxury.'*

LURING AN AUDIENCE (BELOW) *with exotic surroundings, live entertainment and star-studded film previews was Sid Grauman's answer to competition. At his ornate Chinese Theatre in Hollywood, built in 1927, movie stars were also invited to record their hand and foot prints for posterity in the concrete paving of the forecourt.*

The movie experience

During the 1920s shrewd theatre owners realized that they would increase their profits if movies could be made to appeal to a wider audience, the prosperous as well as the poor. One way of doing this was to make the audience more comfortable. In the cities new cinemas were constructed on a grand scale. Cinemas like the Roxy in New York, Grauman's Chinese and Egyptian theatres in Hollywood, the Gaumont in Paris and the Odeon, Marble Arch in London were designed in spectacular architectural style, and with extravagant and exotic interior decor. Luxurious cushioned seats replaced the old wooden benches, and pianos were replaced by mighty organs or full orchestras. These new cinemas became known as 'picture palaces', and offered a new taste of luxury.

John Anderson was a student in Boston in the 1920s, and got a job as one of more than thirty ushers at the Metropolitan, which seated 4000 people. He remembers the trouble that was taken to make movie-goers feel good. 'I was on the main floor, just inside the door. Outside, there was another usher all dressed up, with a dickey shirt front and a lovely jacket....The outside man had a swagger stick, and opened the door as the people were passed in to the second usher, who showed them to their seats.'

Cy Locke, who also lived near Boston, worked at pitching hay to earn enough money to go to the movies. 'It was really an experience,' he recalls. 'You would be treated like a king or queen. You were ushered into an enormous lobby of marble and gilt, with huge stairways leading up to the balconies. All the carpets were at least an inch or two thick. Everything was done in there to make you feel comfortable, to make you feel very important.'

In Scotland a young pianist, Rita Wooton, found work playing in the orchestra at the new Strathclyde cinema in Glasgow after passing her audition. She was impressed both by its size and by the facilities it provided. 'It had a very big balcony, a big vestibule too at the entry...and also a huge stage, of course. It had a grand piano for myself in the band pit. There were violins, cellos, saxophones, trumpets, trombones, drums, everything!'

NEWS HORIZONS (BELOW) *The Biograph Company produced weekly newsreels offering viewers the 'Latest events from all parts of the world'. These became regular features in cinemas, and for the first time people could see for themselves events that took place far away. For George Williams in Britain they were an important part of the show. 'The cinema was the only place where you picked up what went on elsewhere in the world, that's where we picked up most of our news.' The Pathé Gazette, produced by the leading French film company, also brought popular newsreels to international audiences from 1909.*

Barry Johnson's family decided to enter the film business in 1920. They bought a cinema in London. 'It was a medium-sized cinema seating about four to five hundred people.' He helped his father as projectionist, while his mother looked after the cash box. He recalls how after the shows, 'We had to go round and sweep up all the orange peel and the peanuts, with a screwdriver in one hand and a brush in the other, because the children would get so excited that they would literally shake their seats to pieces.'

One of the things that made the cinema so exciting was that it opened people's eyes and minds. As Danny Patt says, 'We didn't have radio then, there was no way for one town to communicate with another....By watching the silent movies we were able to see what was going on in the rest of the world. It was a wonderful thing for these small towns to be able to get that education.'

SETTING THE SCENE (ABOVE) *As the possibilities of film making grew more ambitious and challenging, directors began to explore new subjects and ways of dealing with them. Taking a lead from the Italian film industry, which began making historical, biblical and mythological epic films, Hollywood produced its own film extravaganzas.* Intolerance, *made in 1915, used elaborate settings like ancient Babylon to explore people's attitudes to others' beliefs. Although it was one of the most expensive films to be made at the time, it was not a commercial success.*

THE AMERICAN EPIC

THE WILD WEST, with its intrepid pioneers and heroic cowboys, became one of the most popular film subjects. First featured in Thomas Edison's first Kinetoscope show in 1894, the Western adapted to every shift in the fashions and fortunes of the movie industry. In the era of silent film, tales were told through cowboys such as Tom Mix, who fought black-hatted villains against a backdrop of breathtaking scenery. He was followed by singing cowboys such as Gene Autry, Roy Rogers and Hopalong Cassidy.

The essence of all Westerns was the conflict between good and evil, and the audience's enthusiasm to see the struggle resolved through action-packed drama. George Williams remembers his first experience of Westerns as a child in east London in the 1930s: 'When the film showed the white-hatted cowboys everybody cheered, when they flashed onto the bad cowboys, everybody booed.' The conflict could be set between white men and native Americans or Mexicans, between ranchers and homesteaders, or any individual against the community.

The first Westerns portrayed simple moral stories. By the 1930s some were beginning to explore more subtle types of conflict. *The Robin Hood of El Dorado* in 1936 and *The Oxbow Incident* in 1943 demonstrated the brutality of lynch law in the Old West, and asked searching questions about the racism and cruelty of Western expansion. In 1952 *High Noon* was interpreted by many people as an attack on the victimization of communist sympathizers at that time.

Above all, cowboys represented the most prized American virtues: independence, endurance, honesty and courage. These were epitomized by John Wayne as the classic hero in films such as *Stagecoach* and *She Wore a Yellow Ribbon*. Westerns, with their action-packed drama, spectacular settings, idealized heroes and moral resolution appealed not only to Americans, who could recognize the story of their own society on the screen, but thrilled cinema audiences in all parts of the world.

COWBOY STAR *Tom Mix, renowned for his skilful horsemanship, in a scene from* Rough Riding Romance.

People were even more delighted when talking pictures were introduced, though audiences accustomed to booing and hissing the villains and shouting when they felt excited had to learn to behave differently and keep quiet in order to hear what was being said. Now audiences in different countries needed the help of dubbing or subtitles to understand foreign language films.

Sound was not welcomed by everyone. The musicians who had accompanied silent films, which nobody wanted to watch any more, lost their jobs. It was a sad occasion for Danny Patt. 'When *The Jazz Singer* came out every little town throughout the United States...had a piano player or an organist or somebody playing for the silent movies....I realized that part of my career was nipped in the bud. I was full of grief.' Rita Wooton felt the same. 'The advent of the talkies was a tremendous blow to all musicians.... There must have been hundreds in Glasgow who were employed in the orchestra pits.'

Many of the small, older cinemas were also badly affected. They lacked the facilities and the space to show the new movies, and often could not afford the extra equipment. As Barry Johnson remembers, it meant 'all the average-sized silent cinemas closing down, one by one', including the one his family owned.

The cinema held a special attraction for young courting couples. Franco Ricci, who grew up in Rome, recalls, 'We didn't have cars...our refuge was the cinema. Nobody paid any attention to what other people were doing, no one was scandalized.' For the young Cy Locke in Boston, 'To go to the movies and not hold hands was absolutely out of the question. If you sat in the back row, that was fine, and it wasn't beyond the realms of possibility to try and sneak a kiss now and again.'

As well as being a refuge, the cinema was a school for lovers. Nimmal Vellani was shocked when she first saw people kissing on the screen. Most Indian films at the time were very chaste. She claims romance came into her life through movies. 'If there was one young girl falling in love with a nice-looking man, I would imagine myself doing the same thing. And it actually happened in my life that way. If I had not gone to the cinema so often, I would not have had romance in my life. I would just have been married off like an ordinary girl to the man of my grandfather's choice.'

A ROMANTIC SCENE *from the 1927 Hollywood film* Flesh and the Devil, *starring the Swedish actress Greta Garbo and John Gilbert. The cinema brought romance to viewers across the world, and millions of young men and women learned new ways to kiss by imitating lovers on the screen.*

BROADWAY MUSICAL
With the new sound came a new kind of film – the musical. This first musical, Broadway Melody, *was made in 1929; it was also one of the earliest films to use Technicolor in some of its sequences. Experiments with colour film processes continued during the 1930s.*

The Hollywood dream

By the 1920s audiences around the world were flocking to see American films. The American film industry was not only making more films, it also exported them successfully, producing films that had enormous international popular appeal and subtly sold the view that American capitalism offered the best way of life. Like many others, Kathleen Green liked American films best. 'They were very lively and full of fun, and the British films seemed rather slow...not much in the way of chorus girls or happy times.' In Italy Lisetta Salis also remembers their fascination. She and her friends were struck by the great freedom that American girls seemed to enjoy, such as going out with their boyfriends, and she remembers their clothes as 'more revealing than what would have been worn in any other country'. She first saw a telephone, a car, and a skyscraper on the screen. 'Really the cinema was a great emotional experience! Of course later we became accustomed to these things, but the first moments were so exciting.'

Some people had mixed feelings about the wealth and luxury they saw in American films. Luigi Cavaliere remembers his mother's surprise that industrial workers in the United States owned cars, and Lisetta Salis feels that although people were very curious about American films, 'At the same time they were showing us how backward we were, because in the films they were wealthy...they were successful, happy, lively, well-dressed. The idea of being poorer and less elegant made us feel wretched.'

The American film industry was expanding from its base in Hollywood in California, where cheap real estate and reliable sunshine provided an ideal setting for massive film production. It was Hollywood and its stars that fascinated millions of people across the world, becoming synonymous with glamour, drama and romance. American fashions and new trends were successfully exported through its films.

In some countries attempts were made to resist the dominance of the American film industry. In Britain and Germany quotas were imposed, so film

The fan magazine

FILM FANS EVERYWHERE *could buy specialist publications about the cinema and its stars. In them, people could read the latest gossip about the public and private lives of their favourite screen stars, and could choose from an array of publicity photos for their scrapbooks. The first film magazines were published in the United States in 1911; other countries soon began to produce their own versions.*

THE STAR SYSTEM

THE FIRST MOVIE STARS were not names but faces. Actors and actresses in early silent films were not credited, so fans identified their favourite artists simply by their looks or by the studio that employed them. In 1909 Carl Laemmle, head of Universal Pictures, took the unprecedented step of naming the 'Biograph Girl' as Florence Lawrence. In a blaze of publicity he also hinted (untruthfully) that she had been killed in an accident. There was a public outcry. Studios began to realize the value of publicizing information about their actors, and a network of promotion and publicity was set up. The star system was launched.

Studios exploited the public's fascination with the stars by carefully feeding facts and gossip to magazines and newspapers. William Fox, founder of 20th Century Fox, promoted a

tailor's daughter from Cincinnati as 'Theda Bara', an anagram of 'Arab death'. He circulated rumours that she was the daughter of an Arab sheikh, and portrayed her as a mysterious, exotic seductress.

There were also comic stars like Charlie Chaplin and the Frenchman Max Linder. The greatest, most romantic film stars of all were the swashbuckling swordsman Douglas Fairbanks and his wife, Mary Pickford; she became known as 'the world's sweetheart'. The couple were idolized by millions of fans. The cinema usher John Anderson remembers, 'Everybody was fascinated by movie stars, and especially by Douglas Fairbanks'. He recalls the public excitement when the star couple visited Boston. 'I stood there for hours waiting in line just to get a short glimpse of him when he went by in his limousine....He was my

favourite movie star and I saw every single picture that he played in.'

While the stars were expected to parade the trappings of stardom – palatial mansions with huge swimming pools, limousines, and glamorous social lives – they were used by the studios as capital assets. A star's name would guarantee an audience, and would put a 'trademark' value on a film. But in return for astronomical wages, the studios imposed strict controls on their stars' lives. Stars could be loaned out to other film companies, or suspended without pay if they turned down a part.

The Hollywood system proved highly successful as a way of promoting films; the stars provided a dazzling diversion to their fans.

companies had to produce a certain number of home-grown films before foreign imports were allowed. This was only marginally successful because many of the film companies simply rushed through the production of cheap, poor-quality films in order to reach the quota. These films became known as 'quota quickies'.

Ever since the movies had first reached a public audience, church groups and other establishment figures had feared that they were immoral and that their influence would be corrupting. The liberated way of life portrayed by Hollywood films added fuel to this debate. Some people were scandalized by any suggestion, let alone portrayal, of sexual activity. Kathleen Green remembers the impact of one scene in a film she saw as a child. 'The man came out of the bedroom and there was an awful fuss.' She recalls that she and her friend were very innocent, and did not understand the sexual implications. 'We came to the conclusion that he had gone to bed with his shoes on.'

Pressure on Hollywood to improve its moral standards intensified, and a code of practice was established setting out what was and what was not permissible, both on the screen and off it. The Hays commission hoped to fend off state censorship through its new production codes, which were particularly concerned about sex. 'There could be no kisses with two people in bed together, even if they were husband and wife,' recalls Arthur Abeles. To counteract the adverse publicity arising out of scandals about the behaviour of Hollywood stars, a major public relations campaign was launched to emphasize the importance of the movies to American life. In other countries, which had their own censorship codes, concerns over film content varied, sometimes including portrayals of religion or politics. Whatever the moral dilemma, nothing seemed to lessen the grip Hollywood had on the public imagination. The popularity and power of its films remained undiminished.

GLAMOROUS STARS

Jean Harlow (LEFT) *and the celebrity couple Douglas Fairbanks and Mary Pickford* (BELOW LEFT) *were among the stars who captivated the attention of millions of fans. Their carefully shaped public image was often matched by their exotic private lives. But the fantasy did not last. Douglas Fairbanks and Mary Pickford divorced in 1936, as their careers were fading, and Jean Harlow died of ill health the following year.*

THE SMOULDERING SEXUALITY *of Jane Russell in* The Outlaw *proved too much for the censors. A cut version was finally released several years after the film was first made in 1943.*

RAJA HARISHCHANDRA
(ABOVE) *was the first Indian feature
film. Based on ancient Hindu texts, it tells
the story of a king who gives up his earthly possessions to gain
salvation. Its female roles were played by men. When Rajam
Ramanathan (ABOVE RIGHT) saw it as a young girl, she says,
'It was like God actually appeared in front of us….My
grandmother would even pat her cheeks as penance whenever
Rama or Krishna showed up on the screen.'*

EXPRESSIONS OF ANGST (BELOW) *in Fritz Lang's 1931
film – M – about a series of child murders. It was the first film
in which the leading director used sound. These nightmarish
scenes were characteristic of German expressionist films.*

National cinema

Hollywood exerted a powerful influence, but many countries had also been developing film industries of their own, with their own character. In India the film industry was begun by one man, Dadasaheb Phalke. Inspiration struck when he went to see a movie called *The Life of Christ*. 'I was mentally visualizing the gods, Shri Krishna, Shri Ramchandra and Ayodha. Would we, the sons of India, ever be able to see Indian images on the screen?' Spurred on by what he had seen, Dadasaheb Phalke worked day and night for six months with equipment he had bought in Europe until, in 1913, he produced the first Indian movie, *Raja Harishchandra*. He had laid the foundations for what would later become one of the world's most prolific film industries.

Indian movies soon found a widespread and enthusiastic audience. Older people were astonished by the new medium, and mythological films in particular had a huge impact. Vanraj Bhatia recalls how his great-aunt, who was ninety-two years old, reacted when she went to her first movie, which was about Krishna. 'She went absolutely berserk, she wept and prayed and she prostrated herself, and she thought God had finally arrived.' People took off their shoes before entering the cinemas, he says. 'It was as though they were going to a temple or something.'

PLAYING FOR POWER

ILMS WERE UNIQUE in their power to play on people's credulity and to manipulate their emotions. Almost from the start, the immense impact that films had on those who saw them was turned to political purposes: dictators and totalitarian governments used film for propaganda.

In Italy the fascist government exercised great influence in the film industry through subsidies. When people went to the cinema they became a captive audience for the documentary films that were screened as a regular addition to the programme. Some people enjoyed watching them, but others found them an imposition. Mario Coarelli's family lived in fear after his father had been attacked for his anti-fascist feelings. He remembers that 'All the movies were mainly propagandist....Whenever they spoke, it was all for propagandist aims: "Long live fascism!"...and you sat there and were taught what they wanted you to learn. You had to watch it.'

In Germany entertainment was used as the way to spread the Nazi message. Uninspiring feature films were superseded by sentimental 'waltz dreams', stories of mountain climbers, comedies and lavish historical films, all celebrating the pomp and splendour of Germany's past. Powerful documentaries promoted the Nazi ideals of supreme military order and the superiority of the Aryan race, and viciously anti-Semitic films were also made – all effective ways of shaping the minds of the German people.

During the Second World War the persuasive power of film was exploited in many nations. In the United States a series of seven documentaries was made to explain *Why We Fight*. Cy Locke was the projectionist at his army base and ran all seven of them, including *Know Your Enemy – Japan*. 'Its intent was to make us hate the Japanese,' he remembers. 'They were our enemy and we were supposed to destroy them, and the film certainly served its purpose....I have to fight with myself about that because I was really indoctrinated.'

While American soldiers were being taught to hate the Japanese, audiences in Japan were being shown 'national policy films' that taught them about their war responsibilities and the glories of military life. Nationalistic fervour in the Soviet Union was stirred up by documentary films such as *The Defeat of German Armies Outside Moscow*, which showed thousands of bedraggled, humiliated German soldiers, defeated by the Russian forces.

Film was also used constructively. Racial attitudes in the United States were helped to change by a highly influential film made in 1944, *The Negro Soldier*. Compulsory viewing for all soldiers, black and white, and shown to civilian audiences in 5000 cinemas across the country, it showed the most positive image of black Americans ever seen on screen up to that time – a positive result of film's power to change the world inside people's heads.

PROPAGANDA FILMS *Scriptwriter Carlton Moss recalls how the United States military authorities tried to boost morale among black soldiers in the army, who were still segregated. 'They had to do something on this black question...film was one of the things they were going to use.'*

In Germany the local film industry was also flourishing, especially in the studios that had developed out of the propaganda industry of the First World War. After the war German films reflected the prevailing mood of the time – they were full of pain and foreboding. In the Soviet Union, too, a vigorous film industry developed that reflected the political flavour of Soviet life. Films were used to support the revolution and its achievements, and played a vital part in mythologizing it for the people. They went to the cinema not for escapism or to canoodle in the back row, but to participate in the new socialist culture.

A world of make-believe

The harsh realities that were reflected in German and Soviet films soon became part of real life elsewhere. In 1929 the world was plunged into a devastating economic depression, and the next decade brought great hardship to millions of people. Cinema could offer a brief escape from the real world.

Arthur Abeles, who worked for the American film company Warner Brothers, recalls how competitive the cinemas had to be to draw in their audiences. 'Nobody had any money, so we had to attract them with gifts, things like that....Some people put on variety acts on the stage....But the only way really to get people into a cinema, and they'll come whether they're broke or they're not broke, is a good film.'

The films produced by Hollywood during the Depression were among the most extravagant and spectacular of all time, in dramatic contrast to most people's experience of life at the time. Kitty Carlisle Hart, who appeared with the Marx Brothers in their comedy *A Night at the Opera*, remembers how people responded to the glamorous films that were being shown. 'They were make-believe,' she says. 'They were the world that people didn't have, but that they wanted. And that's why they were so popular.... People were living in terrible circumstances; this was total escape.'

Although most people lacked money to buy warm clothes and struggled to pay the rent, they still flocked to the American movies to see film stars in elegant gowns and well-tailored suits, living in sumptuous apartments with expensive furniture. Cy Locke remembers what the Depression was like for so many people. 'The main square in the town would be filled with little kids shining shoes, selling papers, people wandering aimlessly around,' he says. 'I think that what movies did for these people and for us was to brighten what was virtually an intolerable situation.'

Comedy films were also very popular. Laughter was therapeutic, and as Mary Evelyn Hults, who grew up in New York, remembers, people needed it more than ever. 'It was very cheap to go to the movies in those days. But thinking about what kind of money

GOING FOR GLAMOUR *at the cinema in the 1930s provided relief from reality. Cy Locke* (ABOVE) *recalls how 'Many people would take what I assume was their last dime or their last quarter, and go see Ginger Rogers and Fred Astaire just to escape for a couple of hours.' The dancing duo,* (BELOW) *in the comedy musical* Carefree, *also initiated new dance crazes and fashions.*

"*Just going and laughing for a little while at something that might be totally ridiculous was very important. It was a therapy really in many ways.*"

MARY EVELYN HULTS

HOLLYWOOD FANTASIES
*offered audiences lavish ballroom scenes (*LEFT*) as escapism or the alternative world of horror in monster movies like* King Kong *(*RIGHT*). Large crews were needed for the elaborate studio sets and special effects, providing jobs at a time of widespread unemployment.*

GAME FOR A LAUGH (BELOW) *The Marx Brothers captivated audiences with their hilarious eccentricity in their 1935 hit* A Night at the Opera. *The American comic trio were originally part of a family vaudeville act with their mother and two other brothers, and staged successful plays on Broadway. Groucho's wisecracks and the chaotic activities of Chico and Harpo were at the heart of all their films.*

QUEUEING UP *for the Saturday morning cinema show in Britain in the 1940s was necessary if you wanted to be sure of a seat. 'You might have to go there half an hour or even an hour before it started, if it was a very popular picture,' remembers Ena Turnbull. 'We didn't mind how long we queued as long as we got in.' Cinemas continued to show films during the war to people who were much in need of entertainment. During air raids the screen would flash a warning sign at the audience.*

we didn't have, it was a very special treat. It was a difficult time for people....Just going and laughing for a bit at something that might be totally ridiculous was very important.' People loved the Marx Brothers, with their anarchic humour, and when Charlie Chaplin's latest comedies, *City Lights* and *Modern Times*, were released they were instant successes.

During the Second World War, too, films offered refuge from misery, and even provided inspiration. In German-occupied France the Nazi censors had approved a film called *The Night Visitors* as a simple love story set in the Middle Ages. To French audiences the heroine, Anne, represented France; the Devil, the night visitor, was Hitler. The Devil turns Anne and her lover into stone, but is finally defeated when he realizes that whatever he does, he cannot stop the beating of their hearts. The film's huge emotional impact helped to give Michel Lequenne the courage to join the Resistance movement, and fifty years later, as he re-reads that passage in the script – 'But it's their hearts that beat,' the Devil exclaims, 'That never cease to beat, that beat, beat, beat!' – he is still overcome with emotion: 'Look, I'm crying all over again'.

Boom and decline

Immediately after the war there was a boom in cinema attendance in Europe and in the United States. In Rome, Luigi Cavaliere remembers, 'Everybody wanted to have some fun, and the only thing available was the cinema. Television was not yet available. Everybody would eagerly wait for a new and beautiful film to watch. In these theatres, even if they were not well equipped, people would queue up anxiously waiting to watch the show.... Kids brought pans full of food from home while waiting for the theatre to open. Going to the movies was a party...everybody wished to forget about the ugliness of the war.' George Williams used to go to the cinema with his friends in London. 'The queues were so long, at times it was necessary to split ourselves up into ones and twos and just take whatever seats became available.'

During this time European film studios began producing better quality films than ever before, and local audiences started to identify with movies made by home-grown directors, first in Italy, then in Britain, France, Sweden and eastern Europe. International

ANIMATED IMAGINATION

WHEN A SMALL, mischievous mouse named Mickey first skipped across American cinema screens in 1928, animated film was catapulted into new realms of popularity. Walt Disney's *Steamboat Willie* was the first cartoon made with synchronized sound, and its star, Mickey Mouse, was to become an international celebrity.

Walt Disney played an enormous role in popularizing animation, but he did not invent it. Animation had existed before film itself, but moving pictures gave it a new lease of life. The camera could lie; film could bring life to the inanimate. Using a basic 'stop–motion' technique, films could record sequences of static images (drawings, puppets or models), each slightly different from the one before. When these images were projected in quick succession, the illusion of continuous movement was created.

Early cartoons tended to be short, commercial products designed to precede feature films, but a series of technical developments soon enabled them to stand as films in their own right. In 1913 Earl Hurd patented the use of a transparent medium bearing the moving parts of the cartoon over an opaque background. This technique used celluloid, and made the whole process of animation much quicker. Raoul Barre introduced the 'slash' system, which saved unnecessary drawing. The motionless parts of the characters were drawn only once, while the animated parts of the characters were drawn separately in many different positions. These drawings were then superimposed one at a time onto the background and photographed before the sequence was put together.

The arrival of sound in 1927 and the introduction of colour in the early 1930s allowed animators to create new worlds of magical fantasy. Walt Disney gave life to a cast of much-loved characters who became familiar all over the world to people of all ages. Cartoons were the ultimate escape, recreating a lost world of imagination for adults, and allowing children to revel in fantastic adventures that would be unthinkable in the real world.

MICKEY MOUSE *in his starring role as the sorcerer's apprentice in Walt Disney's phenomenally successful 1940 feature film,* Fantasia. *A whole generation of children were introduced to classical music by the film's cartoon figures, who were drawn to move to the music of Bach, Stravinsky and Tchaikovsky.*

PUBLIC SCREENINGS *at outdoor cinemas were held in postwar Europe at special festivals of international cinema. The huge screen in the courtyard of the Old Oberhaus Castle near Passau in western Germany needed new projection equipment, and special loudspeakers were used to relay films to the 40 000-strong audience. Film festivals awarded prizes and attracted distribution deals.*

film festivals meant that film makers could share new films and exchange new ideas and techniques. In Europe there was a move away from the glamour and fantasy of Hollywood. Italian 'neo-realist' films showed what real life was like. Mario Coarelli liked the new realism. 'They were so beautiful because they showed the same life we were leading,' he says. Franco Ricci appreciated them too, but felt that 'the majority of Italians did not accept this because they said that your dirty clothes should be washed in the family home and not shown abroad'.

Hollywood films were still popular, and as influential with their audiences. George Williams remembers that he learned from American films how to smoke, how to wear the collar of his overcoat pulled up round his ears, and how to kiss. He also remembers being impressed by the material comforts the Americans seemed to enjoy in the films. 'Their rooms always seemed so massive and the apartments so well lit, so luxururious. They had refrigerators, which I'd never seen....The cars were always flash – great big limousines.' Children were encouraged to imitate the child star Shirley Temple. Ena Turnbull was one of them. 'Her hairstyle, her voice, her pretty little face – all mums tried to dress their little girls like Shirley.'

The postwar golden era for Hollywood was not to last. The monopoly of the big studios was challenged, and the film industry was shaken by accusations of communist influence. American movie audiences had reached their peak in the late 1940s, and gradually the fans began to drift away. Many of the sumptuous picture palaces closed and were refurbished as supermarkets or stores. Cy Locke remembers the changes. 'I still liked going to the movies, but there was a sadness...seeing half-empty theatres, and theatres that were starting to degrade in terms of upkeep.' In his view, cars contributed to the fall in audiences. 'Drive-ins were starting to flourish after the war,' he remembers. 'People could get out again, had enough gas to go places.' As people moved out to the suburbs they seldom went to the movies in town, and many young people tended to stay at home once they married and had

WIDESCREEN *processes like Cinerama and Cinemascope (*ABOVE*) were the film industry's answer to television in 1953. Films such as* Tarzan *used new techniques to widen the audience's field of vision and give a heightened sense of movement and realism. This film poster also promotes the use of colour, gradually introduced in the late 1940s.*

PLANES, TRAINS AND CARS (OPPOSITE) *converge at a drive-in cinema in West Virginia, where people watch the big screen from the relative comfort of their cars.*

children. The baby boom spelled the end of the movie boom. Mary Evelyn Hults remembers, 'We had our first child and we seldom went out to the movies'. In Britain, too, as Arthur Abeles recalls, 'People got out of the habit of going twice a week, and they became more selective'. Cinemas and film companies introduced new tactics to draw back their audiences, from 3-D glasses to wider screens and even Smell-O-Vision, and an increasing number of films began to appear in colour.

These innovations were no match for the new entertainment medium. Television now caused a sensation that equalled that of 'the talkies' some twenty-five years earlier. For Ena Turnbull it meant the end of her cinema-going days. 'Television came in and that's when the cinema started to decline,' she says. All the cinema offered, and more, could now be enjoyed simply by turning a knob on the little box in the corner of the living room. People continued to watch films, but more often on television than at the cinema.

In countries where television was not yet available the film industry continued to flourish. India produced more feature films than any other nation during the 1950s. Many of these films, like those made elsewhere, were purely for entertainment, and the music in them was as important as the story. The film composer Vanraj Bhatia believes the songs were their lifeblood. 'With bad songs an Indian movie cannot succeed, no matter how good it is. But there have been bad films with good songs, and they have become hits.' The film industry in Japan was growing and also thrived during this period, as it did in China and South America.

Although the 1950s saw a decline in cinema attendance in some countries, it was still enriching many people's lives. Film had changed the way people saw the world, and to some extent the way they lived in it. 'It was everything,' declares Duilia Bartoli. 'It was about how to live, how to behave oneself, how to talk and walk and how to be courted....For me, it has been everything.'

A NEW DIMENSION
Three-dimensional movies made during the 1950s required audiences to wear 3-D glasses, with transparent lenses, one red and one green to match the double image on the screen. The glasses, first introduced in 1935, had the thrilling effect of bringing the flat screen to life, but as Arthur Abeles describes, they presented practical problems. 'They had to be collected after each performance, cleaned and given out at the next performance.'

WAITING FOR THE SHOW (RIGHT) *in Calcutta. While cinema queues in Europe and the United States were dwindling in the 1950s, the Indian film industry boomed.*

Master Race

THE NAZIS RULE IN GERMANY

WITH THE PRIDE AND precision of veteran soldiers, an apparently endless column of uniformed men moved through the dark streets of Berlin. They marched like conquerors under the Brandenburg Gate, then turned right into the Wilhelmstrasse, the heart of German government and German militarism. Yet these were not soldiers but well-drilled, fanatical supporters of national socialism. As they marched they carried flags and torches. The red and white banners displayed the symbol of the Nazis, the black swastika.

This was the night of 30 January 1933. The men were marching to the Chancellery, and there on the balcony to greet them was their leader, their Führer, Adolf Hitler. Above the blare of the marching bands rose the cheers of the watching crowds. Josef Felder, a socialist opponent of the Nazis, was among them. He remembers 'A sea of swastikas. We were out in the streets and went to the Brandenburg Gate, and watched the Nazis marching into power. People were drinking, there was a huge commotion. We were shocked by this incredible upsurge and the sudden swing to the Nazis' side.'

The Nazi propaganda machine beamed their victory throughout the nation. 'Like a blazing fire,' a radio announcer declared to his listeners, 'the news spreads across Germany: "Adolf Hitler is chancellor of the Reich!" A million hearts are aflame! The nation rejoices and gives thanks!' This was a colourful exaggeration, typical of the manipulation of public opinion that played such an important part in spreading Hitler's message across Germany.

Millions of Germans had opposed Hitler, millions had good reason to fear him. Yet it is also true that for many Germans at the time Hitler's strange grasping of power was a thrilling moment. After the First World War German pride had been badly wounded, and the country's prosperity shattered. By 1933 many Germans felt that only Hitler could give them back their jobs and their security, and restore the greatness and honour of the German people. He promised that he would make the world acknowledge the Germans as a master race, and many believed him.

ORDERED RANKS OF NAZIS *march triumphantly through the streets of Berlin.*

Democracy in crisis

Hitler rose to power in a period of chaos in Germany. In the early months of 1918, fifteen years before, imperial Germany seemed to be on the eve of a crowning victory against the Allied armies in the First World War. Instead, it was the German army that broke. Then the emperor abdicated and fled to Holland, and a republic was proclaimed. For the first time democracy was introduced in Germany under the Weimar Republic. But the country was on the verge of revolution. For a few weeks in 1918 and 1919, political extremists fought in the streets of Berlin, while the Allies imposed a vengeful peace that was to prove disastrous to the German economy.

The new government had to contend with grave difficulties arising from military defeat and a collapsing economy, problems that were not of its making but for which it was blamed. Moderate government seemed to be weak; democracy powerless. Then, with the help of American loans and investments, the economy began to revive. For five short years, from 1924 to 1929, in spite of everything, the Weimar Republic succeeded in restoring order. But the world recession was to bring further disaster. In each of the winters of 1930–31 and 1931–32 over six million people were unemployed; in one of every two German families the breadwinner was out of work. In their frustration and despair, many Germans turned to extremist parties for their salvation.

However, Hitler did not come to power as the result of an overwhelming popular vote. In the 1932 elections only a third of the electorate voted for the Nazis. Millions of people not only did not support what they stood for, but dreaded a future under Hitler's leadership. They had good reason to be fearful. As soon as Hitler took power, he quashed all opposition to Nazi rule. Political opponents were put in concentration camps, and trade unions were banned.

BEGGING IN BERLIN
Still wearing his Iron Cross, the highest decoration for bravery, this ex-officer was one of many Germans who had offered their lives for their country during the war, but for whom their country was not able to provide any work in peacetime.

SCAVENGING FOR FOOD
in the streets of Hanover. This was one way to get enough to eat – not always easy in the harsh reality of life during the economic crisis of the 1920s.

WHEN MONEY WENT MAD

THE HYPERINFLATION OF 1923 had a more profoundly disastrous effect on German society than any of the other hardships that befell the German people in or as a result of the First World War.

In 1914 4.2 gold marks equalled one United States dollar. By 1921 one dollar was worth 250 marks. The following year the rate was 1460 marks to the dollar, and in 1923 the inflation simply went crazy. In the summer the rate was 48 000 marks to the dollar. On 4 October it was 440 million, on 23 October fifty-six billion and by 17 November it was two and a half trillion. A solution was then found by issuing the new rentenmark, guaranteed against Germany's assets – land and railways. The government waited until the exchange rate was 4.2 trillion marks – in other words, until the old mark was worth one-trillionth of what it had been against the dollar in 1914. One trillion old marks could therefore be exchanged for one new mark, and the inflation disappeared overnight.

In its crazy course of little more than a year, the hyperinflation had done appalling damage. It reduced to nothing money hoarded during decades of hard work. Women could no longer save for their dowry, and worried about whether they could get married without one. Postage stamps were overprinted with seven, eight or even nine zeros. Banknotes were used as fuel for stoves. People paid for meals in restaurants before they ate because the price would have gone up before they had drunk their coffee. Others carted their savings to the baker's in wheelbarrows. Those with assets in land, in factories or in foreign currency became rich beyond their wildest dreams, while wages and salaries were worth almost nothing. Many Germans blamed the Weimar government, as malnutrition, hunger, fear and despair became the daily experience not only of those who already knew the effects of poverty, but also of many people accustomed to prosperity.

THE LAST STAMP (ABOVE) *to be issued during the period of hyperinflation. Its value was 5000 million marks.*

BUNDLES OF BANKNOTES (LEFT) *may have been almost worthless, but they could still come in useful as building bricks.*

Hitler's new vision

Hitler skilfully manipulated people's desire to regain what they felt they had lost: pride in Germany's past, hope for its future, a sense of adventure, a sense of security. He would make Germany great again; all the German people were required to do was...do as they were told. Many people were relieved to find a leader with such confidence and strength, and were prepared to accept his belief that in the name of national unity and the restoration of order party politics should be abandoned, that only a strong government could take the harsh measures that needed to be taken. One of the

FROM FAILURE TO FÜHRER

Before the First World War, Adolf Hitler was a lonely, embittered, feckless young man. None who knew him then would have predicted his rise to power. A school dropout and failed art student, arrogant, lazy and aloof, he lived in a men's hostel in Vienna. He had squandered his inheritance, and had to paint picture postcards that earned him a pittance. Most children grow out of playing war games; in his teens, they were still Hitler's favourite occupation. The war offered him a chance to play these games for real: he could now become a hero. He was given the dangerous job of battalion runner and was decorated three times for bravery. He was regarded as an eager and dutiful soldier, but failed to be promoted because of his subservience to his officers and arrogance towards his fellow soldiers.

When the war ended Hitler, like the rest of the German army, was shocked by defeat and by the demoralized society he found when he returned. His own past humiliations and failures now became identified with Germany's fate. Many of the elite storm troopers (fast-moving, lightly but lethally equipped soldiers) joined the Freikorps, irregular units that were encouraged by the army high command to fight revolutionaries and communists, to invade Germany's lost eastern territories and to attack radicals and Jews.

After the war Hitler discovered his abilities as an orator among the disillusioned young men of Munich, particularly Freikorps members, anti-Semitic ideologues and right-wing plotters. He joined the German Workers' Party, the DAP, later renamed the National Socialist German Workers' Party (NSDAP or Nazis). Within a year he had become its undisputed leader. In November 1923 he leapt onto a table in a Munich beer cellar and proclaimed his plans for a coup. He was to march on Berlin and overthrow the Weimar Republic. Instead he was arrested and imprisoned.

While he was in prison Hitler wrote his political manifesto, *Mein Kampf*, 'My Struggle'. Many of his ideas had been gleaned from political pamphlets published before the war; now he infused them with his own hatred, anger and desire for revenge. The book was anti-Semitic, anti-communist, anti-Versailles, full of extreme nationalist sentiments. It laid out all too clearly this provincial politician's plans for taking over the state, reviving Germany as a power and destroying the Jews and all others whom he saw as his enemies. At the time, these ideas seemed so outrageous that few people took them – or their author – seriously.

Hitler undoubtedly had gifts: an extraordinary ability to influence and persuade, powerful appeal as a demagogue, a superb memory for detail, great skills as an actor who had total control of his voice. The extreme political and economic situation in postwar Germany provided circumstances in which these gifts, devastatingly combined with Hitler's complete ruthlessness and lack of compassion, were to sweep this unlikely leader to power.

Reaching out to Hitler *An enthusiastic crowd surges towards Hitler, cheered by his promises to make Germany great again.*

ways in which Hitler gained support was to confirm people's view that the difficulties they endured were not of Germany's making, but were really the fault of politicians, the Allies, the communists, bankers, speculators and Jews. He offered them scapegoats – and promised to deal with them.

At the same time, Hitler seemed to offer a new vision, of Germany restored to all its former glory. His ideal was rooted in Teutonic myth, harking back to a time when German knights had been honourable and chivalrous, and their ladies beautiful and pure. Germans were flattered to be told that their Aryan ancestors had been a superior, uniquely cultured race. They were assured that they could regain this lost quality if they followed Hitler, who would lead the drive to turn the German people into the heroic race they deserved to be – the master race.

Hitler's rhetoric was an inspiration and a balm to those who shrank from the hardships, horrors and uncertainties of twentieth-century reality, with its wars and revolutions. They found refuge in the reactionary paradise Hitler offered them: an idealized German community that would be peopled only by pure, honest, beautiful, strong Aryans, unpolluted by the presence of modern ideas, or by Jews or Slavs. In particular, he drew on old hatreds, old jealousies towards the Jews.

"Today our people know our will was stronger than the German crisis. After fifteen years of despair a great people is back on its feet."

ADOLF HITLER

A VAST CROWD *watches as massed troops parade in front of Hitler at a rally in Nuremberg. Deliberately magnificent in scale, and held in dramatic and imposing settings, the rallies reflected the Nazis' obsession with power and order.*

AN ELECTION POSTER (ABOVE) *for the Nazis depicts the misery of unemployment and urges people to turn to Hitler as 'Our last hope'.*

REINHARD SPITZY *and his wife fulfilled all the necessary conditions to marry and to breed Aryan children. The state gave loans to healthy couples to help them raise larger families, and even awarded medals to unusually productive mothers.*

THE IDEALIZATION OF MOTHERHOOD (OPPOSITE) *was part of the Nazis' reshaping of society. Posters such as this gave almost religious overtones to the important task of raising healthy Aryan children – against an idyllic rural background. Women were expected to fulfil only traditional roles as their contribution to the creation of the master race, and were discouraged from taking part in public life.*

Hitler convinced many people that he could make things better. Reinhard Spitzy, an officer of the SS (Hitler's elite body-guard) from 1931, was one of them. 'What he said was what we all felt: he would get rid of the unemployment and the hunger of the Depression, and the injustice of the Versailles peace treaty and the reparations.' Flattered to be chosen for the SS, to be among those who would form 'the future, aristocratic backbone of the German nation', Reinhard Spitzy shared the Nazi dream of a new German kingdom, a Third Reich. He feels the resentment against the Jews was understandable. 'They were much slyer in business than the normal German and Austrian, and they were so excellent in literature and in theatre, and in cinema, and in science. More than fifty per cent of the medical doctors in Vienna were Jews, more than seventy per cent of the lawyers. Of course all that made for a strong and hardline anti-Semitism. But nobody thought that we would end by killing Jews and throwing them out.'

Walter Mühle, an Austrian who was also selected to join the SS, remembers: 'For us, the Führer was the highest thing that existed...people adored him. The people responded to him like a pop star today. My beautiful years were the peace in Berlin. That was the nicest time in my life...look how many apartments they built for the workers; industry was rebuilt.' It is true that as Hitler poured money into armaments, into housing and other public works such as roadbuilding, Germans became more prosperous. The number of people unemployed fell from the six million of 1932 to 0.3 million in 1939. Freedom was the price they paid for security. Trade unions were banned; instead all workers had to join the German Labour Front (DAF). No opposition was allowed.

Helping the farmers

The German Labour Front was only part of the drive for support in both the towns and countryside. Farmers had also suffered in the Depression, and were given financial assistance. They were also swept into well-managed demonstrations that brought people and party together. Harvest Festival became a mass celebration. Luise Essig, an education officer for the Nazi agriculture ministry, still remembers these occasions. 'Thousands of farmers...and young people from all over Germany travelled in special trains and then

Unterstützt das Hilfswerk

Mutter und Kind

TAKING TO THE ROAD

THE 'PEOPLE'S CAR', the Volkswagen, was Hitler's idea for a cheap, mass-produced vehicle that would make motoring available to all German citizens at a time when cars were a luxury for the rich few. Ferdinand Porsche, later famous for his sports cars, designed the car according to Hitler's specifications. It was to carry two adults and three children, and to look like a beetle. According to Hitler, 'You have to look to nature to find out what streamlining is'.

As part of his huge public works programme, Hitler aimed to build a road network that would be the finest in the world. His grandiose plan included 4000 km (2500 miles) of autobahns. The network eventually provided rapid links between cities, helping to boost the German economy. At first there was also a more immediate military purpose: to move troops and munitions quickly between the western and eastern borders.

The scheme gave work to thousands of unemployed Germans, whose energy and commitment was held up as an example to others – this was national socialism in action. Asked by a radio reporter to tell listeners about their work, one man replied enthusiastically, 'We're building bridges like you've never seen before. What we're building is reliable. We're proud of our work.' The workers' pride was shared by thousands of people who witnessed the opening ceremony as new stretches of motorway were completed, or who heard the radio reports heralding the work as a great German achievement.

In contrast to the willing German workforce whose skills were so widely celebrated, the gigantic Volkswagen factory was built and operated by non-Aryan labour. Seventy per cent of the workforce on the factory floor was made up of forced labour, adults and children, German and foreign. These workers were kept in labour camps, suffering varying degrees of deprivation and harsh treatment according to a precise racial hierarchy. Discipline was rigorously enforced by SS factory guards.

Hundreds of thousands of Germans eager to acquire their own Volkswagen took part in the government savings scheme. They put aside five marks a week towards the purchase of their car. It was an exciting prospect. However, the factory was not ready until 1938, and it was soon converted to make military vehicles. The only 'Beetles' made before the Second World War were obtained by SS officers and other members of the Nazi elite. The people were cheated of their savings. Despite this, after the war the 'people's car' became extremely popular – a triumph of German design and manufacture.

marched for hours to get as close to the front as possible. We all felt the same, the same happiness and joy. The Harvest Festival was the "thank you" for the fact that we farmers had a future again. Things were looking up. I believe no statesman has ever been as loved as Adolf Hitler was then. It's all come flooding back to me. Those were happy times.'

Luise Essig put into practice the new ideal of the Aryan German as self-disciplined, fit, healthy and pure. She developed a training programme called 'Faith and Beauty'. Fitness and the revival of rural crafts were linked with racial purity and the sanctity of the soil. Thousands of young people in the Young Girls' League were taught through the scheme. Gradually a whole generation was taught to live the model life the Nazis prescribed.

Persecuting the Jews

Not everyone was part of this shared national 'folk' experience. The belief that held up pure-bred Aryans as the ideal Germans excluded Jewish people and condemned them as an inferior race.

Horst Slesina worked as a radio reporter. He still remembers how propaganda taught him 'that the Jews are in all the influential positions in the economy, in banks, in cultural areas'. At the time he was persuaded that 'they were ruining our Germanness'. Now he reflects: 'It was a process which developed gradually and took over whole sections of the population who had never thought about it before. A lot of them just talked about not necessarily believing it. But gradually their brains became fogged and they started to say "the Jews are our misfortune".'

Official persecution of Jews began as soon as Hitler took power. Children were excluded from the state education system. Simply because they were Jewish, many thousands of people were expelled from their jobs in law, in the civil service, in universities and elsewhere, or could no longer practise medicine. Both marriage and extramarital relationships between Jews and non-Jews were forbidden. These were not random acts but deliberate Nazi policy, formalized over several years in a series of increasingly harsh decrees, the Nuremberg laws.

'SAVE FIVE MARKS A WEEK (LEFT) *if you want to drive your own car' reads this slogan promoting the savings scheme for the Volkswagen.*

SALUTING THE FÜHRER (BELOW) *Construction workers drive past Hitler at the official opening of a new 1000-km (620-mile) stretch of autobahn.*

'ALL GERMANY HEARS THE FÜHRER' *declares the poster advertising the People's Receiver (Volksempfänger). As Horst Slesina remembers: 'Propaganda gave people a big boost in confidence for the first time'; it played a vital part in Hitler's success. The development of broadcasting as an instrument of the state was masterminded by Josef Goebbels, who believed that 'A good government cannot survive without good propaganda'.*

GERDA BODENHEIMER *as a girl with her family in their garden in Berlin in the 1930s. Only Gerda (with her hand on her father's arm and today,* TOP*) looked Jewish. The family thought of themselves as Germans. It was thanks to the foresight and courage of Gerda's mother that the family emigrated and survived.*

For most German Jews this sudden blast of official hostility was all the more bewildering and painful because, in spite of an undercurrent of anti-Semitism, they had always felt it was their country. A Jewish Berliner, Hans Margules, explains. 'We felt ourselves to be German before the Nazi time. We had German-Jewish beliefs, we were Germans.'

The critical moment, for Hans Margules and for millions of other German Jews, was Kristallnacht, the night of broken glass. On 9 November 1938, 'I was decorating the shop window with my boss and then we heard breaking glass everywhere, all over; it just didn't stop. We looked out into the street and saw a mass of people and we saw that the neighbouring shop, all the Jewish shops had been broken into. The people who were smashing the windows, they weren't even in uniform, they were just young boys with sticks who were enjoying themselves enormously. That was the end of Jewish business in Germany.' The owners of the 7000 businesses destroyed were never compensated; their insurance payments were confiscated.

As many as 30 000 Jews were arrested during Kristallnacht. Yet Hans Margules shows understanding towards the Germans. 'The German had to feed his family. He wasn't anti-Semitic, but he had to do what the party desired, he had to belong to the party to carry on his job, to feed his family, and as it was repeated that the Jews...are terrible, that must have gone into people's heads. They must have thought – well, maybe that's right. You can't judge all the German people...everyone had to speak quietly... fear...it was a dictatorship.'

JEWISH REFUGEES *on board the* St Louis *in 1939. The liner crossed the Atlantic to Cuba, but it was turned back and had to return to Europe. Many of the passengers were later killed. In 1938 and 1939 about 120 000 Jews left Germany to make a new life. It was not easy for them to settle elsewhere, as many countries were reluctant to accept them.*

'JEWS NOT WANTED HERE'

JEWS HAVE BEEN PERSECUTED IN EUROPE for hundreds of years. Their history has been punctuated by hostility; their economic and cultural contribution regarded with suspicion, envy and superstition. In the late nineteenth century animosity towards Jews took a new form: it became an ideology. Jews were blamed for the assassination of the Russian tsar, Alexander II, in 1880. As a result the government officially reimposed restrictions on Jews and unofficially encouraged murderous pogroms. Jews were accused of ritual murder in Hungary in 1882. In that year an international anti-Semitic congress met in Dresden. The new anti-Semitism was also growing in the West. Jews excelled in many fields – as lawyers, writers, musicians, journalists, intellectuals, businessmen and bankers. Their success was often resented. An economic crisis in 1873 was blamed on 'Jewish financiers', and anti-Semitic politicians became popular in Germany and Austria.

In France and in Russia false accusations of Jewish conspiracy were widely circulated and believed. Many people were frightened by the rapid economic and social changes of the late nineteenth century, and some Jews seemed to represent the uncertainties of a bewildering future. Jews were also viewed with suspicion as both socialist revolutionaries on the one hand, and capitalists on the other.

In Germany the desperate situation after the First World War fed an angry search for scapegoats. First among them were the Jews, despite their patriotism during the war. Adolf Hitler drew on his own violent anti-Semitism to play on people's fears and whipped up the potential for hatred. As soon as he was in power, he ordered a national boycott of Jewish-owned businesses.

Further persecution was to come. Within two years the Nuremberg Laws had set out the exclusion of Jews from German society. They were deprived of German citizenship, their status reduced to that of 'subjects of the state'. They were not allowed to vote. More and more careers became closed to them; their children could not attend school; they could not employ domestic servants of German blood. Their passports were stamped with a distinguishing red 'J'. A decree in 1938 deprived Jewish communities of their legal status. The Nazis used the framework of the law systematically to remove from the Jews the protection that the law should provide for all its citizens.

COMING OUT OF SCHOOL *An illustration from one of the children's books published under the Nazis that were designed to help Aryan children identify Jews, and encouraged hostility towards them.*

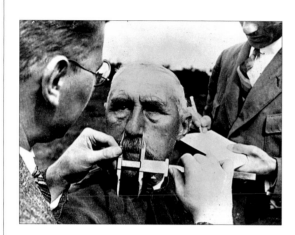

TAKING PRECISE MEASUREMENTS *of people's noses and noting other physical characteristics such as eye and hair colour were part of the pseudo-scientific categorization of individuals into more or less desirable racial types. Germany was not the only country in which questions of eugenics – race care – were being considered at this time. Darwin's ideas about the 'survival of the fittest' shaping the evolutionary process were applied to theories about the best way of ensuring healthy human populations. In Germany these theories were used to justify the Nazis' policies, which were designed to lead to the elimination of non-Aryan peoples.*

Enforcing racial purity

The persecution of the Jews was only one aspect of the Nazis' determination to create the master race. They wanted to purge the German community of all those who they feared could weaken the Aryan breeding stock. This meant the persecution of people who offended social norms and were considered alien, degenerate and unproductive, including gypsies, homosexuals, prostitutes, criminals, alcoholics, vagrants, the workshy, the disabled and the mentally ill.

Many non-Nazi and even anti-Nazi social scientists at this time, in Germany and elsewhere, enthusiastically called for policies to 'improve' the genetic stock. What was different about the Nazis was the ruthlessness with which they pursued their own extreme version of these 'eugenic' ideas. At first the Nazis decided to lock away the 'genetically unhealthy' and sterilize them. By 1945 a total of between 200 000 and 250 000 people – gypsies, schizophrenics, alcoholics among them – had been sterilized.

Anna-Maria Ernst's family were gypsies living in Germany. She remembers her childhood in the early 1930s as a happy time. The gypsies had their caravans and horses, and they could wander wherever they liked, pitching their camps in a forest or by a lake. 'It was a beautiful life,' she reminisces, 'wonderful. There were happy celebrations, dancing – the women were full of vitality. Marriages were arranged. We had real gypsy weddings, which lasted for six or seven days. We loved living life as free as a bird in the sky.'

Gypsies had been roughly treated by the police before. But in 1935 they were described in a commentary on the Nuremberg decrees as aliens. To the Nazis they were an antisocial nuisance. They were now catalogued, categorized, harassed. Anna-Maria Ernst recalls sadly how things changed. 'Everybody had to sell their caravans and their things and move into flats. We had to settle down permanently and register....The wonderful life was over.'

When war began in 1939 the gypsies were rounded up and despatched to concentration camps. Anna-Maria Ernst was sent to Auschwitz. There too the gypsies danced: the SS would burst into their hut in the middle of the night and order them to dance and sing. Some gypsy girls were sterilized without anaesthetics. Many people died in the camps. At least 15 000 of the 20 000 gypsies in Germany were murdered, as were some 500 000 gypsies in other parts of Europe. Anna-Maria Ernst could not understand why they were treated so viciously.

In 1936 Hitler first challenged the other European states. He reoccupied the Rhineland, a demilitarized zone since the First World War. He offered two more challenges in 1938: he forcibly united Austria with the German Reich, and in the late summer annexed the Sudeten German fringes of Czechoslovakia. In 1939 he took over the rest of Czechoslovakia, and then invaded Poland. This time his bluff was called: Britain and France declared war. With the coming of war, Hitler's dictatorship became harsher, its methods even more grim.

Immediately before the war, the Interior Ministry sent round a confidential circular ordering the registration of children who suffered from congenital deformities. By early 1940 these children were being systematically killed or starved to death. In the summer of 1939 Hitler had personally ordered one of the leading Nazi doctors, Dr Leonard Conti, to organize what was called a 'euthanasia' programme (in fact a programme of mass murder) for adult patients suffering from a number of conditions, including schizophrenia and epilepsy. At first the victims were given lethal

A bewildered woman *is questioned by researchers. Gypsies, like other minority groups, were graded into categories. They were forced to register with the authorities and to settle permanently in one place.*

injections. In January 1940 the first patients were gassed, and thereafter the numbers executed increased steadily.

The reality of Hitler's racial policy was brought home to thousands of families, who learned with horror that a relative they believed was being cared for in a hospital or asylum had in fact been murdered. One of these was the Rau family. Marie Rau's mother suffered from depression and anxiety. Diagnosed as an incurable schizophrenic, she was eventually taken to a clinic at Hadamar. Here, in groups of sixty, patients were led down to a cellar and choked to death with carbon monoxide gas. The Rau family were told that their mother had died as a result of 'complications from a wart on her lip'. They learned the truth only after the war. As Marie Rau now says, 'The fact that these people were murdered is a disgrace for our whole society.'

Terrible suspicion hardened into certainty. Judges raised questions, but were told that the programme had Hitler's express authorization. A Protestant pastor objected in person to Hitler. Roman Catholic bishops also protested; Pope Pius XII published an order condemning the 'direct killing' of innocent persons. Count von Galen, bishop of Münster, preached a sermon against euthanasia. It is said that Hitler himself witnessed a demonstration against the transportation of mentally disabled children. In August 1941, when he ordered an end to the gassing, some 71 000 people had been killed; the programme continued by other means.

'The Jew will be exterminated'

In January 1939 Hitler had made a prediction that sounded to many at the time an ugly but idle threat. If 'Jewish financiers', he told the German parliament (the Reichstag), 'should succeed in plunging the nations once more into a world war, then the result will not be the Bolshevization of the earth, and thus the victory of Jewry, but the annihilation of the Jewish race in Europe.' Eight months later, Europe was at war and Hitler was in a position to put his bloodcurdling prophecy into effect.

As the Nazis moved into country after country, they isolated the Jews. News bulletins solemnly told Germans at home that in Poland 'the hardest task for the Germans is the Jewish question'. Their rhetoric represented a systematic policy of death. There

The yellow star

THE STAR OF DAVID *had traditionally signified God as protector of the Jewish people. When the Nazis forced all Jews to identify themselves by wearing the star it became instead a symbol of humiliation and a target for hatred.*

THIS DAILY NEWSPAPER *in Hanover carried an article on Wednesday 25 February 1942 written by Hitler himself. The subheading reads* Der Jude wird ausgerottet – *'The Jew will be exterminated'. Hitler was confident enough to make his intentions public.*

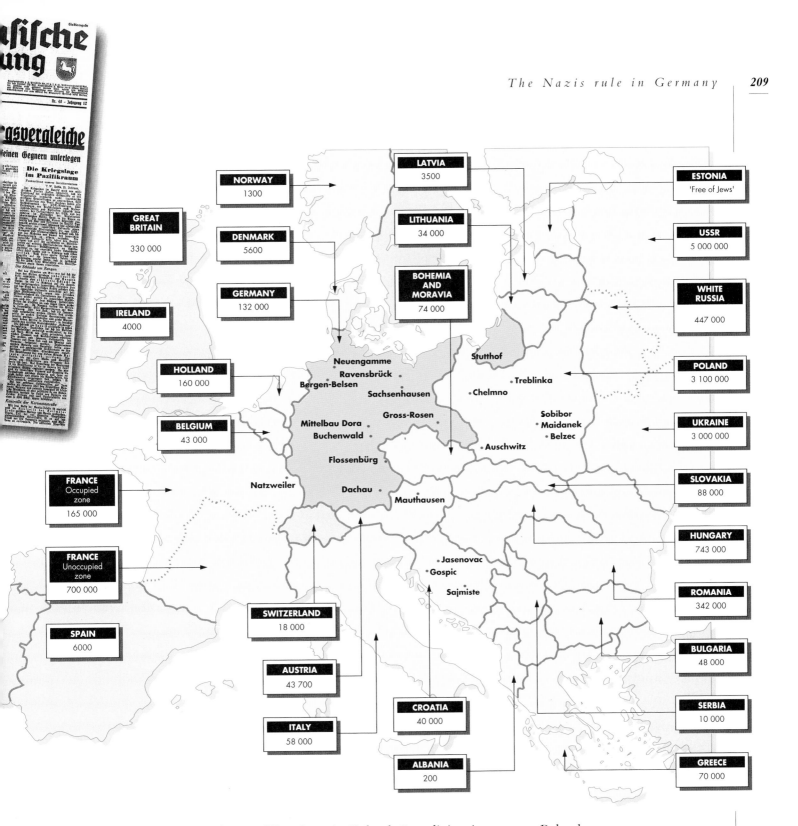

NORWAY 1300	**LATVIA** 3500
GREAT BRITAIN 330 000	**ESTONIA** 'Free of Jews'
DENMARK 5600	**LITHUANIA** 34 000
IRELAND 4000	**USSR** 5 000 000
GERMANY 132 000	**BOHEMIA AND MORAVIA** 74 000

GREAT BRITAIN 330 000
IRELAND 4000

NORWAY 1300
DENMARK 5600
GERMANY 132 000

LATVIA 3500
LITHUANIA 34 000
BOHEMIA AND MORAVIA 74 000

ESTONIA 'Free of Jews'
USSR 5 000 000
WHITE RUSSIA 447 000
POLAND 3 100 000
UKRAINE 3 000 000

HOLLAND 160 000
BELGIUM 43 000

Neuengamme
Ravensbrück
Bergen-Belsen
Sachsenhausen
Mittelbau Dora
Buchenwald
Gross-Rosen
Flossenbürg

Stutthof
Treblinka
Chelmno
Sobibor
Maidanek
Belzec
Auschwitz

FRANCE Occupied zone 165 000
FRANCE Unoccupied zone 700 000
SPAIN 6000

Natzweiler
Dachau
Mauthausen

SLOVAKIA 88 000
HUNGARY 743 000
ROMANIA 342 000
BULGARIA 48 000
SERBIA 10 000
GREECE 70 000

SWITZERLAND 18 000
AUSTRIA 43 700
ITALY 58 000
CROATIA 40 000
ALBANIA 200

Jasenovac
Gospic
Sajmiste

EUROPE'S JEWISH POPULATION *was listed in detail by the Nazi leaders at a conference in January 1942. The major concentration camps are named on this map. Most of these were forced labour camps; those in Poland were set up specifically as extermination centres.*

were three million Jews in Poland. Jews living in western Poland were driven east and herded into ghettos in the towns, especially in Cracow, Lodz and Warsaw, a process that was carried out with the utmost brutality.

Tadeusz Pankiewicz, who worked in a chemist's shop in the Cracow ghetto, saw what took place there. Thousands of people were in the square waiting to be deported. The Germans searched the empty houses, shooting anyone who had stayed behind. In the silence, in bright sunshine, a young and elegantly dressed woman

> *"The worst things that could possibly happen in the world happened in the ghetto... It was hell that those people lived through."*
>
> TADEUSZ
> PANKIEWICZ

CHILDREN OF THE GHETTO *shared their parents' suffering. In Warsaw the Germans allowed themselves 2300 calories a day. The Poles were allowed 900 calories a day; the ration for Jews was only 183 calories. This was deliberate starvation.*

walked forward. 'I could hear her footsteps. As she approached the people who were to be deported she passed the Germans, Gestapo men, who were standing by with whips and pokers....They beat her in the face, in the eyes. All she wanted to do was to say good-bye to her mother, who was standing in one of the rows. She got to her mother, and they said their farewells. At that point the Germans pounced on her, dragged her back to the place she came from, beating her and kicking her mercilessly.' He speaks for all the ghettos when he observes, 'The worst things that could possibly happen in the world happened in the ghetto – unimaginable, indescribable murders.'

With the German invasion of the Soviet Union in June 1941, Nazi policy also crossed a line. Jews had been pitilessly mistreated; now their extermination was to be the final solution. At first the SS tried to get local anti-Semites to do their work for them, with some success. But it was not enough. Soon four special motorized SS murder units,

ROUNDING UP JEWISH FAMILIES *in the Warsaw ghetto. This was where the process of destruction began for Polish Jews. The frightened small boy in the foreground was the only one of the group to survive. One of the guards was later identified from this photograph and prosecuted for war crimes.*

each 1000-men strong, fanned out behind the advancing army. Their mission was to kill communist commissars by the hundred, and Jews by the hundred thousand. Sometimes they simply dug a grave, lined the Jews up in front of it, and shot them, in row after row, so they fell on top of each other into the grave. Sometimes they took them to nearby dunes or pits and shot them there.

Zvi Michaeli lived in Eishishky in Lithuania. Some 3500 Jews lived in the town. They were herded to the pits that had been dug in front of the old cemetery. Zvi Michaeli was sixteen years old; he went with his father and younger brother. He still weeps as he remembers that day. 'When we all undressed...when I saw Rabbi Zushe undressed, I thought this was the end. His glowing face...the verses from Psalms that he recited in our ears...up to then I'd been confident that we wouldn't die. And my father was

RESISTING THE NAZIS

'WHAT WE HAVE WRITTEN and said is in the minds of all of you, but you lack the courage to say it aloud.' These are the words of a twenty-year-old student, Sophie Scholl, who was executed for resistance to the Nazis. Although there was little effective opposition to the Nazis, a heroic minority of Germans from many backgrounds – Christians, both Lutheran and Catholic, socialists and communists, students and trade unionists, civil servants and army officers – did have the courage to resist. And it took courage: telling an anti-Nazi joke, hiding a Jewish friend or listening to a foreign radio station could lead to torture and death.

In 1936 and again in 1941 there were widespread demonstrations against Nazi orders to remove crucifixes in Roman Catholic districts, part of Hitler's campaign against religion. Clergy and doctors objected to the euthanasia programme set up in 1939 for patients with mental illnesses, and in February 1941 there was an uproar in Absberg,

Franconia, as mental patients were being taken to their deaths.

Throughout the period of the final solution there was only one case of open protest by Germans on behalf of Jews, and incredibly, it worked. In February 1943 the Gestapo, cracking horsewhips and shouting 'All Jews out!', broke into homes and factories to round up the last 10 000 Jews in Berlin. Some 8000 of them were immediately sent to Auschwitz and the remaining 2000 people, Jews married to Aryans, were held at Rosenstrasse 2-4, a Jewish centre in the heart of the city. For ten days and nights their husbands and wives gathered outside, shouting 'Murderers!' at the SS guards. According to one witness, 'the accusing, demanding cries of the women...like passionate avowals of a love strengthened by the bitterness of life', could be heard above the traffic. Goebbels, fearing that the secret of the final solution might leak out, authorized the release of the Jews still being held in the Rosenstrasse centre.

ON THE BRINK *between life and death, a gaunt victim awaits the bullet that will send him into the pit. In the wake of the advancing German armies, special murder units of SS men spread out across the occupied European countries. Their instructions were to find and kill Jewish people. Whole communities of men, women and children were rounded up and murdered in this way.*

saying, "You will live, don't be afraid. You will live and take revenge." My brother David...he clung so tight. And the shots of the machine gun....There was a mixture of voices, of people crying, and children, and the shots...and the dust...and everything mingled together...I found myself inside the pit. I felt my father give me a push and lie on top of me. He wanted me to live.' And live he did, escaping to the woods, covered with his own and his father's blood.

In the first year, the death squads murdered 750 000 Jews in the territories captured from the Soviet Union. Two German marksmen alone, helped by Ukrainian 'packers' who arranged the bodies of the dead, shot more than 33 000 Jews from Kiev in the ravine at Babi Yar. Over the next year, the SS were responsible for the deaths of one and a half million people. Altogether, two and a quarter million Jewish men, women and children were killed, either hanged or more often systematically lined up and machine-gunned so that their bodies fell into pits, where they were destroyed by fire or with quicklime or simply covered with earth.

Even worse was to follow. Although the Nazi leaders attempted to keep details of mass shootings secret, they themselves had no moral compunction about them. However, this way of killing people did cause psychological problems among the soldiers who carried out the executions. Some of the men in the firing squads became openly sadistic; others were overcome by fits of crying and suffered breakdowns in their health. Some of them even became deranged, and shot wildly at their comrades.

Mass shootings were not an efficient way to murder millions of people. As that was just what Hitler was determined to do, his dire purpose to exterminate the Jews was now transformed, with bureaucratic thoroughness, into an enormous operational plan: the extermination, not just of the Jews living in Poland and Russia, but of the entire Jewish population of occupied Europe, some eleven million people.

The SS turned to a more scientific weapon: gas, which had already been pioneered in the killing of mental patients in 1940. In December 1941 Jews were transported to the camp at Chelmno, in the German-occupied part of Poland. They were killed by being herded into vans that were then filled with exhaust gases. In

CROWDS OF DEPORTEES *arrive at Auschwitz. The bustle gives the scene an air of normality, but for these passengers the destination meant death.*

March 1942 killings began at a camp at Belzec, this time in gas chambers filled with fumes. In May mass exterminations began at a new camp at Sobibor, and on 23 July at Treblinka the Germans started gassing the Jews from the Warsaw ghetto.

At Auschwitz in southern Poland a concentration camp for political prisoners had been extended to house forced labour for a large local factory. The commandant's deputy, ordered to execute political prisoners and Russian commissars, found that Zyklon B gas killed people with hitherto unattainable efficiency and in unprecedented numbers. Both Auschwitz and its adjoining camp, Birkenau, were linked to the main railway network. All was now ready for the greatest crime in history.

The final solution

Jews were being transported to the camps from all over occupied Europe. Hans Margules had earlier fled his own country, but he was caught by the Germans in Holland and forced to help with deportations. He explains his duties. 'At six in the morning we had to fetch the people who were on the transport list....If they couldn't walk we had to take them on stretchers to the trains. No one had any idea that there were extermination camps, otherwise

HANS MARGULES *closing a railway wagon door. He was forced to organize the departure of Jews from a camp in Holland on their long train journey to the death camp of Auschwitz.*

MUSICIANS OF TEREZIN

IN JUNE 1944 A DELEGATION from the International Red Cross travelled to Czechoslovakia to visit the Nazi concentration camp at the walled town of Terezin (in German, Theresienstadt). The Nazis used Terezin as a show camp in an attempt to disprove international reports of the existence of extermination camps.

The entire town, built around its medieval castle, had been turned into a camp through which 140 000 Jews passed, most of them on their way to Auschwitz or one of the other death camps.

Conditions in the camp were so harsh that one in four inmates died. Yet they were allowed a degree of apparent freedom. As a result Terezin became at once a parody of Jewish cultural expression and a place of intense artistic activity.

There was a coffee house in Terezin and a café-concerthall. There was a symphony orchestra, several chamber music ensembles, and even a jazz band called the Ghetto Swingers. More remarkable still, music of lasting quality was composed in the camp by Jews who found the courage to work creatively under sentence of death. Viktor Ullmann, a pupil of Arnold Schoenberg, wrote over twenty pieces there. Other Terezin composers included Pavel Haas, a pupil of Leos Janácek, and Hans Krasa; his children's opera *Brundibar* was so popular in the camp that the jazz band played selections from it in the main square. The Nazis featured the band in a propaganda film.

CREATIVITY IN CAPTIVITY *In the Terezin coffee house a group of prisoners listens to music played on violin, trumpet and accordion. The sorrowful expressions of the listeners are a reminder of the reality that lies outside the café window.*

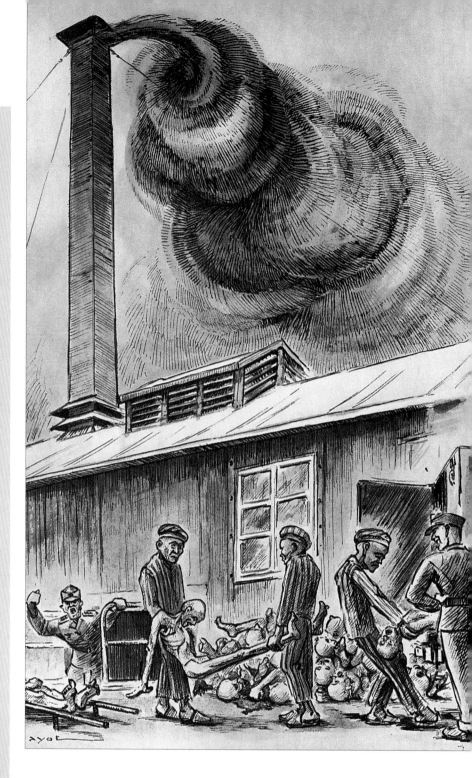

there would have been a panic and the process wouldn't have gone so smoothly. We had to shut the doors. The SS stood behind me and gave the orders. It was very difficult to say no. How could people in our position oppose an SS man?'

The train journey to the camps was itself a terrible ordeal. Norbert Lopper was a Viennese prisoner forced to work on the ramp where the trains stopped. 'We opened the carriages and the people fell out of them. They had just suffocated. Many had been badly wounded. With some of the transports, the SS went onto the roofs of the wagons and shot right into the carriages. Blood was all over the people. We had to get them out of the wagons and carry them to the trucks....This was the most dreadful thing I had to endure. These people were blue and puffed up...they had been crushed to death.'

As the prisoners arrived at Auschwitz in the trains, doctors divided them, some to the right, some to the left: those who were strong enough to go to the work camp, to live at least for a time; those who were to be taken straight to their death.

Dora Schwartz arrived with a group of mothers and their children; they were immediately sent to the gas chamber. 'When we arrived we didn't know where we were. We suspected this was a place of death. We saw the smoke from the chimneys. The sight made you shudder. This was going to be our fate. I was lucky. After the selection another official saw me and pointed for me to go with the others, with the ones who were allowed to live.'

At the time none of the prisoners realized the implications of the selection process. Those who were being sent straight to their deaths were told they were going to have a shower. Only when they had been lulled right up to the gate of the gas chamber, still clutching their towels, did the SS drive them in with beatings. Ten minutes after the gas was released, a doctor would look through a peephole. If everyone was on the floor, it was over. Gangs of prisoners then pulled the dead bodies out and loaded them onto trucks to take them to the crematoria.

Not all Jews went quietly to their deaths. People living in the Warsaw ghetto in April 1943 bravely resisted deportation to Treblinka, selling their lives dear for a month. There was also an uprising at Treblinka itself in August, and another in October at Sobibor. Almost a year later there was a mutiny among working prisoners at one of the crematoria at Auschwitz; they succeeded in blowing up the crematorium before they were overpowered. Riots were not uncommon, and on one occasion a contingent doomed to the gas chamber seized the guards' weapons and shot at them. This probably did not happen more often because of the prisoners' anguished mental state and dreadful physical condition by the time they reached the camp. Men, women and children, weakened by hunger and disease, and exhausted by the long journey crammed together in cattle trucks, were shepherded to their deaths with elaborate cunning by ruthless, heavily armed men.

BILLOWING SMOKE (LEFT) *from the crematorium chimney dominates this drawing by an inmate of prisoners under guard having to carry the bodies of their fellow inmates to be burned. As Wolfgang Gebhardt, whose father worked at the local factory, remembers, 'You could see the prisoners, and you could smell the crematoria. The question was, how did they kill people? Did they just leave them starving and burn them, or did they do something else? These people were starving, everybody could see that. My father was suspicious that people were killed. But he never asked because everybody was afraid to know too much.'*

A MOMENT OF ANGUISH *for a woman prisoner attacked by a guard dog in the camp, sketched by a fellow prisoner. The last words of several Jewish women were written down, and discovered years later hidden in a jar. One woman said, 'I am still so young. I have not really experienced anything in my life. Why should death of this kind fall to my lot? Why?'*

FACING THE TRUTH *When the concentration camps were liberated, Germans living nearby were brought in to see the terrible truth for themselves. These civilians confront the shocking sight of a trailer loaded with emaciated corpses in the camp at Buchenwald.*

RAISING THE SOVIET FLAG (OPPOSITE) *on the roof of the Reichstag, in Berlin on 30 April 1945. Within an hour, and less than a kilometre away, Hitler committed suicide. He had promised to rebuild Germany, but instead its cities had been reduced to piles of rubble.*

The terrible truth

The tide of war turned against the Germans in November 1942. In 1943 Soviet tanks began the long, bloody process of rolling the Nazi armies back, across Russia, out of Russia into Poland and back into Germany, while American and British forces fought their way towards Germany from the west. The master race was master no longer.

As the war ended, the true cost of the Nazis' delusion of a special racial destiny was exposed. On 26 January 1945 Auschwitz was captured by the Red Army. Just 7000 skeletal survivors were found. The SS had burned twenty-nine large storehouses before they fled. In the six that remained the Russians discovered, among other things, 836 255 women's dresses.

In mid-April British tanks entered the concentration camp at Bergen-Belsen. They found 30 000 prisoners in the last stages of starvation, and the remains of 35 000 more. Two weeks later the Americans liberated the camp at Dachau, where there were some 33 000 survivors. The emaciated bodies of the dead were piled 'like a heap of crooked logs ready for some infernal fire', as one witness described it. The American troops were so angry that they shot all 500 SS guards within the hour.

No one knows exactly how many people died in the war Hitler began. His insane venture was a disaster – not only for his enemies, but for his supporters too. He had promised to establish Germans as the master race. Instead, he had gambled with their country, and lost.

Years later, scraps of evidence were found, illuminating the human pain that was the price of the catastrophe. After the war, for example, in the ruins of the Gestapo headquarters where many hundreds of Hitler's opponents were interrogated and tortured, a piece of paper was discovered. On it, Harro Schulze-Boysen, an air force officer who had joined a left-wing resistance movement, had scribbled a poem. The last verse read:

Die letzten Argumenten	The final arguments
sind Strang und Fallbeil nicht,	are not noose and guillotine,
und unsere heut'gen Richter sind	and our judges today are
noch nicht das Weltgericht.	not yet the world court.

10

Total War

THE EXPERIENCE OF THE SECOND WORLD WAR

THE WAIL OF THE AIR-RAID sirens came at the end of a bright, sunny spring day in Plymouth on 20 March 1941. Betty Lawrence, a trainee midwife, was on night duty preparing for a difficult delivery when a bomb struck the children's ward next door. 'There was dead silence, and then you could hear these children crying. Then the next minute, a whoosh right down through the maternity block, and the lights went out and the debris was falling down.... I had to deliver this baby by torchlight, with muck and dirt and dust.'

The following day she walked through the devastated, skeletal city. 'The smell and the stench and the smoke and the fires still burning – I imagine that's what hell would look like....It was utter despair. I still remember the smell, an acrid, smoky smell....You couldn't even find the road. I felt my youth was gone.'

Margarete Zettel can still recall the confusion and horror of the air raid on Hamburg in July 1943, which produced a firestorm throughout the city. 'When we came out of the shelter it was just a pure inferno, chaos, an unbelievable storm, it's something that you can't really imagine....The first thing we noticed was this horrible smell, a smell I still have in my nose even today. The neighbouring house was just a pile of rubble. People were buried in it. There was the smell of blood and cement and burning all mixed together – it was horrible, revolting. It took me a long, long time to get over that.'

The Second World War was total war; a war in which civilians were targets and their homes became the battlefields. During the First World War soldiers had dug trenches at the front; now the civilians were doing the digging, preparing the shelters they hoped would protect them from aerial bombing. As the war escalated, the forces of both dictatorships and democracies mercilessly attacked each other's civilians. The years of fear became a grim test of endurance among whole populations; for many unarmed people it meant fighting for their lives against terrible odds.

BOMBED OUT *Civilians make the journey to work brick by brick through the smouldering ruins of their homes.*

GAS ALERT (ABOVE)
An air-raid warden wearing a gas mask clatters his warning rattle during a civil defence exercise. Masks were issued for all adults, children and even babies, but people's fears of gas bombing were not realized: it was not used during the war.

Preparing for the worst

When Britain and France declared war on Germany two days after Hitler's invasion of Poland, no one knew what to expect. For people on both sides of the conflict, the shadow of the First World War still loomed. Margarete Zettel, a teenager in Hamburg, was too young to have experienced the first war, but shared her parents' memories: 'We felt very sad and really afraid at the same time...because in the First World War my family lost a number of people.' Horst Westphal, who was only nine, was aware that people in Germany were 'quite euphoric at trying to stop the Germans from being suppressed in Poland – that was the version presented to us in the media. But people were very unhappy that the war had started.' In Britain the news marked the end of distant negotiations by politicians abroad and the beginning of tangible fear at home. Betty Lawrence was at a dance in Plymouth when people started pouring onto the streets. She remembers, 'They were saying, "They're going to announce the war"....Everybody was very, very frightened.' She had heard about the First World War, but this time she felt it would be different 'because we knew there was going to be more bombing'.

During the 1930s there had been frightening predictions of what modern weaponry, and particularly aerial bombing, could do to civilian populations. Bombs had been used by the Japanese on Shanghai in 1937 and by the Germans at Guernica during the Spanish Civil War. Above all, people feared that poison gas would be used, as it had been in the First World War, but this time in bombs dropped over cities rather than shells in the trenches. Gas masks were issued to the entire British population, and in France to all those who lived in towns and cities. In Germany only civil defence workers, Nazi party members and civil servants were supplied with gas masks. People were instructed to carry their masks at all times of the day and night.

Other measures were taken to protect civilians. In France and Britain women with babies, and children both individually and as whole schools, were evacuated from Paris and London to unknown guardians

VISIONS OF HELL
A baby screams desperately for help after the Japanese air attack on the Chinese city of Shanghai in 1937. Japan's merciless bombing raids provoked a sense of moral outrage and horror in the West, and the terrible reality of the Chinese experience fuelled the Europeans' fear of what the war would bring.

DIGGING IN (LEFT)
Families in Britain assemble their Anderson shelters. The shelters were issued free to those who earned less than £250 a year.

and destinations in the countryside. As the British government started to build large air-raid shelters, thousands of householders were issued with their own Anderson shelter. Donald Alder was a child living in Plymouth at the time, and remembers, 'My step-father made ours up at the bottom of the garden. We put a bed in there, and I always felt safe in that shelter.'

The government also issued advice about how to protect homes from aerial bombardment, and instructions on how to seal doors in the event of gas attacks. People bought scrim, a fine canvas, to paste onto windows to prevent the glass shattering. Practising the air-raid drill became part of the daily routine in offices, shops and schools. Some areas were better prepared than others. Betty Lawrence recalls that at the hospital where she worked in Plymouth, 'We were told to get a wash bowl for each patient to put over the patient's head in case of an air raid'.

Throughout Europe a black-out was imposed so that cities and towns could not be identified at night. From the outset, people in Britain, France, Germany and Poland learned to manage in the dark. With no neon signs or illuminated shop windows, neighbourhoods were immersed in darkness after dusk and people relied on torches, which had to be pointed downwards, to find their way. Donald Alder remembers, 'Anyone who showed a light was taken to court and fined as much as two pounds....Even the cars, and there weren't many of them about, even the buses had half the headlamps blacked out and the light was made to show only on the ground.'

Despite the lengthy preparations, and the wail of sirens signalling only a false alarm within minutes of the declaration, aerial bombing remained a distant threat in Britain during the early months of war. Along the Belgian and French borders with Germany, British and French forces waited for German attack in concrete bunkers, but there was so little fighting on the Western Front that the period was dubbed the Phoney War. Elsewhere the picture was different. In Poland fears were borne out by the Germans' fierce bombing of Polish towns and the daunting reality of occupation; in October the Soviet army invaded Finland with air attacks on civilians. By spring 1940 western Europe, too, was in the firing line.

WAITING FOR THE TRAIN *A boy receives his destination tag as he waits with his school group in a queue of subdued young evacuees. At the start of the war the British government organized billeting for children from the cities with families in 'safe' areas. Country people were shocked by the condition of some young refugees from poor areas, who were unwelcome guests. Many were homesick, and returned within a few months to cities still free from raids. Two more waves of evacuation followed during the war.*

REFUGEES TAKE TO THE STREETS *in Belgium as their bombed houses burn. Those who went by car had to abandon their vehicles when they ran out of petrol. Most people went on foot or by bicycle, salvaging what they could and not knowing when or if they would return.*

UNEQUAL PARTNERS
A poster of 1941 urges Norwegian civilians to join the Waffen SS, Hitler's elite combat troops, 'against Bolshevism'. After Hitler's blitzkrieg campaigns German propaganda chiefs played on the patriotism of men in occupied Denmark, Norway and the Netherlands to form their own Viking Division within the SS, and in so doing attempted to gain support for the attack on the Soviet Union.

Living under fire

With the lightning war, or 'blitzkrieg', people in northern Europe experienced the full force of the Nazi war machine smashing into their towns and villages. In April 1940 German troops invaded Denmark and Norway. Denmark fell in a day; Norway, supported by Anglo-French forces, held out until June. In May the German armies invaded Belgium, Luxembourg and the Netherlands. German tanks and troops swept towards the English Channel, and by the end of May Hitler was ordering his troops to Paris.

Pierre Rondas was living in the Belgian town of Louvain. He had just received his call-up papers when a raid began, and he found himself in a long column of people trailing from the town to seek safety at the French border, under the threat of German aircraft. 'Most of the people walking on the streets were civilians with horses, trucks, carriages....The people fleeing had a lot of luggage with them, but along the way, as the trip was long and difficult, they were beginning to abandon it....There were lots of abandoned cars....What is happening behind you or next to you, you don't look at it and you don't remember. You just look forward. There was a lot of misery there.'

Exposed on the open road, everyone was a target for the German air force. 'You heard the noise of the planes and then the noise of the machine-gunning. We heard the whistling of the bullets and everybody rushed off the roads to find cover in the ditches. Once the planes had flown on, the people just crawled out of these ditches again...tried to grab all their things back together, all their suitcases and bags, and then they walked on....There were people who were injured falling off trucks. They had blood on their bodies and their clothes, but few people could help because they wanted to get away.'

When Belgium surrendered just eighteen days later Pierre Rondas began to feel safer. 'I heard it from a German army car radio that was stationed at some farm where I was sleeping....We were now part of Germany.'

In June 1941 Germany launched a new blitzkrieg on the Soviet Union, in one of the largest military assaults in history. The German army, supported by Finnish and Italian troops, swept across Belorussia and the Ukraine, heading for Moscow and

TOTAL GLOBAL WAR

THE SECOND WORLD WAR was the first global war, involving almost every continent in the world. Colonial links meant that many territories and sea-lanes far from the warring powers were also drawn in. Among the Allies, Britain included its empire, notably Australia, Canada and New Zealand, and for France the war involved its territories in West Africa and Indochina.

Among the few countries to remain neutral throughout the war were the Irish Republic, Sweden and Switzerland. Some countries changed allegiance during the war. Under the fascist dictator Benito Mussolini, Italy was a founder, with Germany, of the Axis powers ranged against the Allies, initially just Britain and France. Mussolini supported Hitler's invasion of France and then the Soviet Union, but after his fall from power and Italy's surrender to the Allies in 1943, Italy declared war on Germany. Northern France came under German occupation in 1940; the Vichy government there

collaborated with Germany until 1943, while the Free French army supported the Allies. The Soviet Union, unsure of British and French intentions, had agreed with Germany before the war on the joint division of Poland, and supported Hitler's invasion from the west with its own attack on eastern Poland. The Soviet Union also supplied Germany with raw materials until it was itself invaded in 1941.

The struggles between these countries were rooted in the domination and ambitions of powerful leaders. While Hitler embodied the most awesome totalitarian threat, ruthless expansionism also motivated Mussolini and the Japanese warlords. By the time war was declared in Europe, the Sino-Japanese war had already signalled Japan's territorial aims for its Greater East Asia Co-Prosperity Sphere, and the atrocities it was prepared to inflict to achieve them.

The war expanded dramatically when ambitions in the east collided with those in Europe, culminating in

Japan's attack on the American fleet at Pearl Harbor, Hawaii. As a consequence of the pact made weeks earlier between Japan and Germany, Hitler now declared war on the United States, precipitating active American support of the Allies.

A series of events marked the turning of the tide against Germany after its early successes in achieving a Nazi-controlled Europe. Among them were disastrous decisions made by Hitler himself, who kept personal control of his armies. His invasion of the Soviet Union started a war on a second front that he could ill afford, while his declaration of war on the United States – until then an unmobilized economic giant – gave massive impetus to the Allies. Decisive battles, especially in the Atlantic and the Pacific, and the Allies' re-entry into Europe gradually signalled the defeat first of Germany and then of Japan.

WORLDWIDE CONFLICT *The war was fought in east and west, on land, at sea and in the air.*

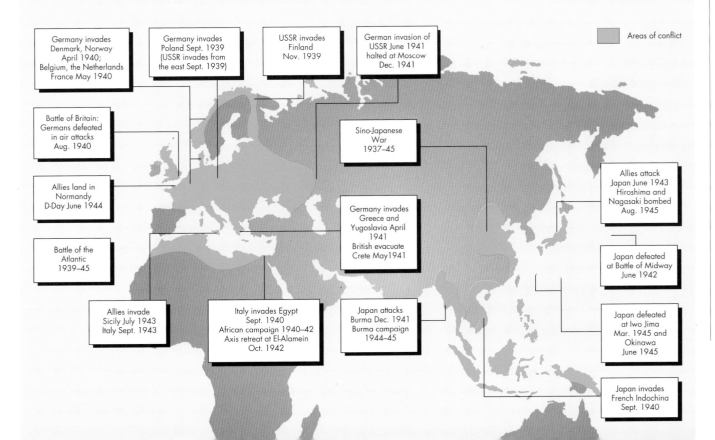

Germany invades Denmark, Norway April 1940; Belgium, the Netherlands France May 1940

Germany invades Poland Sept. 1939 (USSR invades from the east Sept. 1939)

USSR invades Finland Nov. 1939

German invasion of USSR June 1941 halted at Moscow Dec. 1941

Areas of conflict

Battle of Britain: Germans defeated in air attacks Aug. 1940

Sino-Japanese War 1937–45

Allies attack Japan June 1943 Hiroshima and Nagasaki bombed Aug. 1945

Allies land in Normandy D-Day June 1944

Germany invades Greece and Yugoslavia April 1941 British evacuate Crete May1941

Battle of the Atlantic 1939–45

Japan defeated at Battle of Midway June 1942

Allies invade Sicily July 1943 Italy Sept. 1943

Italy invades Egypt Sept. 1940 African campaign 1940–42 Axis retreat at El-Alamein Oct. 1942

Japan attacks Burma Dec. 1941 Burma campaign 1944–45

Japan defeated at Iwo Jima Mar. 1945 and Okinawa June 1945

Japan invades French Indochina Sept. 1940

Leningrad. In parts of the Ukraine the invading armies were welcomed as liberators from communism. But the Nazi view of Slav peoples as sub-human led to terrible atrocities.

Behind German lines Soviet partisans organized resistance, and paid the price of reprisals. Serafima Schibko lived in fear of both sides. She saw her village near Minsk burned several times. The men were taken away to execution or to provide forced labour for the Germans. In desperation people ran to take refuge in the woods. 'No one stayed in the village when it was burned for the last time,' she says. 'When we came back, we saw only burned ruins....We were glad to have survived....We weren't able to feel anything more, we were just trying to save our children.'

The early months of blitzkrieg had dramatically increased Hitler's gains in Europe. After advancing through France the German army had forced the retreat of British and French forces from the coastal town of Dunkirk in May 1940. France had been divided into the occupied north and west and the unoccupied south and east, with a puppet capital at Vichy. With the Germans just across the Channel the British prime minister, Winston Churchill, broadcast a sombre warning: 'The battle of France is over...the battle of Britain is about to begin.'

"Those who could tried to run away. I had five children with me...where could I run to, having so many children with me?"

SERAFIMA SCHIBKO

SHOCKING AFTERMATH
A woman huddles alone in the charred ruins of her home. Whole communities in the Soviet Union were the victims of arson attacks by German soldiers, who had been taught that the people they were killing were less than fully human.

NO THROUGH ROAD
(RIGHT) *Fire erupts as German forces turn a street in the Ukraine into a war zone. Hitler's invasion of the Soviet Union, supported by the Finnish armies that had been victims of the Russian invasion two years before, was a repeat of his blitzkrieg tactics in Europe. But with the winter weather, the German army and its transport froze to a standstill and troops resorted to hand-drawn sledges. The German defeat at Stalingrad later confirmed the formidable capacity for endurance of civilians under siege.*

"We all hated the Germans at that time....An eye for an eye, a tooth for a tooth. I thought if they can do this to us, do it to children, we should do it to them. **"**

BETTY LAWRENCE

DAILY DEATH TOLL *People gather round a noticeboard listing casualties on the morning after an air raid in Plymouth, anxious to find out whether anyone they know has been killed.*

Under bombardment

In summer 1940 the aerial bombing of cities was becoming a reality in Britain. The Battle of Britain between the British and German air forces over the English Channel reached its peak in August; the German air force also began to attack urban targets. An all-night bombing raid on London on 23 August marked the beginning of the blitz. In September heavier raids began, and in mid-October nightly bombing intensified. During one of the worst periods, Londoners sheltered for seventy-six consecutive nights in the passageways and on the platforms of underground stations. Raids on other British cities followed. On 14 November the German air force launched a heavy raid on Coventry, an important centre of the war industry, destroying about a third of the city, killing about five hundred people and causing more than 1400 casualties.

Plymouth, with its large naval dockyard, was the most densely bombed city in Britain. More than one thousand people were killed there, and more than three thousand were injured. Sid Newham was at the cinema one evening when the noise became overwhelming, and people in the audience were advised to make their way home as best they could. 'When we got outside I had the shock of my life,' he remembers. 'The place was an inferno. Every other building seemed to be alight and the bombs were coming down.' Minutes later, a bomb hit the shelter in his back garden. He found himself staring at the open sky in a shower of dust. 'I could only free myself down to my waist, because there were big boulders resting on my legs. When I got the top part of my body free, I started pulling away at the rubble in front of me until I came across a woman's head. I smoothed her hair, cleared round her neck and patted her face. I said, "That you, Mum?" You couldn't tell because her face was just black. And she says, "Yes, it's me, Sid. I'm all right".'

Later that night Sid Newham was discharged from hospital with bandages on his injured legs and a walking stick to lean on; the beds were needed for the following night's raid. His grandmother and his sister died from the bombs, and his father, aged forty-two, was paralysed from the waist down.

Like the German air force, the British air force had tried to

COMMUNITY SPIRIT
(RIGHT) *Residents of Islington, London, shelter in a basement during an air raid. For people without a garden, church crypts, cellars and coal holes became places of refuge. The frightening wait underground was alleviated by determined attempts to boost morale.*

A DAZED MAN (BELOW) *sits among the remains of houses in Plymouth reduced to matchsticks during a night-time raid. The thousands of people made homeless during the blitz were advised to 'make their own arrangements'; many stayed with relatives, neighbours or friends.*

Decoration for heroes

THE GEORGE CROSS *recognized the heroic efforts of civilians in living up to the defiant slogan 'Britain can take it' during bombing raids by Germany. Introduced by King George VI in 1940, it was awarded mainly to civilians for 'acts of the greatest heroism or of the most conspicuous courage in circumstances of extreme danger'. The honour ranked second only to the Victoria Cross, Britain's highest military decoration.*

SIGNED UP *Sid Newham joined the Royal Air Force soon after losing his sister and grandmother in the blitz. 'I wanted revenge,' he says. 'I thought to myself, "This has got to stop, I've got to do my share".'*

SIGNING OFF *A member of a British air crew chalks a message on a bomb to his anonymous German enemy.*

hit strategic targets at first, but precision bombing had proved impossible and they too resorted to 'area bombing' to cripple industry and make workers homeless. Despite prewar concerns from leaders in both Britain and the United States that bombing should not be used against civilians, in 1942 Winston Churchill was boasting to his Soviet ally, Joseph Stalin, 'We hope to shatter almost every dwelling in almost every German city'.

The raid on Hamburg in July 1943 was unprecedented in its intensity. It created a firestorm, with hurricane-force winds and temperatures reaching 1000 degrees centigrade. Suction uprooted trees and flung people through the air over a sea of fire. About 42 000 civilians were killed in Hamburg – more than all the deaths during the blitz in Britain.

Horst Westphal immediately realized that the bombing was 'a completely different, new kind of bombing...flares were sent down by parachutes and lit up whole districts of the city...there were special bombs to break the windows, and then incendiary bombs came....The fire from the bombs was able to go wherever it wanted because there was no protection anywhere, there were no windows, no doors, everything had been blown out.'

Margarete Zettel remembers that during the days following the bombing, 'The sun never really managed to get through, you just saw a huge red fireball and there was smoke and this horrible stench, there was darkness everywhere, but not like night time. You could see the contours of the houses, it was very spooky. We were afraid from that point onwards....It was certainly a kind of total war. I can't imagine it being more total than that.'

People painted signs on bombed buildings to tell relatives where they had gone, while thousands more gathered at the railway station to be evacuated to areas where there were medical supplies and food. And the clean-up operation began. Horst Westphal recalls, 'An organization called Todt used to arrive with lorries; they piled the corpses on and took them to one of the mass graves at Ohlsdorf....Concentration camp prisoners were sent in with flame-throwers to burn the corpses, and the streets were walled up at the ends so no one could go in, because they were afraid of infection. It was a horrible chapter.'

SOLDIERING ON (LEFT)
*Civilians carve a path
through ruined buildings in
Hamburg. Both in Britain
and in Germany, people
tried to maintain a pattern
of daily life.*

WAR EFFORT *Margarete
Zettel* (ABOVE) *was awarded
the Cross of Honour for her
help rescuing people during
the raids on Hamburg. 'After
the attacks people were closer
to each other but we were
broken at the same time,' she
says. 'Resistance grew a little
bit against Hitler because
people were saying, "What's
the sense of it all?"'*

BOOSTING MORALE

ENTERTAINMENT was a valuable commodity during the war, and one that did not need to be rationed. It was also a vital means of strengthening morale, and the popular media of cinema and radio made it available to everyone.

Cinemas had closed at the start of the war in Britain because of the fear of bombing on such concentrated civilian targets. But when they re-opened they became oases of escapism and encouragement. Most people under the age of forty used to watch at least one feature film a week, and most of the films were American. After the entry of the United States into the war Hollywood began to play a more active role in morale-boosting, adopting the slogan 'Morale is mightier than the sword'.

In the United States, too, people flocked to see patriotic musical extravaganzas such as *Star Spangled Rhythm*, *This is the Army* and *Yankee Doodle Dandy*, a celebration of the American way of life starring James Cagney. There were dramas such as *Meet Me in St Louis*, a hymn to the good old days starring Judy Garland, and *Since You Went Away*, a tribute to the 'unconquerable fortress' of 1943 – the American family during the war. Hollywood

was more popular still among the troops serving abroad. In the United States armed services 630 000 men and women were watching a movie every night by 1943. Star performers travelled overseas to make personal appearances behind the battle lines, or to promote the sale of government war bonds.

The radio was a source of both information and reassurance. People in occupied countries risked their lives in listening to the British Broadcasting Corporation, while British civilians relied on it for Winston Churchill's speeches to the nation, and for the weekly edition of *Sincerely Yours*, hosted by Vera Lynn, whose signature tune became *We'll meet again*. The Japanese took advantage of her popularity to sap morale among British prisoners by announcing that she had been killed.

Entertainment also came direct to people at work and at play. Ousted from their grander venues by the threat of bombs, city musicians staged concerts in public parks, factory canteens and aircraft hangars, while provincial theatres declared with pride, 'We Never Close'.

MAKING DO *A harmonica player improvises for factory workers on a makeshift stage at a lunch-time concert.*

LAUNCHED INTO BATTLE *A Liberty cargo ship begins its journey from the West Coast to the open sea. A total of 2770 such ships were built in the United States in an effort to keep pace with their equally efficient destruction by German submarines during the war. As the war in the Pacific and the Atlantic raged on, thousands of troops lost their lives at sea.*

The war of production

A new chapter in the war began on 7 December 1941 when the Japanese attacked the United States Pacific fleet at Pearl Harbor in Hawaii. In 1941 President Roosevelt had banned the sale of raw materials to Japan because he wanted to help China in the war against Japan. By the following year negotiations were embittered and the Japanese were ready to take Pacific territories, rich in raw materials, by force. American volunteer pilots had already helped Britain's defenders during the Battle of Britain in 1940, but Pearl Harbor was the catalyst that turned the tide of American opinion from reluctance to indignant determination.

With the entry of the United States into the war, the world's greatest economy was converted to war production. It became the principal supplier to the Allies of machinery, aircraft and ships for the wars that were raging in the Soviet Union, North Africa, China and the Middle East. For people in the United States the Japanese invasion never came, but the war did change lives and landscapes as new factories were built and people found work.

California was one of the areas most affected. Shipyards there competed to produce Liberty ships in record time for the battle of the Atlantic. With the new urgency came innovation in manufacturing, as prefabricated parts and assembly-line production were introduced to keep pace with the demand.

Victor Cole worked at the Kaiser shipyard in Richmond, near San Francisco. He recalls the proud moment when a ship that had been built in a record few days was launched; there were 'people all over the shipyard and almost shoulder to shoulder, standing around and cheering and waving their hats. Everyone's mood was

ALL HANDS ON DECK *Victor Cole, pictured here with his wife Marge celebrating the completion of the '556th' ship, was part of the American battle of production at the Kaiser shipyard in Richmond, California. 'The mood there was, "We're winning",' he remembers.*

ROOTED IN SHOCK *Men at the United States naval base watch incredulously as a fireball erupts from the boats anchored on 'battleship row' in Pearl Harbor. About a hundred warships and 500 aircraft in the nearby airfields were sitting targets, and some 2500 Americans were killed in the attack.*

'WASTE NOT WANT NOT' *was the slogan of the home front in Britain, as household rubbish and iron railings were salvaged to make war machinery. There was an overwhelming response to the government's plea, 'Women of Britain, give us your aluminium…we will turn your pots and pans into Spitfires and Hurricanes.'*

"This is an impossible thing that we have done, and yet we can do it again, and so we have great pride".'

With every resource being poured into the war, the United States government introduced rationing for fuel and some foods. 'The things we normally thought would always be available were not,' says Victor Cole. 'It was hard to get whisky.…There was always enough rum around, so they would make you buy a bottle or more of rum every time you got a bottle of whisky.'

Food rationing was imposed everywhere. Goods that were usually imported from other countries were no longer available. The restrictions led to a flourishing black market. People in rural areas could grow more of their own food so they fared better than those in cities, who were dependent on the food supply. In Britain football pitches and lawn tennis courts were dug up to make way for vegetables and allotments sprang up on every available patch of suburban land. Everyone was given a ration book; as government intervention influenced the national diet, many families were eating better than they had done before the war.

Women were vital to the war effort. In March 1941 women in Britain were called to factories and farms to fill jobs previously occupied by men; in December national service was introduced for all unmarried women between the ages of twenty and thirty, and by mid-1943, 90 per cent of single women and 80 per cent of married women were employed in the armed forces or in industry.

In Germany the number of women working rose, but less dramatically. The Nazis were concerned that the 'psychological and emotional life' of women might be affected, and so might their ability to bear children. Even so, the 1941 Women for Victory campaign brought many German women into factories, and many more were called up for *Arbeitdienst*, work service.

The Germans also raided their conquered territories in Europe for workers to boost the war effort. There were three million foreign workers in Germany in 1941, and by 1944 there were seven million, 20 per cent of the workforce. They worked in aircraft and chemical factories, in quarries and on fortifications. Alexandra Sakharova was sent from Leningrad to a farm in Germany, where she worked fifteen or sixteen hours a day to help cut hay with a sickle, to harvest potatoes and to feed the piglets.

WOMEN'S WORK *in a German engineering plant. The war brought more women into factories, where they did highly technical work; onto the streets as postmen and transport workers; and onto the land as farm workers.*

She was paid a pittance, and given potatoes to eat. 'If anybody needed me, they just called out, "Russian Pig",' she says. 'Of course it was not very pleasant, but I was Russian. I was proud that I was Russian.'

The Japanese drafted children as young as ten from their own country to work in factories. Katsumoto Saotome was eleven years old in 1944. He had to work in a steel plant, shovelling scrap metal into trolleys and pushing them along railway tracks. 'The school wanted us to feel like military people,' he says.

Even unborn babies were regarded as part of the war effort. Yoshiko Hashimoto remembers, 'Before my first child was born I was issued with a maternity certificate....Where it should say "Scheduled date of birth" it says "Scheduled date of production". Looking at this, it makes me very angry, because the life of one person is considered as a commodity, an article. That's the way the government thought about people.'

Like the Germans, the Japanese wanted an empire and were prepared to consider other peoples as a mechanical means to that end. Japan imported one and a half million Koreans to work, mining coal, digging tunnels and building fortifications. The recruitment itself was brutal. Yan Pyun Tou was planting rice on his neighbour's farm in Korea when a stranger abducted him. He was locked in a prison cell and shipped to Japan, where he was put to work at a hydroelectric plant. 'Our bosses were very hard on us,' he says. 'We were beaten almost every day...they didn't see us as human beings.'

CHILD LABOUR *Children in many Japanese schools were sent to work in ordnance factories, where instead of schooling they were taught allegiance with the help of a military drill and patriotic slogans. Katsumoto Saotome paraphrases the wording on the bandanna he wore round his head. 'No matter what happens, Japan will win the war, because we are a land derived from the gods'. Children were part of the war effort in other countries too: in Germany members of the Hitler Youth went round their neighbourhood collecting bones from the Sunday roast to make explosives.*

"We were there twenty hours a day…we dug trenches in the ice. We lost people all the time because the Germans were constantly in the air bombing us. **"**

LEONID GALPERIN

THE ROAD OF LIFE
Leonid Galperin worked around the clock to guard, maintain and improve the 56-kilometre (35-mile) route across Lake Ladoga. 'It was very difficult and very monotonous,' he says. An army of ten thousand civilians worked on the huge frozen lake, including nurses who helped drivers already weakened through hunger and injured by bombs.

Life under siege

As total war brought new privations to civilians in the combatant countries, no city experienced more hardship than Leningrad. By September 1941 the German and Finnish armies had encircled the city, and a thirty-month siege began. Rather than launching a full-scale attack, Hitler's tactic was now to starve the city out while continuing to bomb and shell its inhabitants. Civilians of all ages became involved in defending the city, and waging their own desperate battle against starvation as supplies dwindled. Elena Taranukhina, a piano teacher, helped to dig anti-tank ditches, and worked in a hospital nearby. As an exceptionally bitter winter set in, temperatures fell to minus 40 degrees centigrade, and she and her friends slept in their fur coats. There was no wood – they had burned all the furniture they had, and even their books – and no water. 'We couldn't wash ourselves,' she recalls, 'because we were only strong enough to fetch water to drink.'

The bread ration was cut to 125 grams a day – a slice and a half. When flour ran out, the bread was made from wood cellulose and sawdust, and soup was made from carpenter's glue. Elena Taranukhina would start to queue for something resembling food at four o'clock every morning. 'All the birds died because of the frost. We tried to catch them but it was very difficult.…We ate grass, all kinds of grasses. We made soup. I brought the horse dung home, and I wanted to eat it.' Cats, dogs and mice disappeared from the city, and the sight of dismembered corpses bore haunting testimony to suspicions of cannibalism.

The deathly cold did bring one benefit: the huge Lake Ladoga froze over, creating a lifeline to the east. On 17 November two reconnaissance groups set out on foot, roped together and wearing life-jackets, to test the thickening ice. A few days later a 7-kilometre (4-mile) long column of 350 horses pulling sledges set out. The horses, which were also weak from starvation, were hardly strong enough to pull their sledges. But the convoy got through to bring back essential supplies.

Leonid Galperin helped to maintain the vital road across the frozen lake, and he

remembers, 'We called it the opening of the road to life. The road did not stop for a moment….When the ice became stronger, lorries and even tanks could get through, though they removed the upper layer of ice. At last Ladoga was working on a full scale.'

The road to life was under constant threat of death. Leonid Galperin remembers, 'We lost people all the time because the Germans were constantly in the air bombing us. Our anti-aircraft cannons didn't function but we were there around the clock and had no place to hide.'

Fragile epitaphs

SCRAPS OF PAPER *torn from an address book read as a litany of death, the names and dates recorded by an eleven-year-old girl in Leningrad as her mother, brothers and grandmother died around her.*

ACTS OF RESISTANCE

THE RESISTANCE, the movement against enemy occupation, involved civilians in activities from spying and sabotage to guerrilla warfare. It was always risky. When activists were captured they were tortured for information, but the German army was often undiscriminating in its reprisals. In one of the worst incidents, German troops in Greece responded to the discovery of two murdered soldiers by killing thirty elderly villagers and thirty-eight young children in the village of Klissura.

In the Soviet Union the resistance forces, or partisans, were formidably organized, constituting a guerrilla army that operated in the forests, with radio links to its own army commands. Governments exiled in London helped to support partisans in other invaded countries, sometimes with dramatic results. In August 1944 the home army in Warsaw, supported by the Polish government in London, tried unsuccessfully to oust the German army and seize the city before it was occupied by the advancing Soviet army. But when the Soviet advance halted, German reprisals resulted in more than 20 000 deaths. General Charles de Gaulle also operated from London, and his volunteer army, the Free French, fought alongside the Allies. In France his emissaries vied with the communists in organizing sabotage campaigns, painting road signs black and planting ambushes.

Resistance was also a matter of individual courage. Volunteers landed by parachute or by boat in occupied countries, bringing with them escape route maps and forged identity cards hidden in chess sets, which they smuggled into prisoner of war camps. Others organized convoys to ferry prisoners home. All over Europe people were engaged in spying: railway clerks reported on goods being sent, while waiters picked up careless talk among German customers. People in Denmark and the Netherlands, horrified at the brutal treatment of the Jews during the German occupation of their country, held demonstrations in protest, and many Dutch families concealed Jews to prevent their deportation to concentration camps.

Yugoslavia was the one occupied country in which resistance succeeded in liberating the people. The communist leader Josip Broz Tito led a partisan army against Italian and German troops, and also fought a savage civil war against non-communists, capturing towns and establishing local governments in the areas they liberated. Here, as elsewhere, the price paid in lives and misery was very high.

A NEW IDENTITY *These false French identity papers were prepared for a British air force officer. Forged papers became a lifeline for pilots who had been shot down in occupied countries and for prisoners of war attempting to escape.*

The Germans failed to break the lifeline, but people in the city still grew weak and many collapsed and died of starvation in the streets. Elena Taranukhina, like thousands of others, dragged her dead mother on a sledge to her grave.

In the midst of all this horror, the people of Leningrad heard that the great composer Dmitri Shostakovich had written a new symphony dedicated to the city. The city orchestra's conductor searched for members of the orchestra and found that only twenty-seven were still alive: many of them had died of starvation. Determined to stage the symphony, he arranged special rations for the musicians and persuaded the army to release musicians to play with them. Each rehearsal lasted forty minutes – people were too cold, tired and weak to play any longer.

On the day the symphony was performed the Red Army created a diversion to draw away German fire. Lubov Zhakova was one of the hundreds of people in the audience. She remembers 'the feeling of enthusiasm, of celebration, in the fact that this Shostakovich symphony was devoted to Leningrad. Everybody realized that. People appeared here straight from the battlefields with their rifles.' At the end of the concert there was complete silence, and then tumultuous applause. Lubov Zhakova was pushed towards the conductor to hand him a bouquet of flowers, an astonishing sight during the war. She had picked them from her grandfather's garden in commemoration of the remarkable event. The symphony became an emblem of Leningrad's resistance, and marked a moment of human victory. The concert was broadcast across the country.

The siege was finally lifted in January 1944, when the Red Army broke the German stranglehold. By that time more than 630 000 civilians had died of cold, hunger and disease, and a further 200 000 had been killed by the German armies.

In June 1944 Allied armies broke into Hitler's Europe with an invasion that had been planned for more than a year. In the D-Day landings, forces of American, British and Canadian troops in an armada of 4000 Allied ships and 10 000 aircraft swooped onto the beaches of Normandy in France, beginning a series of battles towards Germany and the recovery of Europe. For civilians in Europe and the Far East, the battle of morale was not over.

RITE OF PASSAGE (OPPOSITE) *With bowed heads, a couple pulls a dead victim by sledge to the cemetery in Leningrad. In a diary written during the siege one entry reads: 'Taking a body to the cemetery exhausts the last vestiges of strength from the survivors. And so the living, in fulfilling their duty to the dead, are brought to the brink themselves.'*

REPRIEVE *Survivors of the Leningrad siege crowd round for tickets to hear the symphony dedicated to the city. 'We were carried away by the feeling that we were winning after the terrible winter...we hadn't expected to live,' remembers Lubov Zhakova. 'It was a real ceremony for us, a feeling of joy, a very serious victory.'*

Utter destruction

By spring 1945 the bombing of cities reached new heights. In February British aircraft launched an attack on the German city of Dresden that killed some 50 000 people, and resurrected debate about the morality of the indiscriminate killing of civilians. On 10 March American B-29 bombers, built to carry 'the greatest weight of death ever lifted into the skies', launched air attacks on Japan. Half a million incendiary bombs were dropped on Tokyo to force the Japanese to surrender.

Katsumoto Saotome, who was living in Tokyo, remembers, 'Nobody ever dreamed there would be such an air raid. We still believed we could put out the fires, that was what we were told, what we were taught....There was heavy punishment for the people who ran away from houses that caught fire.'

On the night of the Tokyo raid there was a strong northerly wind. Sumiko Morikawa, a mother with three young children, recalls, 'I was worried because of the wind....Later that night the sirens started going off continuously. Looking out from our window, I could see red. It was as if the clouds were burning.' When the bombs began to fall she strapped her twin babies on her back, took her four-year-old son by the hand, and with thousands of other desperate citizens hurried to the park, where 'fire just erupted everywhere around our feet'. She tried to put out the fire

A CITY LAID WASTE
Only concrete buildings were left standing in Tokyo the morning after the March raid. The city was a tinderbox of wooden houses and shops, which were reduced within minutes to funeral pyres. People fled from their underfloor shelters to the canals, but even the water could not quench the raging firestorm.

RAIN OF TERROR *An American B-29 drops its deadly load. In the same month as the Tokyo raids, kamikaze pilots flew suicide missions in planeloads of explosives to sink Allied ships off the Pacific island of Okinawa.*

with water from the lake but resorted to jumping in. 'Fire was actually coming into the pool,' she recalls.

Yoshiko Hashimoto ran to the river carrying her baby. 'There were people who had become fireballs themselves and were rolling over...it was like hell,' she says. 'I decided to jump into the river. As I jumped I saw my mother's face; it was very sad. I'll never forget that face.' Two young men pulled Yoshiko Hashimoto into their boat. 'We stayed overnight on the river. It was full of corpses....I was so tired I hardly knew whether I was alive or dead....In the morning the two men took me and my baby to hospital.' The Tokyo raids killed 120 000 people, more than any other single action in the war.

United States forces had seized islands in the Pacific in order to secure bases for their raids on Japan. Fighting lasted for weeks on Iwo Jima, and thousands died. On the island of Okinawa, some Japanese took their own lives rather than suffer the ultimate shame of surrender. Shigeaki Kinjo remembers, 'The men were given two hand grenades each....The sergeant who was passing them out explained that, if you came across an American soldier, you should throw one at the American and use the other to commit suicide... we were told it was an honour to die for the emperor.' He and his eighteen-year-old brother felt it was their responsibility to make sure that everyone in the family died. 'The first person we killed was my mother,' he says. 'We used a rope in the beginning. In the end we used rocks to stone her head. I was crying. It is a terrible, terrible experience to kill your own mother.'

Five months later, total war reached its climax. On 6 August United States aircraft dropped the first atom bomb on Hiroshima. It killed about 78 000 people. Those near the centre of the blast were vapourized; thousands more suffered horrific burns, and radiation sickness signalled the beginnings of lifelong illness. Three days later, a second atom bomb killed about 40 000 civilians at Nagasaki. Japan surrendered unconditionally on 15 August.

Some Japanese committed suicide, and Yoshiko Hashimoto recalls, 'There were many men crying because Japan had lost the war.' She felt differently. 'I held my baby, I held my sister with the burns, and I cried with happiness. I thought, "I never want to see another war".'

> *"These aircraft were things that I'd never seen before....It was like a devil coming from somewhere out of this world."*
>
> KATSUMOTO SAOTOME

MAKESHIFT REFUGE *A lonely survivor sits in the blasted wasteland that was the city of Nagasaki.*

Coming home

By the time Japan surrendered, the war in Europe was already over. As troops returned to euphoric crowds and happy families, millions of refugees were starting the long, slow journey home, carrying their meagre possessions in bundles and hoping to find something left of their homes and their families. Alexandra Sakharova and her workmates had been freed in April 1945 when American troops arrived at the German farm where she had worked. She made the journey home barefoot. When she reached Leningrad a month later, she found both her aunts and her mother alive. They had not expected to see each other ever again. 'Nothing else was left for me,' she says, 'just quite unbelievable joy.'

WELCOME BACK *An ex-prisoner of war arrives from the Far East to a rapturous greeting from his wife and son in London. In Britain single-storey 'prefab' housing had provided a temporary solution to being bombed out. Soldiers all over the world returned to grown children, changed circumstances and unfamiliar surroundings.*

THE ROAD HOME
(OPPOSITE) *Belgian, Dutch, French and Polish survivors edge their way over the river Elbe along a railway bridge destroyed by the Germans to halt the advancing Red Army. For thousands of refugees the journey home took weeks of trudging through landscapes mutilated by war.*

The war had cost more than fifty million lives worldwide. For the first time in the history of war, more civilians had been killed than soldiers. The Soviet Union suffered most losses, with twenty million deaths. Poland lost six million people, 15 per cent of the population, including three million Jews. The war cost Germany about four and a half million deaths, while 450 000 British people lost their lives and 120 000 died for the British empire. In financial terms, the United States had contributed almost half of the Allied war effort, and Germany had spent more than Italy and Japan combined. And the price of war continued to be paid by survivors now learning to live with the consequences.

As communists joined hands with capitalists over the ruins of fascism, the mood was for many people one of subdued shock rather than of triumph. The discovery of Hitler's concentration camps added to the known horrors of the war. The moral victory of freedom against totalitarianism, and the overwhelming relief that the years of siege and destruction had ended, was tempered by the knowledge of the terrible methods of the war and the means employed to bring it to an end. Many of those who had witnessed the use of complex technology and of fellow human beings as instruments of mass extermination now fervently hoped that in future the dread of such extremes in war would bring about peace.

11

Brave New World

THE
COLD WAR
YEARS

'EAST AND WEST HAVE met,' declared the radio commentator excitedly. 'This is the news for which the whole Allied world has been waiting. The forces of liberation have joined hands.' It was on the afternoon of 25 April 1945 that soldiers of a United States army patrol first saw the Soviet lines near Torgau, south of Berlin on the river Elbe.

Alexander Silvashko and William Robertson were two of the first soldiers to meet. They both remember the excitement and comradeship of that moment. As Alexander Silvashko says, 'We met like brothers. We had defeated a common enemy. We were united in fighting fascism, and together we had won. The Americans gave us cigarettes and food. They gave us whatever they had, even watches, as souvenirs. The atmosphere was unbelievable.'

The Russians' exhilaration was equalled by that of the Americans. William Robertson recalls, 'There was the great curiosity of actually meeting Soviet soldiers. We knew they were a powerful army, but we didn't know them as individuals – and here they were shaking hands with us. It progressed to a great celebration of a very significant event. They were good people. There was the relief that the war was coming to a close, and that the Allies had won the war. We were just plain thankful that we were there and breathing.'

The photograph of the two lieutenants was seen around the world. It became a symbol of the victorious alliance between the communist Soviet Union and the capitalist West. However, within weeks it became apparent that fraternity was not to be the key to the postwar relationship between East and West; in the very moment of triumph a new conflict was being born. Popular hopes for peace were again to be disappointed. The Soviet Union and the United States, now elevated to superpower status, nursed a mutual hostility that divided most of the world into two armed camps. This led to a new kind of war – the Cold War – that was to have a profound effect on the lives of a whole generation.

THE WARM EMBRACE *between William Robertson and Alexandr Silvashko became a symbol of peace and hope.*

Emerging from the war

As the peoples of Europe emerged from the rubble of war and began to rebuild their lives, they knew that the victors represented two fundamentally different political systems. The differences had been buried in the urgency of the need to defeat fascism, but as soon as victory was assured, they resurfaced. The British, Soviet and United States leaders had met at Yalta in February 1945 to discuss the future of Europe, and particularly of Germany, when the war ended. At Potsdam near Berlin in July 1945 there were further negotiations, with the United States president, Franklin D. Roosevelt, and Britain's prime minister, Winston Churchill, both trying to restrain Joseph Stalin's demands for Soviet domination of Eastern Europe. The Soviet Union had suffered most during the war, with the loss of more than twenty million lives, and Stalin was determined to make sure that his country could never again be threatened by Germany. To allay his fears, he sought to extend communism to the countries of Eastern Europe, which lay on the Soviet Union's western borders.

The Allies agreed that Germany should be divided into four zones, administered by Britain, France, the Soviet Union and the United States. The capital city, Berlin (which was situated within the Soviet zone) was similarly divided. The trust and cooperation this arrangement required was soon to be tested, and the goodwill that had characterized the ending of the war did not last.

Anatoly Semiriaga, a Soviet army officer, was in Berlin in the early days after the war, liberating people from concentration camps and helping local townspeople to find food, water and shelter in the shattered city. He remembers his orders: 'I was told, "Captain, your job is to see to the population of this area, at least to find bread for them." People emerged from caves, from their hiding places to welcome us. You had to care for these people. They had to be lodged somewhere...you had to encourage them. They were under tremendous shock.' But within days the humanitarian effort was to be coloured by politics. 'We were called in by our officers and told: "Listen, the Germans were not solely responsible for

COMING HOME TO BERLIN *Many of Berlin's citizens had been evacuated from the city towards the end of the war to escape Allied bombing. When they returned they found their homes reduced to rubble, their ruined city in the hands of the enemy.*

> *"A whole avalanche of these unfortunates were coming back to the east, and people were also moving to the west. These two currents were meeting. You had to care for these people."*

ANATOLY SEMIRIAGA

ANATOLY SEMIRIAGA, *an officer with one of the Soviet army units that defeated the German army near Berlin, felt compassion for the thousands of freed prisoners, refugees and homeless citizens he was instructed to look after in the early days of peace.*

REBUILDING WORK IN DRESDEN *being carried out by the patient labour of the city's inhabitants. The task of feeding, clothing and housing the bewildered citizens of Germany was a major concern of the occupying forces in the early years after the war.*

this war. It wasn't just Hitler, it was the imperi-alist system. And who are the representatives of imperialism now? The allies we fought on the same side as against Hitler." We were taught that the defeat of fascism was one important step towards the victory of socialism all over the world. Since the Red Army had liberated Eastern Europe, sooner or later socialism would be established there.'

Paul Nitze, who went on to become one of the United States' expert commentators on the Cold War, was also in Berlin when the war ended. He witnessed the Soviet efforts to gain compensation from Germany for the damage that had been done to the Soviet Union during the war: 'I watched what the Russians were doing. They were pulling up the railroad tracks and seizing every bit of everything they could find and moving it out of Berlin, straight back to Russia.' He was in regular contact with the Russians in Berlin, and remembers that 'Their unwillingness to compromise, to work out any workable deal, was something very frightening. You got the feeling these were difficult people who were going to be impossible for us to get along with.'

Soviet troops had freed the countries of Eastern Europe from the German armies. Now they introduced their ideology to

RETURNING HERO *A GI describes his wartime adventures to an admiring audience in his local store. For many Americans, this was an era of greater spending power and consumer choice than they had ever experienced before – as magazines (ABOVE RIGHT) and the advertising industry (ABOVE) were eager to remind them.*

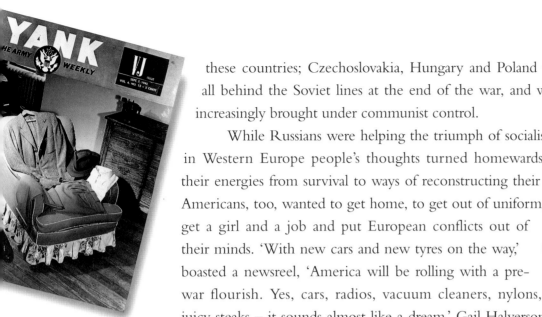

these countries; Czechoslovakia, Hungary and Poland were all behind the Soviet lines at the end of the war, and were increasingly brought under communist control.

While Russians were helping the triumph of socialism, in Western Europe people's thoughts turned homewards, and their energies from survival to ways of reconstructing their lives. Americans, too, wanted to get home, to get out of uniform, get a girl and a job and put European conflicts out of their minds. 'With new cars and new tyres on the way,' boasted a newsreel, 'America will be rolling with a pre-war flourish. Yes, cars, radios, vacuum cleaners, nylons, juicy steaks – it sounds almost like a dream.' Gail Halverson, who had been in Europe as a bomber pilot, agrees. 'It's like a new life. It's like walking from one scene of a tragedy into a musical,' he explains. He was eager to get home, to 'go back to see my girl-friend, plan for what we were going to do after the war. All the worry and concern was just obliterated,' he remembers, 'and we disbanded our military. We just disbanded very rapidly. Now it was time for peace.'

'DADDY'S COME HOME!'
A newly discharged US soldier greets his happy three-year-old daughter on his return home to New York. For families on both sides of the Atlantic, peace brought reunion and the chance to rebuild family life.

From allies to enemies

By the autumn of 1945 it was becoming obvious to the strategists in Washington that the Soviet Union was already no longer an ally but a potential enemy. On 9 February 1946 Stalin made a speech in Moscow that sounded, as Paul Nitze recalls, like 'a delayed declaration of war against the US'. A few days later an expert in Soviet affairs, George Kennan, despatched from the United States embassy in Moscow what became known as the 'long telegram', arguing that the United States must 'contain' Soviet power.

The British were also concerned about Soviet intentions. Only a few days after Kennan's telegram had been received, the British statesman Winston Churchill visited the United States. At a small college in Fulton, Missouri, he sounded his own warning. 'From Stettin in the Baltic to Trieste in the Adriatic,' he growled, 'an iron curtain has descended across the continent. Behind that line lie all the capitals of the ancient states of central and Eastern Europe – Warsaw, Berlin, Prague, Budapest – and all these famous cities, and the populations around them, lie in what I must call the

Soviet sphere.' The Russians did not want war, he said; no, all they wanted was 'the fruits of war and the infinite expansion of their power and doctrines'. Churchill called upon the English-speaking peoples to adopt a policy of strength and a close alliance that would resist Soviet ambitions. There was a hostile reaction to his speech, but it helped to change the public mood. The press had once portrayed an alliance of three equals; now, Joseph Stalin was shown as a despot forcing whole countries into submission.

By the spring of 1947 Churchill's prophecy of a divided world was coming to pass. There was Soviet pressure on Iran, on Turkey and on Greece. Things were 'happening in a hurry', the United States president, Harry Truman, wrote in a private letter to his sister. On 27 February the president appealed to congressional leaders for a united effort. The secretary of state, General George Marshall, said: 'It is not alarmist to say that we are now faced with the first crisis of a series which might extend Soviet domination to Europe, the Middle East and Asia.'

To challenge the Soviet initiative, in March Harry Truman spelled out what became known as the Truman Doctrine in a solemn speech to a joint session of Congress. 'I believe that it must be the policy of the United States to support free peoples who are resisting attempted subjugation by armed insurgencies or by outside pressures. I believe that we must assist free people to work out their own destinies in their own way.'

TUG-OF-WAR IN BERLIN
Without a common language, this Soviet soldier and German woman have misunderstood each other's intentions. The money the woman has just been given was not a gift, but payment for the bicycle the soldier wanted to buy from her. Fellow civilians look on in some discomfort at this minor incident in a world that was filled with mistrust and misunderstanding.

THE IRON CURTAIN *that came down across Germany divided the countries of Europe into two very different political, economic and military groups. In 1949 the North Atlantic Treaty Organization (NATO) was founded in the West, matched in 1955 by the Warsaw Pact. In the postwar settlements the Soviet Union had gained substantial territories along its western boundaries, and absorbed the previously independent Baltic states of Estonia, Latvia and Lithuania. The peoples on either side of the Iron Curtain were taught to feel fear and hostility towards those on the other side.*

Members of NATO

Countries under Soviet influence

--- Pre-1945 borders

PLANNING FOR PEACE

WHILE THEIR MEN were still fighting, leaders in the United States, the Soviet Union and the other 'united nations', as the allies against Germany were known, lay the foundations for the charter of a new international peace-keeping organization, the United Nations Organization. One of its goals was 'friendly relations among nations'. After negotiations in Washington and then at Yalta, the UN charter was signed in San Francisco on 26 June 1945, at a conference attended by representatives from twenty-six nations across the world. The United Nations formally came into being in October that year, with fifty-one members.

Like its predecessor, the League of Nations, the UN was founded on the principle of collective security for the peaceful settlement of disputes. It required its members to act together in a global effort to prevent war. Britain, China, France, the Soviet Union and the United States became the five permanent members of the UN's Security Council, which was responsible for maintaining international peace through collective security, economic sanctions or, as a last resort, military intervention.

As collective security depended upon agreement among the main powers, the UN charter ruled that decisions made by the permanent members of the Security Council must be unanimous. But with the increasing divide between the Western powers and the Soviet Union, the machinery of peace was weakened. When conflicts arose, the Soviet Union frequently exercised its power of veto, rendering the Security Council powerless. The only time the UN used military intervention in its early years, to settle the Korean conflict, the Soviet Union was absent from the council and therefore unable to veto the decision. The UN had been set up by the wartime victors to protect future generations 'from the scourge of war'. Now the conflicting interests of the two world superpowers prevented it from fulfilling this function.

The UN's principles of international peace may have been weakened by ideological and economic disputes, but it held firmly to its belief in equal rights and self-determination for people of all nations. It provided a new platform for the establishment of international humanitarian standards. Specialized agencies were set up. These initially dealt with postwar problems of refugees, rehabilitation and resettlement, and were then extended to cover issues such as slavery, religious intolerance and detention without trial.

Other agencies were set up to safeguard and promote better opportunities in employment, education, science and medicine. Through the newly established World Bank and the International Monetary Fund the UN was able to fund projects in developing countries, building roads and railways, and introducing telecommunications.

STARTLED BY THE UNITED CHORUS *from postwar leaders, the United Nations cradles the infant charter. This 1946 cartoon reflects the popular disbelief that the victors would be able to set aside their differences and work together for peace through the international organization they had themselves established.*

The changing relationship between the two former allies was demonstrated in an American newsreel at the end of the year. 'Soviet Russia was expansively stabbing westward, knifing into nations left empty by war. On orders from the Kremlin, Russia had launched one of history's most drastic political, moral and economic wars – a cold war. The United States was obliged to help Europe safeguard its traditional freedoms and the independence of its nations. Gone was the spirit of wartime unity that reached its peak on that historic afternoon in April 1945 at the Elbe river in Germany. Here two worlds actually met, but this coalition was to be torn asunder.'

The suspicion the West felt towards the Soviet Union was mirrored in Soviet fears about the intentions of the West. A Soviet feature film also recalled the meeting on the Elbe; in their version it was the Americans who were trying to take over Europe. Alexander Silvashko was now a schoolmaster in a remote village, and was disappointed when he went to see the film. 'I thought I'd find my character played somewhere in it. I was terribly upset when I realized that it was completely untruthful.' He remembers, too, that at that time 'there was an atmosphere of fear. Children liked my tales of the war but I never told them about the meeting on the Elbe. If I had discussed openly what had happened, I would have been in trouble. I would have been pulled in and questioned by the secret police.'

Ordinary Soviet citizens did not believe all they were told about the West. Nevertheless, as Anatoly Semiriaga explains, they did believe that Churchill's Fulton speech, the Marshall Plan set up to aid Europe's economic recovery, and the North Atlantic military alliance were designed 'to enslave Europe and set it against Russia'. Similarly, Westerners might not believe everything they were told about the Soviet Union, but they were still highly suspicious. One of the Americans who had met the Soviets on the Elbe was Elijah Sams. He appeared on a television programme, *Strike It Rich*, and decided to spend the money he won on visiting the Soviet Union to 'help peace efforts'. The State Department advised him not to go. His friends and neighbours 'thought we were kind of out of our minds'. When he returned he was questioned by the Federal Bureau of Investigation (FBI) on suspicion of being a communist.

Mutual hostility was reflected in political cartoons. Most Western cartoonists systematically dehumanized and demonized 'commies', 'reds' and 'pinks'. Their Soviet counterparts, who might have been banished to a forced labour camp if they failed to show enough enthusiasm in their work, understandably in their turn dehumanized and demonized Westerners.

'**DARWIN CORRECTED**' *reads the title of this cartoon from the satirical Soviet magazine,* Krokodil. *The ape is pointing to a picture of Heinrich Himmler, Hitler's deputy, emphasizing the likeness between him and the grim-faced, bloodstained American soldier.*

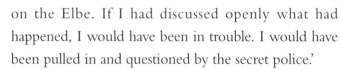

THE RED MENACE *of Stalin (*RIGHT*) looms over Europe. In this French cartoon he is poised to take over France, having already plunged the communist knife into the states of Eastern Europe and into China. The musicians accompanying his dance are leading French communists.*

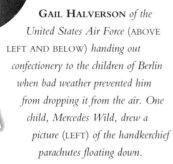

GAIL HALVERSON *of the United States Air Force* (ABOVE LEFT AND BELOW) *handing out confectionery to the children of Berlin when bad weather prevented him from dropping it from the air. One child, Mercedes Wild, drew a picture* (LEFT) *of the handkerchief parachutes floating down.*

The Berlin blockade

All the pressures of the postwar world converged on Berlin in 1948. The city was the spearhead of Soviet penetration into the heart of Europe, and at the same time a Western capitalist outpost deep inside the communist world.

In West Germany, the Western powers had introduced the currency reform that would shortly set off the *Wirtschaftswunder*, the economic miracle. They wanted to extend the reform to their sectors of Berlin. The Russians angrily refused permission. The atmosphere in Berlin was taut to breaking point when, on 23 June 1948, the Western powers announced that they were extending the currency reform to West Berlin anyway. The very next day the Russians began their blockade of Berlin.

Anatoly Semiriaga was now a Soviet liaison officer there, and remembers, 'The blockade was prepared weeks in advance. We had done everything we could to make the Allies leave West Berlin voluntarily, because it was a mote in our eye. So in the end we decided to force them to leave by making life intolerable for West Berlin.' They cut off the power, blocked the highways, stopped an American military train. But now the West, which had watched and done nothing as Stalin cemented his power across Eastern Europe, decided to act. Regardless of cost, they began to supply the city by air. The pilots who had bombed Berlin a few years earlier were now called back to feed its people.

Gail Halverson was one of these pilots. 'A telex came in and says we want four of your planes to leave Mobile, Alabama and go to Frankfurt within four hours, and we want crews for that. And I volunteered. We knew the dire straits that the people of Berlin were in.'

For many people in the West, the blockade confirmed all that they had been told about the Russians. To Gail Halverson it all came down to a simple comparison between good and evil. He was impressed to find that the children in Berlin spoke about freedom and did not ask him for anything. So he took to dropping them chocolate, fastening it to little parachutes made out of hand-kerchiefs. One young girl, Mercedes Wild, was at school when she saw the parachutes floating down. She did not get any chocolate, so she wrote to Gail Halverson: 'Dear Chocolate Uncle, Please

AIRLIFT TO BERLIN

THE CITY OF BERLIN, an island of capitalism well over a hundred kilometres inside the communist Soviet sector of Germany, became a besieged city as the blockade took effect. The Soviets were determined to starve Westerners out of Berlin; the Americans were determined to stay whatever the cost, and were instructed to respond as though the city was a beleaguered garrison.

The air corridor was the only remaining link between Berlin and the West. It became a lifeline for the two million inhabitants in the Western sectors. American aircraft – freighters and bombers – returned to Europe. The air forces of the United States and Britain flew round-the-clock operations that involved hundreds of aircraft. Berlin's two airports could not cope with the volume of traffic, so a third airport was rapidly built with the assistance of 19 000 volunteers.

It was dangerous and exhausting work for the pilots, who snatched sleep between flights on sacks in the aircraft hangars. There were so many flights, the aircraft were loaded to capacity, landing controls were primitive – it was a situation that could have brought disaster. But of the 272 000 flights that landed in the city in 321 days there were just twenty crashes. The most intensive flight schedule ever was a triumph of organization.

The skies above Berlin were constantly filled with the roar of aircraft; one landed on average every ten minutes bringing food, fuel and medical supplies. Most of these were everyday essentials, though the effort to maintain a degree of comfort was extended in December to Christmas trees and boxes of chocolates. The record delivery reached 13 000 tonnes of supplies one day in April 1949 – the average was 4000 tonnes a day for civilians and another 500 tonnes for military personnel.

The blockade was a political disaster for the Soviet Union, which failed to lure West Berliners into the Eastern sector despite offers of Soviet food and fuel rations. As a result of their endurance, the people of Berlin were seen to be choosing a future with Western values. The airlift continued until September, four months after the blockade was lifted. It hastened the division not only of Berlin itself but of Germany, and had highlighted the real dangers of the dangerous game of brinkmanship in the Cold War.

A CROWD OF WEST BERLINERS *watches an American aircraft, heavily loaded with essential supplies, flying in to land at Tempelhof airport during the blockade of the city.*

throw a parachute into the Hennelstrasse, you will recognize the garden because of the white hens.' He could not see the chickens, so he sent her some chocolate by post instead. The first piece, she says, was 'heaven on earth'; she put it on the windowsill and ate it bit by bit for a long, long time.

On 12 May 1949 the Russians finally gave in, and ended the blockade. By this time, the North Atlantic Treaty had been signed in Washington, and later that same month the West German Parliament voted through the *Grundgesetz*, the new constitution of a new sovereign West German state.

Life in the Soviet Union

The Soviet climbdown over Berlin turned a crisis for the West into a triumph. The Soviet people were told nothing. Their only task was to follow their leader. Millions were taught that central planning and collective work in unquestioning obedience to Stalin were the only ways to build a modern, just society. They sat through lessons where they were taught: 'We read the life of Comrade Stalin and we lift our heads. We clench our fists, we believe in our todays and our tomorrows. We believe in the battle led by Joseph Stalin.'

On Stalin's seventieth birthday in 1949 his people were summoned to celebrate the victorious march of socialism. Tamara Banketik, then eleven years old, was chosen to congratulate him. Among a group of children clutching bouquets, and in front of a huge crowd in Moscow, her voice rang out: 'We are the children of Lenin and Stalin. We strive to the summit of learning. Teacher, leader, beloved friend: Father Stalin, welcome!' She remembers now: 'I was transported into a fairy tale. He had such kindly eyes. It was as if he was my father.' Like the girl in the fairy tale, after the grand occasion Tamara Banketik had to give back her pretty dress. For her family, as for many others, reality was different. 'We lived in terrible conditions. It wasn't a house but a little shed. There was no running water or electricity. Each day I only had money for one ration of bread. I had to fight myself to stop eating it before I got home and shared it with my mother.'

From childhood, Russians were constantly reminded of the sacrifices that had been made in the Great Patriotic War, as the

A MOMENT OF GLORY *for Tamara Banketik as she makes her speech and presents flowers to Stalin. Like so many others, she bore the hardships because 'we always hoped that around the corner there would be a better life. Now I realize there was nothing around the corner.'*

Second World War was called, and of the economic sacrifices they must now themselves make in order to prevent the suffering ever happening again. More than 60 per cent of the country's budget was spent on defence, so the people endured continuing hardship while the armed forces were built up. Young Russians of Tamara Banketik's generation were brought up to see the West as decadent and dangerous. 'We knew our society was just and that capitalism was terrible. That's what we were taught. It did not matter how badly I lived now. I hoped it would get better.'

Russians lived in a closed world where all information about the West was ruthlessly controlled, and often distorted. Soviet newsreels painted the United States in garish colours, as a place where lynching was common, art and entertainment debased, and where millionaires kept their dogs in great luxury while the unemployed queued for food.

MAY DAY IN MOSCOW
The military might of the Soviet Union parades through Red Square in front of large crowds. A huge standing army was maintained to ensure the defence of the nation at a time when it felt under threat from the West.

"At that time everyone had to conform. Everyone had the same hairstyle, the same clothes. I never thought I would be a jazz man, but to me it was part of being a dissident."

ALEXEI KOZLOV

ALEXEI KOZLOV *began to play the saxophone in 1957, when he was twenty-two years old. His interest in the culture of the West was dangerous, but nevertheless he listened to the Voice of America radio station and from it learned all the American and British songs. He also took the risk of approaching visiting Americans in the street so that he could acquire otherwise unobtainable American clothes.*

The spying game

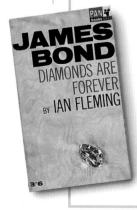

SPIES AND COUNTER-SPIES *infiltrated popular fiction during the Cold War. One of the most successful of them was the British secret agent James Bond, who pursued a glamorous career in espionage. Intrigue, adventure and suspense, as well as Bond's own flamboyant personality, made him a hero and the books an international success, selling millions of copies in a dozen languages.*

It was extremely difficult to gain access to Western ideas, though radio stations did broadcast over the Iron Curtain. Alexei Kozlov was one of the listeners. 'The radio was our only access to the West, and neighbours could denounce you for listening to those stations.' Like many others he had a special interest: it was not ideology, but jazz. 'I tried to learn English by listening. I bought myself a dictionary because I was so interested in what Nat King Cole was singing in "Walking My Baby Back Home". But you had to be so careful. If you said you loved Impressionism, or Louis Armstrong, you could be tried under the article "Idolators of the West".' In the Soviet Union jazz was banned, and the propagandists had a saying: 'Today he plays jazz, tomorrow he betrays the nation'.

Stalin did not rely on propaganda alone to maintain control over his people. All over Eastern Europe the new communist governments mounted show trials at which alleged 'traitors' were intimidated into making confessions, and their downfall then widely publicized. 'These curs planned invasions of the Soviet Union and Poland,' screamed a judge on a Soviet newsreel. 'I call for the death penalty. Crush him with an iron fist. There must be no mercy.' There was none. In Eastern Europe and in the Soviet Union itself, thousands of people were executed and millions more sent to suffer hunger and exhaustion in the forced labour camps.

Fear in the United States

Soviet propaganda against the West was matched by the hostility and fear with which the communist world was portrayed in the United States. Conventional Soviet military forces were far greater than those of the United States, and *Life* magazine devoted almost one whole issue to showing how large the gap was – 2 600 000 men in the Red Army to 640 000 GIs, thirty Soviet armoured divisions to just one American division. The military supremacy of the United States rested on its nuclear weapons. Even this was now to be challenged. On 18 September 1949 a United States aircraft flying over the North Pacific detected exceptionally high levels of radiation. 'Grim news,' a newsreel reported solemnly. 'The communist bloc also has the atom bomb. Behind the Iron

CONTAINING THE COMMUNISTS

THE PEOPLE of the Soviet Union were taught to fear and mistrust the world beyond their borders. The American diplomat George Kennan's analysis of this was reflected in the 8000-word message he sent from Moscow to the government in Washington. 'Wherever it is considered timely and promising,' he warned, 'efforts will be made to advance official limits of Soviet power....At the bottom of the Kremlin's neurotic view of world affairs is a traditional and instinctive Russian sense of insecurity.'

Kennan's view was very influential. In July 1947 he published an article in which he urged the United States to apply 'a long-term, patient but firm and vigilant containment of Soviet expansive tendencies'. He urged that the United States should maintain their own forces wherever necessary to counterbalance the Soviet threat. Kennan, who admired and liked the Russian people though not their leaders, later insisted that his 'containment doctrine' had been taken out of context, and in particular that he had recommended political rather than military containment.

The more the United States sought to limit Soviet expansion in order to contain the threat of communism, the more the Soviet leadership felt justified in its fears of domination by the West. The more the Soviet Union built up its military strength so that it could resist the perceived threat from the United States, the more the Americans feared Soviet power, and sought to limit it.

In April 1950 President Truman discussed with his National Security Council a proposal for a massive American military build-up if the containment of communism were to be more than a bluff. He was advised that defence expenditure would have to be more than tripled, to $50 billion a year, and was reminded that 'the Cold War is in fact a real war in which the survival of the world is at stake'. As more countries were gradually drawn into the superpower struggle, people throughout the world came to understand the nature of this new reality – that the activities of the two superpowers now shadowed the lives of everyone.

CONTAINING THE SOVIET UNION *was the key to United States foreign policy. As well as building alliances with friendly states on the borders of the Soviet Union, the United States also established a series of military bases in them.*

Curtain is the most sobering threat ever to menace free men.' To emphasize the real nature of this threat, the broadcast continued: 'The target area is our North American continent, but the bull's-eye of the enemy's target is you, your family, your home.'

Many Americans now succumbed to paranoia too. They believed J. Edgar Hoover, director of the FBI, when he declared: 'Communism in reality is not a political party, it is a way of life. An evil and malignant way of life. It reveals a condition akin to disease, that spreads like an epidemic and, like an epidemic, a quarantine is necessary to keep it from infecting this nation.' And Herbert Philbrick, an ex-communist who became an FBI informer, had this to say about his former friends: 'They are lying, dirty, shrewd, godless, murderous, determined...an international criminal conspiracy.' The United States became obsessed with the idea of communist infiltration, espionage and betrayal.

The official Committee on Un-American Activities had been investigating subversion by fascists and communists since before the war. Now a new figure, the senator Joseph McCarthy, entered the fray. For the next four years McCarthy occupied the

ON TRIAL FOR SPYING *The United States pilot Gary Powers, whose U2 spyplane was shot down by a missile over Soviet territory in 1960 while on a secret 'reconnaissance' mission at the height of the Cold War.*

spotlight, supported by other conservative congressmen and a whole cast of informers and denouncers. Many of their victims were highly placed officials, distinguished scholars, Hollywood actors and scriptwriters.

Others were caught in the whirling blades of McCarthyism. Manny Fried was a local official with the Machinists' Union in Buffalo, New York state. He was charged with being a traitor. He explains: 'Anything that was taking place, we were interfering and carrying out orders from the Soviet Union, which was nonsense, absolute nonsense. J. Edgar Hoover sent out a team of twenty-five FBI men to get me. They had decided I was a symbol of the left in the community and they must break me. They visited every single friend of my wife's, and one by one pressured them to break off their friendship with us. They wrecked my marriage. The difficulties in the union I could handle, but the difficulties they caused in my marriage were terrible, really terrible.'

Fear spread across the country. To alert citizens to the communist menace, civic leaders in the town of Mosinee, Wisconsin acted out a Soviet takeover for a day. Newspaper editor Bill Sweinler, who helped to organize the event, describes what happened. 'The Russian army came into the school, and burned school books there in a bonfire. I was arrested. They arrested all of the clergy – the community Catholic priest, the Lutheran minister and the Methodist minister; the mayor and the chief of police. They stopped a train. The people of Mosinee thought they had been invaded. Four of us actually broke into Dad's printing office and printed armbands with the hammer and sickle on them. Our school lunch that day was black bread and potato soup. The kids got an education that couldn't come out of a book. It was an education we saw first hand – that we had it pretty good as Americans!'

At the beginning of 1949 the Communist Party gained power in China. In the United States fears grew of Soviet world domination, while in the Soviet Union the news was greeted with delight. There people were assured that world revolution was inevitable. 'Now one quarter of the world is in the socialist

MANNY FRIED *was a union official persecuted for being a communist, and so for being, as this poster declares, an 'enemy of America'. He came under FBI surveillance – shown by this document authorizing the installation of a hidden microphone in the studio over the garage at his home.*

MOSINEE SEIZED BY REDS! *When the town enacted what could happen if communism took over the United States, the local newspaper joined in the exercise by reporting the events taking place that day.*

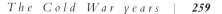

DAILY RECORD-HERALD

WISCONSIN, MONDAY EVENING, MAY 1, 1950 — FIVE CENTS

WEATHER
WISCONSIN—Partly cloudy this afternoon and tonight. Not so cool this afternoon. Tuesday mostly cloudy and warmer.

Seized by Reds!

Security Police Stage Coup While City Sleeps

Proclamations and Regulations of New Regime

Whole World Learns of Red Coup

Commissar

JOSEPH KORNFEDER

Kornfeder and Gitlow Direct Mosinee Coup

Police Chief Executed; Mayor Dragged From Home in Pajamas

Democracy to Be Restored

Main Street Now Stalin Boulevard

Presence of State Legion Leaders Fails To Stop Red Revolt

Red Security Police Halt Train

Communist Cooperation

Pop Makers Must Follow the Red Line

RED SCARE COMES TO HOLLYWOOD *The fear of communism was played out in films such as* Red Planet Mars, *a thinly veiled story about communist invasion. When investigators became suspicious of communist infiltration in the film industry, some great Hollywood stars* (RIGHT), *led by Lauren Bacall and Humphrey Bogart, flew to Washington to protest.*

PERSECUTION IN POLITICS

'ONCE THE DOGS ARE SET ON YOU everything you have done since the dawn of time is suspect,' wrote Raymond Kaplan in a farewell note to his wife before he committed suicide. He was an engineer who had been summoned to give evidence to the Senate subcommittee investigating suspected communists. Another victim was Julius Hlavaty, a Czech-born mathematics teacher. He was being investigated because he had once broadcast over the Voice of America radio station, and the subcommittee feared communist influence there. Asked whether he had ever been a communist, he refused to give evidence, claiming his constitutional privilege against self-incrimination under the Fifth Amendment. As a result, he automatically lost his job.

The subcommittee's chairman was Senator Joe McCarthy. On 9 February 1950 he touched a nerve in the national psyche when he announced – quite untruthfully – that he had a list of 207 communists who worked in the State Department. McCarthy convinced himself that the United States was being undermined by a secret communist conspiracy. He was not alone. The Committee on Un-American Activities was already investigating the alleged influence of communists in Hollywood, in the State Department, among American experts on China and in the labour unions. Caught between the danger of prison for perjury if they denied communist connections, and the certainty of persecution if they 'took the Fifth', many innocent individuals who had joined the Communist Party in the very different political context of the 1930s now saw their lives ruined.

The background to this fear and the persecution which it encouraged was bewilderment. Only a few years before, Americans had returned from Europe after their victorious crusade for democracy. Now the world was apparently already under threat again, this time by the possibility of communist domination, and all American communists were regarded as traitors. It was on this mood that McCarthy capitalized.

After four years, McCarthy overreached himself. In 1954 he organized hearings to investigate the absurd possibility that the United States army was riddled with communist influence. On a live television broadcast he was humiliated by the challenge from Joseph Welch, an elderly Republican lawyer from Boston. 'Have you no sense of decency, sir, at long last?' Welch demanded. McCarthy was finished. He was censured by the Senate and in 1957 died of alcoholism.

DIVIDING THE KOREAN PEOPLE

THE POLICY OF THE UNITED STATES to contain communist expansion faced its first real test in 1950 with the outbreak of war in Korea. Formerly ruled by Japan, the Korean peninsula had been divided between the Allied occupying forces at the end of the Second World War – the Soviets in the north and the Americans in the south. Attempts to unite the country failed, and the United Nations eventually recognized the newly created government of the Republic of Korea, established in the south in August 1948. A month later, the communist government of the Democratic People's Republic was set up in the north. However, each side claimed jurisdiction of the whole country, and thousands of soldiers were killed in border incidents.

On 25 June 1950, exactly a year after the withdrawal of United States troops from South Korea, the North Korean army, well equipped by the Soviet Union, invaded the south. It was as allies that the Soviet Union and the United States had divided Korea in the postwar peace settlement. Now they were political enemies, and another war was fought to keep it divided.

Fifteen countries sent forces to fight against the communist troops of the north after their attack had been condemned by the United Nations, but the United States was the principal contender. This was not just a conflict between North and South Korea, but a war between the United States and communism. When American troops penetrated deep into the north, approaching the Yalu river near the Chinese border, communist China intervened on the side of North Korea, forcing the United States troops to retreat.

The fighting continued for another two years. An armistice was finally reached in July 1953 after prolonged peace negotiations that were influenced by the United States' threat of using nuclear weapons against China.

The Korean war set a precedent for the use of intervention as a means of preventing communist expansion. In this, the United States had succeeded. Most of the 125 000 Chinese and North Korean prisoners of war did not want to return home. But after three years of fighting, cities had been destroyed and air bombing campaigns had devastated many of the industrial areas of North Korea, its transport systems and its housing. Millions of people temporarily became refugees, and more than three million people were killed, a million of them civilians. The people of Korea had paid a high price in the ideological conflict between East and West.

PASSING ON THE ROAD
South Korean civilians fleeing from the war zone meet American soldiers, reinforcements marching towards the fighting.

commonwealth,' declared a Soviet newsreel. 'Now one in three people lives under socialism. There are over a billion of us.'

Into this mood burst the news that forces of the communist republic of North Korea had invaded the south. Western newsreels portrayed the conflict as one between freedom and the Soviet push for world domination. 'It's a weary business,' one report put it, 'chasing Red bandits and liberating a country whose only wish is freedom from aggression. It also calls for sacrifice in lives and blood of Koreans and Americans who are grimly determined to

stop communist imperialism.' A Soviet newsreel painted a quite different picture, reporting that 'American imperialists declare war on peace-loving Korea'. Anatoly Semiriaga remembers that there was a war scare in Moscow, just as there was in Washington. 'The Americans were waiting to destroy us as an island in the turbulent seas of imperialism,' he says. 'We were told no more than that. So everything was simple. There were no doubts. They were our rivals, our enemies.'

Bids for freedom

Joseph Stalin died in 1953. Under the new leadership of Nikita Khrushchev the worst of Stalin's terror ended, though it would take several decades for his influence to fade. Khrushchev urged peaceful coexistence and competition with the West, rather than outright hostility.

Under the new policy Soviet citizens and the peoples of Eastern Europe were still not allowed to travel to the West to see for themselves the differences between the two ways of life. But foreigners could come and experience socialism. Tourism was encouraged. In 1957 the Americans were even allowed to bring an exhibition to Moscow. Thousands queued for hours to see what capitalist goods looked like. Alexei Kozlov, the jazz musician, managed to get into the exhibition. 'The Communist Party lost their hold over so many people by raising the Iron Curtain even for a month,' he says. 'It was as if we were discovering a new planet, stepping into the future. We were stunned. We couldn't believe that people lived like that.'

As the subject peoples of Eastern Europe realized that the tyrant was dead, they began to stir. A few weeks after Stalin's death, building workers in East Berlin rioted and were ruthlessly repressed. In October 1956 there was more trouble when Hungarian students in Budapest protested against Soviet rule. The authorities tried to stop them, but workers and soldiers joined in and a peaceful demonstration instead became a revolution.

Gergely Pongratz was a Hungarian farm worker who had been conscripted into the army, and now he found himself on the barricades. As the Soviet

'THE END OF THE DEMOCRATIC ZONE' *this damaged sign once declared. Taken from the border between the Eastern and Western sectors of Berlin, it is being carried by a worker during a protest march in 1953. The action, at first encouraged as a 'critical demonstration', was suppressed and martial law declared when real protests and strikes threatened to cripple industry.*

infantry followed the tanks through the city streets, darting from doorway to doorway, he says, 'I saw a Russian head looking out. I aimed and pulled the trigger, and saw the Russian soldier fall on the pavement. I started to cry; I had killed a human being.'

After just four days of intensive fighting the Soviet forces withdrew. For a week the Hungarians thought their uprising had freed the country. Talks were even held with the Soviet government about Hungary's independence. As Gergely Pongratz asks: 'Can you imagine how we were feeling at that time? We were in the glories, in heaven.'

Their joy was short-lived; the Soviets came back in force. Western radio broadcasts had talked of freeing those enslaved by communism, but now the West took no action on Hungary's behalf. After ten days, Gergely Pongratz recalls, 'We gave up because we saw we were not going to get any help and what we were doing was suicide'. There came one last despairing radio cry, monitored in the West: 'This is

Burning portraits of their hated prime minister, Matyas Rakosi, Hungarian freedom fighters take to the streets during the uprising in 1956. For a few exciting days it seemed that independence would be granted to Hungary; instead, Soviet forces returned and crushed the revolution.

Hungary calling! The last remaining station....Early this morning the Soviet troops launched a general attack on Hungary. We are requesting immediate aid—' Then the voice was cut off. The people of Hungary felt that the free world had betrayed them. A quarter of a million Hungarians managed to escape to the West. Gergely Pongratz was among them, together with his mother and sister. Overcome with emotion, he describes their departure. 'We crossed the border, we went about fifteen or twenty metres and my mother turned around. She went a few metres back, under the flag, the Hungarian flag, and in a handkerchief she put earth. She is buried in the United States but that earth is under her head – Hungarian earth, Hungarian land.'

The Iron Curtain fell again, and the borders were more and more heavily guarded. There was only one gap – Berlin, where the German inhabitants were still able to move freely between the Eastern and Western sectors of the city. More than three million Germans voted with their feet for the West. But now this freedom was also to be denied.

A **HUMAN WALL** *of East German soldiers on guard in Berlin on 14 August 1961. They are standing shoulder to shoulder on the western side of the Brandenburg Gate, 'protecting' the Soviet sector until the wall itself is built in this part of the city.*

A divided city

On Saturday 12 August 1961, 4000 East German refugees were registered in West Berlin, the highest number recorded. Early on the Sunday morning, 40 000 men began to seal off the Soviet sector. Two Soviet divisions were deployed in a ring round the city, ready to intervene if necessary. At first the 'wall' was a makeshift affair of barbed wire. It became an impenetrable concrete barrier snaking through the city on the line of ancient parish boundaries. On the Tuesday of that first week a photographer captured the moment that one of the East German border guards, Konrad Schumann, jumped for freedom in full uniform. Eventually hundreds more people escaped to the West, jumping from windows, swimming canals. East German guards were under orders to open fire on anyone trying to escape, and dozens of people were killed.

Anita Möller was one of those whose attempt to escape was successful. When the wall was first built she, like hundreds of thousands of other East Berliners, was in despair. 'We thought,

LEAPING TO FREEDOM
This photograph of Konrad Schumann escaping to the West became a famous symbol of the need to be free.

DIVIDED BY THE WIRE
Under the watchful eye of East German guards, a mother and daughter reach out across the new barrier. Many Berlin families suffered enforced separation from their relatives when the wall was built.

ANITA MÖLLER (ABOVE) *escaped to the West with her family, but had to leave her mother (on the right of the photograph) behind. 'The West was portrayed as the evil capitalist enemy, but I had relatives in West Germany and I knew that wasn't the case,' she recalls. Accustomed to travelling across Berlin, she could not believe it when she heard about the wall suddenly being built across the city.*

A FAMILY IN FLIGHT (RIGHT) *The day before the bricked-up homes along the border were due to be evacuated, this family unblocked a doorway and fled to the West.*

"We can't get out. It's all over." ' Her brother was already in the West, however, and he was determined to help her. He and his friends dug a 200-metre (218-yard) tunnel right under the wall. When they were ready they sent her a message to come with her husband and child to a café on the East Berlin side. 'We waited a long time in this café. It was like a spy film. There were secret signs: a newspaper, a party badge, a bag in the right hand. If things went wrong we could be shot. We all knew that.'

It was frightening in the tunnel. 'In the middle, right under the wall, someone had put a sign saying, "You are now leaving the Eastern Sector", and I thought, I'm in the West. Finally I got through and came up on the other side.' Anita Möller could not tell her parents she was leaving because she knew the secret police would interrogate them. Her mother was ill; she died without ever being given permission to visit her family.

In the West the Berlin wall was called 'the wall of shame'. In the East it was the 'anti-fascist protective rampart'. Less than twenty years after East and West had linked arms on the banks of the river Elbe in the moment of victory, they had become two armed camps, divided by two irreconcilable philosophies. The 'just and enduring' peace for which both East and West had fought, the brave new world they had both dreamed of, seemed as far away as ever.

A WATCHER ON THE WALL (RIGHT) *Protected by barbed wire and concrete, East German border guards maintained a constant, vigilant scrutiny of activities in West Berlin. For nearly thirty years the city was to symbolize the mutual hostility and contrasting ways of life under capitalist and communist systems.*

12

Boomtime

The years of prosperity

IN THE UNITED STATES A NEW era of prosperity had begun. When the Second World War ended Americans found that they were members of the world's richest, busiest, most confident nation. American servicemen returning home from Europe found dramatic contrasts: in the United States there was no rationing, cities and factories were undamaged, and shops were full of food and other goods.

In Europe life immediately after the war was very different. 'There was poverty and misery. There was nothing,' explains Gerardo Ciola, who lived in the mountains of southern Italy. 'The only work available was on the land. There were so many people and so little work.'

Life was equally difficult in France, where the orphaned Evelyne Langey was growing up. 'There were still soup kitchens,' she remembers. 'I'd queue up for four or five hours with my jug and come back with millet seed. You'd feed it to the birds now. I was so hungry that for the only time in my life I wanted to steal some steak from a butcher's stall. I could never pluck up the courage to do it. But when you had thoughts like that it just shows how desperate the shortages were, and continued to be long after the liberation.'

Throughout Europe there were refugees, homeless people, little work, little money, little food. By the winter of 1947 the United States government realized that the Europeans needed help. To prepare the public for this, and to draw attention to the Europeans' plight, a special train was sent across the United States collecting food parcels. The food this Friendship Train provided brought new hope to many Europeans at a time of desperate need; they had never seen such plenty. It was accompanied by the message that 'Prosperity makes you free', and allowed people a taste of the good times that Americans already enjoyed.

This was just the beginning. Many of the children of postwar Europe would grow up to a better life than anyone at the time could have imagined, and eventually caught up with their American counterparts. They too enjoyed this era of rapid economic growth and unprecedented opportunity – a boomtime.

THE AMERICAN DREAM *came true as prosperity*
brought a new suburban way of life to many families.

New beginnings

At the end of the war the people of Europe were exhausted. Families were grieving for husbands and sons who had not come home. Cities had been devastated by bombing and by the fighting armies, and with factories in ruins there was little work.

In some countries there was a new mood of optimism. In Britain a Labour government had come to power, and it was promising dramatic change. It was part of Labour's vision to rebuild the bombed cities as fast and as well as possible. In a film about the reconstruction of Coventry, the planners announced that out of the ruins a great new city would arise, and they were not thinking only of its material prosperity. 'This is the people's city,' they declared. 'Coventry is going to be a place to live in where people believe that human life can be good and pleasant. In

PEDESTRIAN PRECINCTS *were an innovation in town planning that helped to make Coventry a popular modern city. It had suffered some of the worst bomb damage in Britain during the war, but with the growing postwar car industry Coventry became a boom town.*

QUEUEING FOR RATION BOOKS *in London in 1951. All over Europe food and other supplies remained in desperately short supply for some years after the war.*

QUEUEING FOR RATION BOOKS *in London in 1951. All over Europe food and other supplies remained in desperately short supply for some years after the war.*

the days to come we must feel that it is not every man for himself, but every man for the good and happiness of all people living.'

The road ahead, however, was a difficult one. As well as the physical devastation that some of them had undergone, whole countries had been reduced almost to bankruptcy, while their weary people were impatient for the new society their leaders promised. The winter of 1946–47 in Europe was the harshest in living memory; in the icy conditions coal stocks ran dangerously low. Rather than recovering from the war, Western Europe was staggering from crisis to crisis. The United States government became concerned, and sent an official to investigate. His report was alarming. He warned that the wartime destruction to the European economy had been greatly underestimated, and that the political situation echoed the economic crisis.

The political situation did seem to be in a state of upheaval. In France and Italy large communist parties enjoyed considerable prestige because of the part they had played during the war in resisting the Germans. Many working people believed that only communism would bring a real improvement in their lives. Fear of communist takeovers in Western Europe like those that had already taken place as a result of the Soviet presence in Eastern Europe helped to persuade the United States government that something must be done. A huge programme of aid for the whole of Europe was launched. Western Europe accepted the offer, but the Soviet Union under Joseph Stalin would not tolerate the countries of Eastern Europe becoming dependent on and grateful to the Americans, and the aid was rejected.

The ration book

RATIONING OF SOME FOODS *continued until as late as 1954 in Britain. Everyone used coupons like these to obtain their fixed allowance of clothing and food.*

**'FREE PASSAGE FOR
THE MARSHALL PLAN'**
(OPPOSITE) *is the message
on this poster promoting
American aid in West
Germany. Marshall Aid
brought hope and new
opportunities to Europe as
well as lifting the barriers of
hunger and poverty in the
aftermath of war.*

Europe's recovery plan

The Marshall Plan, as the aid programme was known, was both an act of generosity and one of enlightened self-interest. Its aim was simple: to make Western Europe prosperous again. The United States had learned some hard lessons in the economic depression of the 1930s, and recognized that in order to continue enjoying its wealth, it must share it. The United States was in need of overseas markets to export to – the healthier the markets, the more the United States itself would benefit. But the scheme was political and ideological as well as economic, as a prosperous Europe would be far less likely to embrace communism as an attractive alternative to capitalist democracy.

The British government took the lead in welcoming the aid, and went out of its way to allay fears about what it meant. In France the Americans were regarded with some suspicion. Wally Nielsen, an American on the staff of the Marshall Plan, thinks that 'the presence of these Americans was an embarrassment and a humiliation'. He describes their reception. 'The Americans came to France with probably quite romantic ideas that we were going to bring this economic help and we would be welcomed with open arms and that the wounds of war would be bound up. We were subjected to a number of jolts of reality. I remember that the first day I went to my office in the hotel I had to fight my way through a line of screaming pickets. They were members of the Communist Party in France. They were picketing the building because of their claim that the Marshall Plan was simply an American scheme to control Europe.'

Wally Nielsen acknowledges that the Americans' affluence might have been difficult for the French to accept, too. 'Most of us who staffed the Marshall Plan came from ordinary backgrounds, but once we got to Paris things were dramatically different. First of all the prices made everything just dirt cheap for us, so here we were having lunch in an elegant restaurant in the middle of Paris, that was pretty heady stuff. There was a luxury aspect of the thing that none of us had anticipated.' It was different for the French. Wally Nielsen remembers eating in a smart Parisian hotel soon after he arrived. 'I had a steak that was so tough I could only eat a little part of it…when I had pushed my plate away and the waiter

'GO BACK TO AMERICA!' (RIGHT) *declares this anti-American French Communist Party poster in 1950. Eastern Europe was not alone in its suspicions of Marshall Aid. Many people in Western Europe saw it as an attempt by the United States government to tighten its grip over Europe through dollar imperialism.*

DIVIDING THE AID CAKE (BELOW) *European recovery depended on cooperation, and the United States insisted on the submission of a joint plan for Marshall Aid by the countries that would benefit from it. After the First World War punitive reparations had been imposed on Germany; in the new spirit of peace after the Second World War American aid was offered to allies and enemies alike.*

Greece $694m

Austria $677m

Belgium/Luxembourg $556m

Denmark $271m

Norway $254m

Turkey $221m

Ireland $146m

Yugoslavia $109m

Sweden $107m

Portugal $50m

Trieste $32m

Iceland $29m

United Kingdom $3176m

France $2706m

Italy $1474m

West Germany $1389m

Netherlands $1079m

removed it, I noticed that he took the remains of the steak and wrapped it in a napkin and carefully put it in his pocket. The hardship of life in Paris at that time was really very severe.'

The Economic Recovery Plan (ERP) – the official name for the Marshall Plan – included both emergency aid to deal with the shortages of food and fuel, and development aid to help Western

A HELPING HAND FOR FARMERS *Tractors such as the one acquired by the Jolivet family had top priority in the early days of the recovery programme. As Raymond Jolivet explains, 'That was the beginning of progress in farming; farming expanded with the availability of high-performance equipment.'*

European countries rebuild and modernize their agriculture, transport and other industries. Sixteen countries benefited, regardless of their wartime allegiance. At first shipments of food – grain and animal feedstuffs – were the most important priority; the first shipment, 9000 tonnes of American wheat, sailed from Texas in the spring of 1948.

The plan also helped European farmers to grow more food themselves. Raymond Jolivet was twelve years old when the tractor arrived on his father's farm – the first one in the district. There was great excitement. 'Lots of people stopped to see what was going on. They wanted to see what kind of work the tractor could do and to take a close look at it, because at the time we didn't see many in the countryside.' He remembers the difference it made. 'The tractor meant that production increased fivefold during busy periods like harvest time. It was easier because the tractor took some of the effort out of working in the fields. You no longer had to walk behind the horses – you always had to follow the animal when you were ploughing, you know, whereas with the tractor you were sitting down, and that made a big difference.'

Marshall Aid made possible some remarkable projects, including hydroelectric dams, land reclamation and irrigation. This was still an age of heavy industry: coal and steel, shipbuilding, and the manufacture of heavy machinery. Money was used to re-equip coal mines in Belgium, Britain, France and Germany, and to build modern steelworks in Britain, France, Germany and Italy. The Italian worker Giovanni de Stefanis recalls the excitement at the arrival of some milling machines from Cincinnati, Ohio. 'It was obvious where they came from. On the front there was a large badge divided in half: one half was the American flag, the other had the initials ERP. We knew it was part of Marshall Aid and we all worked happily. This wasn't second-hand machinery, and it was very efficient.'

In Douai, a town on the French–Belgian border, people turned out to line the streets and watch a giant steel press being delivered from Chicago. 'It was enormous,' says Jean Dubertret, an engineer who worked on it after it had been installed. 'When it was on its way from Le Havre teachers brought pupils of all ages to

watch this monster go by. I'll never forget when it rolled into the
factory. Most of the workmen stopped what they were doing to
come and see this new toy. It was so different from what we'd
known before that everyone was amazed.' The press was used
to make the chassis for Citroën 2CVs.

Marshall Aid was immensely important to Europe. It
totalled $13 billion (worth perhaps twenty times as much
in the money of the 1990s) – 5 per cent of the gross
national product of the United States at the time. And in
addition to public money, the private American relief
parcels that were donated to the Europeans amounted
to a further $500 million – the equivalent of
more than $3 from every man, woman and child

in the United States. But Europe's postwar recovery was not solely due to American help. Their assistance made a major contribution to the work of reconstruction, while the Europeans continued to work towards prosperity for themselves.

The economic director of the British and American zones of West Germany, Ludwig Erhard, insisted on a drastic currency reform in June 1948. This produced almost immediate results. 'The black market suddenly disappeared,' he later explained. 'Shop windows were full of goods; the factory chimneys were smoking; and the streets swarmed with lorries. Everywhere the noise of new buildings going up replaced the deadly silence of the ruins.' Apathy was replaced by hope, in West Germany and elsewhere across Europe.

The reconstruction gradually led to industrial expansion, and was accompanied by social reform. Europe entered an age of political consensus; even in France and Italy, where communist parties were strong, the legitimacy of the system was accepted. Each Western European country introduced its own version of what, when it was pioneered in Britain by the Labour government between 1945 and 1951, came to be known as the 'welfare state'. Industrial productivity and social welfare, the components of the new 'social market' mixed economy, had a direct effect on the lives of tens of millions of people.

In the United States the postwar boom had already freed many Americans from the want and drudgery they had endured during the 1930s. The French engineer Jean Dubertret visited the United States to study American production methods in the early days of the Marshall Plan. He was interested in the American way of work; not just the analysis of costs and processes, which he had learned about from conferences he had attended, but the efforts to improve working conditions and to encourage good relations between the staff – attitudes that were quite different from his experiences in French factories. He was also astounded by the way Americans lived. After the austerity of life in Europe, it seemed almost like a dream. 'We were struck by the fact that everyone could have a car, a house and a garden. They had everything at the time – television, freezer, refrigerator, the lot. Our workers were astonished to find this was available to everybody.'

GETTING PEOPLE BACK TO WORK *in factories that had been rebuilt or had reverted to peacetime production, was an important part of the reconstruction process. American production methods helped European industries to modernize and become more efficient.*

The American dream

The Americans were beginning to enjoy the new opportunities available to them. At the end of the war, Betty DuBrul had been living in New York with her mother as there were no houses or apartments for her and her husband Don to buy in the city. One day they drove out to look at a model house in Levittown. 'We came to the house, walked through it, and Don looked at me and I looked at him and he said, "Shall we?" "Sure, why not?" So we put a hundred-dollar deposit down and this is it, this is our house, this is what we wound up with. It was a perfect little house, and it came with a refrigerator and a stove and a washing machine. For so many young couples, with the men coming back from the war,' Betty DuBrul remembers, 'it was the answer to a dream.'

William Levitt was the Henry Ford of housing. He turned the idea of a detached house for every family from a dream into a real possibility. A house could not be moved along an assembly line, but the process of housebuilding could be broken down into twenty-seven separate operations, so twenty-seven separate teams of workers moved through the houses. Before the war, the typical builder had built five homes a year. Levitt built thousands. He could afford to sell them for $8000 each, and to add a swimming pool for every thousand homes. The men went off to work in the city, leaving the women and the children at home.

These families created a huge new market, and new ways of marketing soon followed them out to

BUYING A LIFESTYLE *not just a home* (ABOVE AND BELOW) *was only one of the benefits offered by the new suburban Levittown complexes, which had their own schools, shopping centres, churches, swimming pools, libraries and community centres. Of the 1400 homes bought on the first day the houses were for sale, some even came with a free television and vacuum cleaner. But the American dream home was not available to all: black people were excluded from them; the houses were for white American couples only.*

Pop-up toast

ELECTRICITY IN THE KITCHEN *brought many new gadgets to simplify domestic chores. The automatic toaster would make sure that 'bread becomes superb toast...not now and then – but always', as the advertisement for this gleaming Toastmaster promised.*

A REVOLUTION IN RETAILING *was introduced with new supermarkets, which appeared first in the United States and later in Europe. Shoppers took some time to get used to the confusing atmosphere of the huge shops with their wide range of foods and household goods at competitive prices, and to the new self-service method of retailing that they heralded. Supermarkets soon became a potent symbol of affluence, creating new patterns in people's lives and offering them greater choice than ever before.*

the suburbs. Discount stores such as E. J. Korvette sold the new labour-saving appliances for the new suburban way of life. One young housewife at the time, Louise Aber, explains why the stores were so popular. 'We were just starting out, and we had to fill the houses up with appliances, television sets, linens, you needed every little thing for the kitchen, you needed towels, you needed clothes for the children. Korvette was a terrific store, it was a discount house that everybody ran to. People came even to do their food

NEW REFRIGERATION METHODS (RIGHT) *enabled housewives to do all their shopping in a single weekly visit to the supermarket. Fridges and freezers quickly became a vital feature of the modern American household.*

BUY NOW – PAY LATER

THERE WAS A TIME WHEN the only people who could borrow money were those who did not really need it. The well-to-do middle classes could take out loans from the bank for major purchases, whereas those who had no money often could not buy what they needed. 'In God We Trust', declared the sign in many American saloons and shops, 'Others pay cash!'

Credit for all became an essential part of the postwar boom, assuring manufacturers of a growing number of purchasers. The American housewife Jackie Sunderland remembers what the new spending power felt like. 'It isn't that you had that much money,' she explains. 'You could charge everything. We didn't save like our parents did – we charged. You worried about paying the bills month after month, but you would spread it out. There is no question that shopping made you feel better.' Credit buying of consumer goods was first offered through hire purchase; then credit cards also encouraged many more people to buy on credit rather than waiting to save their money before spending it.

In consumer credit, as in consumer goods, the United States led the way. The housing boom of the 1950s was fed by easy financing. Car dealers advertised easy credit terms, and extended the repayment period from two years to three. Domestic appliances, televisions, consumer goods and even holidays were sold 'on the never-never'. In 1950 Diners' Club issued the first credit card in the United States. At first made of cardboard, it became plastic from 1955. American Express followed in 1958, and Carte Blanche in 1959. Under the headline 'What a Country!', *Fortune* magazine pronounced in 1956 that, 'Never has a whole people spent so much money on so many expensive things in such an easy way as Americans are doing today.'

For many people in Europe the idea of buying expensive goods in this way was alarming at first, but traditional financial caution was gradually eroded as customers lost their fear of debt. Hire purchase enabled buyers to take their new goods away as soon as the first instalment was paid, though they could be repossessed until one-third of the hire purchase price had been paid. During the 1960s credit cards were introduced in Europe, and rapidly became popular there as well. As people became more confident that their future was financially secure, they became more willing to pile up debts. Easy credit was not just a bubble on the surface of the new prosperity, but an essential part of it.

A TELEVISION *was one of the first items people were tempted to buy with the new credit offers.*

THE HIDDEN PERSUADERS

URING THE Second World War the Coca-Cola Corporation persuaded the US military that the boys overseas needed a Coke to keep up their morale. Coca-Cola emerged from the war as a worldwide symbol of American culture. With its instantly recognizable red and white colour scheme, wavy writing and distinct bottle shape, Coke was also proof of the power of the sophisticated new advertising style that developed after the war.

Advertising created an appetite for goods and services on a new scale, and exerted a powerful image of Western life and Western values that would eventually spread throughout the world. Thirsty workers in Third World countries thought they were sharing in American prosperity when they bought a bottle of Coke; French intellectuals, wary of growing American influence, denounced 'Coca-Colonization'.

Using techniques borrowed from wartime propaganda and from social analysis, the advertising agencies clustered along New York's Madison Avenue identified new markets by targeting particular groups and creating new needs and aspirations. Advertising had once simply shown the product at its best, and given information about where it could be found and what it would cost. By the 1950s advertisements sold an image, pictured a lifestyle, created a mood, and exploited half-acknowledged desires.

Advertisements became increasingly influential, as Georgette

Braga explains. 'The commercial itself actually meant more to me than all these products they were talking about...they depicted all these lovely women – they were all so beautiful. They made you feel that if you bought this product, even though it was a floor cleaning product, you were going to turn into this wonderful creature. I think we were very gullible, and we bought into it because it was new.'

Sometimes the advertisement reassured potential buyers that they deserved to buy what they wanted. Cadillac showed 'the man who had earned the right to sit at this wheel'. The hamburger chain McDonald's slogans ended: 'You deserve a break today'. At the other extreme, admen found that the women who took four out of every five purchasing decisions about consumer goods could be influenced by guilt. To increase their own share of the lucrative washing powder market, Proctor & Gamble and Unilever vied with one another to make women feel their washing should be 'whiter than white'. Sometimes an 'expert' in white coat and horn-rimmed glasses would earnestly advise them...to choose the advertiser's product.

In the 1950s advertising was becoming a huge industry. As people became prosperous, the potential market grew. There were more and more consumers who could be persuaded that what they had never even thought they wanted was really what they needed to prove their success and bring them happiness.

shopping because the food was discounted too.' Louise Aber can remember the evening Korvette first opened in her neighbourhood. 'We had never had anything like that before, and the first day that they opened up there were thousands of people there, the streets were packed, you couldn't get in, you couldn't get out. It was the beginning of a completely different era.'

It was indeed the beginning of a new era: one of prosperity based on cheap cars, cheap gasoline, cheap homes in the suburbs, cheap food and cheap appliances from discount stores. It was also based on the high wages that many more people could now earn, and boundless confidence in the American way of life. A cartoon called 'Meet Joe' spelled out the economic optimism on which the postwar politics of consensus were based. 'Hi folks! Joe's the king because he can buy more with his wages than any other worker on the globe. He's no smarter than workers in other countries. Sure, being an American is great, but how could you be superior to any foreigner when you or your folks might be any one of a dozen races or religions? So, if you're no superman, it must be the American way of doing things that makes you the luckiest guy in the world.'

The 1950s in the United States were a time of widely distributed affluence, of complacency and consensus, and of minimum dissent. In politics, extreme positions to both left and right were out of fashion. Big business and big labour unions worked together to increase productivity and wages. With the benign figure of General Ike Eisenhower as president, it was a period when American men worked for higher wages than they had ever dreamed of, and most American women stayed at home bringing up the big families of the 'baby boom' according to traditional values.

Caryn Pace's parents, like so many others who had lived through the Depression, gave their children what they themselves had missed. 'My mom was a housewife and mother, so she stayed

GOOD TASTE AND GOOD LOOKS *were sold alongside the products in advertisements. Women were used to help sell the goods as well as being targeted to buy them. Many women were intimidated by the new demands of advertising, and the role it imposed on them as keepers of the brightest, best and cleanest homes; they felt that their identity and independence were being undermined. As the American housewife Jackie Sunderland puts it, 'I was the extension of my husband. I was not me.'*

BARGAIN HUNTERS *examine the selection of toasters, irons, food mixers and hair dryers on display at a New York department store sale in 1951. These new domestic appliances met a growing demand for labour-saving devices in the home, and began to reflect people's increasing awareness of style, design and new materials.*

COLOURFUL NEW CARS (OPPOSITE) *sold by General Motors offered their owners easier driving with automatic gear changing. It was important to the American economy for consumers to be able to drive easily and in comfort to the large new shopping malls.*

VEHICLE OF FREEDOM *for Bill Braga (LEFT), a lifelong car enthusiast. His 1958 Oldsmobile opened up new opportunities for himself and his friends: 'You could do what you wanted to do because you had your car, you could get the jobs that paid more money because you could get in the car and go to it. You could build yourself your own world.'*

GAS WARS (BELOW) *between rival stations reduced fuel prices further and further. As more people owned cars, generating new businesses, more gas stations appeared. But despite the cheap fuel, Bill Braga could not always afford to pay for it. Instead, he would sit and listen to his car radio. 'You could be ten minutes away,' as he explains, 'but you still had your own space, that car became your private space.'*

home; my father was a roofer, a blue-collar worker. I was his pride and joy, Daddy's little girl, and he couldn't do enough for me, and neither could my mother. Christmases were really great. I had five or six dolls, maybe four stuffed animals, three games, and a set of drums. One Christmas my cousins came over; they were three boys, and they were harder on things than I was, so all my new toys got broken. The next morning my parents went out and bought me all new toys for Christmas. My parents spent their money on giving me what they had never had.'

Not everyone was as content with their lot as Caryn Pace and her family. It was a time when rebellions of all kinds were beginning to simmer in American life that would boil over in the 1960s: against the authority of the middle-aged over the young, the dominance of men over women, the tyranny of whites over blacks. Like many housewives in the 1950s, Jackie Sunderland felt both happy and dissatisfied. As she recalls, 'I loved my husband, loved my children, I loved a lot about my life, but it was sort of empty. I was doing somebody else's work, and I wasn't doing what I wanted to do. I was a corporation wife. It was "shop until you drop", and this is what we did, with a few committee meetings and a few charity things on the side. We outfitted, we decorated, you know, we just bought.'

Nevertheless, many people found life in the 1950s exciting. Bill Braga was one of them. 'I worked after school in a gas station. I saw the cars come in and out, and picked the one I wanted – I looked for the shiniest, the biggest, the brightest car I could find. I bought myself a 1958 Oldsmobile. We used to ride down the highway with our flashy cars and a loud radio. The girls would turn and look, the car was bright and flashy, you had a date. The fifties were a great decade. Television was brand new. It was the first time that kids, the seventeen- and eighteen-year-olds, had their own music...it was theirs. It wasn't from your parents, it was your own.'

Bill Braga's wife, Georgette, remembers that girls did not have cars of their own, but still noticed the kind of cars the boys drove. 'I mean, who wanted to go to a drive-in movie in some guy's father's station wagon? So you did look for the guy with the flashiest car.'

GENERAL MOTORS
HYDRA-MATIC DRIVE

400,000 Oldsmobile owners, who drive the Hydra-Matic way, are blazing the trai
tomorrow's motorists will follow. They go without shifting—without pushing a clutch
as Hydra-Matic Drive shifts the gears and does the footwork for them. During the pa
8 years, these 400,000 Oldsmobile owners have *proved* the day-after-day dependabili
of GM Hydra-Matic Drive. And today, as Oldsmobile leads the way into a new Golde
Era of progress and advancement, Hydra-Matic Drive is still *first* . . . *automatically*

UTURAMIC OLDSMOBILE

'*You've never had it so good*'

In Europe ten years after the war all the investment and effort, both through American aid and the Europeans' own planning, was beginning to pay off. In West Germany the miracle was delivered by armies of businessmen starting up in improvised offices and workshops, while in France an almost equally dramatic economic boom was credited to the planners and technocrats. By the middle 1950s the battered French railway system had become the most efficient in Europe; the motor manufacturers Renault had been rebuilt, and at Sud-Aviation in Toulouse the Caravelle was being constructed, the first of a new generation of French airliners. In 1948 production in France had been at the 1936 level; by 1955 it was half as high again, and from 1955 to 1958 French productivity grew by 8 per cent a year.

In Italy the economic miracle came a little later and was even more dramatic; it was generated through both public and private enterprise. State enterprises such as AGIP in oil and IRI (a company with holdings in steel, shipbuilding, shipping, radio and television, telephones and banks, and the national airline Alitalia)

Badge of ownership

THE STRIKING SIMPLICITY *of the Volkswagen badge made it easy to recognize. Fixed to the bonnet of every Beetle, the VW logo became a familiar symbol of simple design and distinctive appeal among enthusiastic drivers of 'the People's Car'.*

A COMMUNITY OF EUROPEANS

THE DAY THAT SIX EUROPEAN NATIONS pledged themselves to build an ever closer union was a significant moment in European history. In Rome on 25 March 1957 Belgium, France, Germany, Italy, Luxembourg and the Netherlands set the seal on thirteen years of intensive efforts to create economic ties between the European states so strong that they and their peoples would never again try to destroy each other through war.

The postwar European movement had begun in the wartime Resistance against Hitler. In 1944 fifteen delegates from Resistance groups in nine countries, including German and Italian representatives, had risked great danger to meet in Geneva. There they passed a resolution declaring that 'Resistance to Nazi oppression...has forged between [the peoples of Europe] a community of aims....Federal union alone can ensure the preservation of liberty and civilization on the continent of Europe, bring about economic recovery, and enable the German people to play a peaceful role in European affairs.'

After three-quarters of a century of enmity, the French and the Germans came to recognize that it was in their mutual interests to find ways to end the era of hostility and try to build a future they could share. Their aims were supported by circumstances. For Western Europe to withstand the threat of communism, both from the Soviet Union and from the communist parties in their own countries, it was essential to repair the devastated European economies as quickly as possible; working together to achieve this was seen to be more effective than working alone. American insistence on economic cooperation among recipient countries under the terms of the Marshall Plan reinforced this view, and led to the establishment of the Organization for European Economic Cooperation. The OEEC, with its membership of eighteen European states, oversaw the fair distribution of Marshall Aid funds.

This was just the first stage in a long process leading towards European unity and eventually European union. The French continued to lead the way, establishing the European Coal and Steel Community with West Germany, and inviting other nations to join it. Those countries that chose to accept the invitation – Belgium, Italy, Luxembourg and the Netherlands – became the founder members of the European Economic Community (the Common Market) in 1957.

The founders of European union came from many nations, with different backgrounds and traditions of belief. What they had in common was their conviction that nationalism had led to devastating wars and the catastrophe of Hitler, and that the future of Europe must lie in greater unity. In later years, the European Community would grow both in the number of member countries and in its economic and political power. Some would say it also became cumbersome and bureaucratic. But it began as the dream of young idealists determined to create a new, strong Europe out of the ruins of the Second World War.

READY FOR THE ROAD (BELOW) *Volkswagens at the West German factory, where industrial success was met by a growing demand from customers worldwide. Half of the 330 000 Volkswagens produced here in 1955 were exported.*

A GUIDE AT THE 1958 WORLD FAIR *in Brussels standing in front of the Atomium. Its molecular structure symbolized the newly linked nations of Europe.*

GETTING AWAY FROM IT ALL

FOR CENTURIES you could tell the rich by their white skin, evidence that they had no need to work. In the last years of the nineteenth century this began to change, as Russian aristocrats and rich English people discovered the winter sunshine on the French and Italian Rivieras. During the course of the century, sunshine was to become one of the goods that was marketed and sold to ever larger numbers of people.

When paid holidays first became law for French and British workers, they took their families to nearby seaside resorts. After the Second World War holidays in the sun were something many Western Europeans came to take for granted. In 1950 a million French citizens took camping holidays; by the early 1970s more than five million did so each year.

New travel companies were established to cater for new holidaymakers' needs. Kuoni was founded by Alfred Kuoni in Zurich in 1906, and after 1948 opened offices in Milan, Paris, Rome and Tokyo; eventually it had offices in all five continents. As early as 1951 Kuoni pioneered charter flights to Africa, and to the Mediterranean in 1959. In 1970 the first charter holiday flights to the Far East were introduced.

Another pioneer was Elif Kroager, pastor in the small Danish town of Tjaereborg. He could not afford to take his wife on holiday, so he offered to arrange a trip for a group of local people. In 1950 he took seventy people from the local school to Spain. The business quickly expanded, with package holidays by coach travelling throughout Europe. In 1959 Tjaereborg introduced air travel for its holidaymakers; in 1964 30 000 people applied for a holiday for which only 1000 places were available. By 1973 Tjaereborg had become the largest tour operator in Europe.

Club Mediterranée offered a different kind of holiday: an experience of 'simple village life' for people who lived in cities. Club Med was founded in 1951. Its camps were built on deserted stretches of the Mediterranean coast, in Morocco, Tunisia, Turkey and Yugoslavia. Visitors checked in their wallets when they arrived, and used poppet-beads to buy what they needed. They lived in grass huts near the beach, and newspapers and radios were banned. The recreation of a primitive utopia attracted more and more city dwellers, who were soon in danger of killing the very thing they sought. High-rise hotels replaced straw huts, and crowds polluted unspoilt beaches.

In May 1950 Horizon holidays pioneered the package tour in Britain. When the standard return air fare to Nice was £70, Horizon took groups to Corsica in chartered war-surplus aircraft for two weeks' camping at half that price. Escaping from the regulated atmosphere of package holidays, young people in the 1960s took the 'hippie trail' through Afghanistan to India and Australia; many young Australians and New Zealanders took the same route in reverse on their way to Europe.

Tourism spread Western money, Western fashion and ideas of personal freedom to countries as diverse as Indonesia, Thailand, Turkey and The Gambia. By 1974 tourists were spending $29 billion a year, 6 per cent of the total value of international trade. Generating income in convertible currencies, the world's fastest-growing industry had become a lifeline for the economies of many of the world's poorer countries.

A HOLIDAY IN THE SUN *was once the exclusive privilege of the rich. As tour companies organized more package holidays abroad at reasonable prices, they became increasingly popular.*

modernized rapidly. Family businesses such as Olivetti and Pirelli, and manufacturers of washing machines, motor scooters, clothes and shoes, and above all the giant Fiat car and engineering group, brought modern production techniques to the manufacture of stylish, imaginative new products. Italian industrial production grew at over 9 per cent a year between 1950 and 1958.

Throughout Western Europe the producers of all these new products were also becoming the consumers of what they helped to make. For working people this was a heady experience. The Jordan family, in the English Midlands, could speak on behalf of millions of industrial workers. George Jordan had experienced unemployment before the war. He moved from the Newcastle coalfield to work in a car factory in Coventry. 'It was unbelievable. You could go out, have seven or eight pints, go for a meal, and still have a few shillings left in your pocket. We used to go to the theatre, too. Whatever you wanted to do, you did. You wanted to go out of town, you went out of town.'

The car makers were some of the best paid workers of all. There were five big car factories in Coventry at that time. As George Jordan's son Ray points out, 'If your job didn't suit you, you could move to any one you wanted. I've known people who weren't happy, they'd move to another factory. The work was around. There was money to be had and to be spent. That's what I think money is for: earn a pound, spend a pound.' Easy credit made it possible to spend more even than you earned. And there were new ways to spend it, too – on foreign holidays, for example. 'The first time I went to Spain, when I was eighteen,' says Ray Jordan, 'I think I took £50 with me. I couldn't spend it all.'

Industrial workers in Germany, in the Netherlands and in Scandinavia were also earning incomes that would once have seemed unbelievable. It was the same in France. 'It was a bit like falling in love,' describes Monette Gaunt, who worked as a sales-woman in Paris. 'We called them the thirty glorious years after the war. It was a period of great expansion, of consumption, and there was no unemployment.'

In Italy the first symbol of liberation was not the car but the motor scooter, made by Vespa or Lambretta. Evio Barretti worked in the Vespa factory in the days when scooters were practically made by hand. In 1958 he bought his own. 'It wasn't possible for a working man to buy a car, but with a Vespa you could go to the mountains. I used to go with my wife and pick mushrooms. You could touch heaven with your fingers with your first Vespa.'

All over the north of Italy new factories were going up, and even with the new labour-saving machines they were still hungry for workers. Women as well as men were now needed as workers on the new assembly lines. Edda Furlan went to work in the Zanussi factory. The work was hard. 'They put me in the paint shop. We were spraying, and there was all the dust. We had to

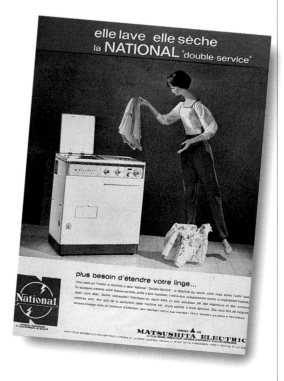

THE 'DOUBLE SERVICE' WASHING MACHINE *produced by the Japanese company National offered French housewives the extra convenience of dry as well as clean clothes. 'Washing machines, televisions with large screens, large refrigerators – all white,' lists Monette Gaunt as she remembers the consumer boom in France. 'It was a fairy tale.'*

FAMILY MOBILITY *in Italy was made possible by the addition of sidecars to the Vespa. In the United States a car cost the equivalent of a hundred days' work for an industrial labourer; in Italy it was equivalent to about a thousand days' work.*

wash from head to foot every day. You just had to put up with it, it was poisonous work, it was very hot, because once we cleaned the machines, they went into the furnaces at 600 degrees. But to have a washing machine is a huge advantage. In the winter I had to go and break the ice in the public wash-house...the washing machine is a great thing.' Edda Furlan regards herself as lucky. 'We found work, while the generations before us – you know how they were. I went into the factory and I worked my eight hours and then came home and did the housework...yes, I was happier.'

In the south there was an even bigger pool of labour eager to go to work in the new factories. Gerardo Ciola grew up in the Basilicata, where the only work was on the land. He did not want to leave. 'It was painful,' he recalls. 'We Italians are very attached to our families. But we had to go. We had to look for work elsewhere.' The first experience of factory work could be daunting. Lillo Montana migrated from Sicily to Turin to work for Fiat in 1969. 'The first day at work was traumatic,' he remembers. 'In our village there were no working rhythms or timetables. This sudden entry into the industrial world was certainly not a pleasant thing. Visually the place seemed to me like one of the circles of hell – there were sparks everywhere, noise, smoke, people running left and right who didn't speak.'

Giovanni Lano was a priest in Turin, and remembers both the sadness and the hope. 'One would see the trains arriving from the south,' he recalls, 'and unloading all these men with their baggage, and above all with their hearts full of expectations and hopes of a better life. Memories of these moments are always a bit sad...that crowd of people who would arrive with nothing and who would find themselves disoriented in a big city. It was the three Ms that made them come north: *mestiere*, a job, in order to get a *moglie*, a wife, and their last dream was a *macchina*, a car. They were not impossible dreams. People just wanted to achieve the standard of living they saw on television.'

GERARDO CIOLA *proudly driving his hard-earned new Fiat. 'I was so excited,' he recalls. 'I had worked and waited such a long time for this car.'*

Gerardo Ciola was one of those men. After a while he could afford a small flat. 'The first thing I wanted in the house was a television, and then the other household goods. Every month there was something else to buy.' Eventually he

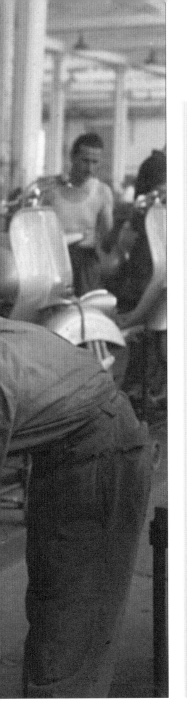

MIGRATING WORKERS

FOREIGN WORKERS flocked into Western Europe during the boom years of the 1950s, attracted by far higher wages than they could have earned at home and the chance to learn new skills. They were prepared to do the boring, dirty or dangerous jobs that the prosperous Europeans were now reluctant to undertake themselves.

There were also 'internal' migrations within Europe. Up to nine million Italians moved from the impoverished region in the south, the Mezzogiorno, to seek their fortunes in the cities of the industrial north. Some twelve million Germans fled from communist East Germany to the West. The expanding West German economy was still not satisfied, and West Germany signed treaties with several countries allowing German companies to set up recruitment offices on their territory. Moroccans, Turks, and Croats from Yugoslavia responded by migrating in their hundreds of thousands. The millionth of these *gastarbeiter*, 'guest workers', was feted as a hero in the press and presented with a motorcycle.

Workers were also recruited in the former British and French colonies. The British National Health Service and London Transport, for example, were particularly active in the West Indies. After the Algerian war in the early 1960s some two million *pieds noirs* (Europeans from Algeria) and another two million Muslims from North Africa settled in France. Foreign workers made up about 7 per cent of the labour force in Britain, France and West Germany; the proportion in Switzerland was 30 per cent.

The newcomers' experience was often disappointing. Immigrants from the West Indies and the divided Indian subcontinent, arriving as full British citizens and expecting to enjoy the superior life they had learned was available to all in Britain, encountered instead cold weather, cold welcomes, discrimination, poor housing and sometimes racial hostility.

Elsewhere, foreign workers received limited rights and short term labour contracts. In West Germany the *gastarbeiter* were denied citizen's rights, could not vote and were often not allowed to bring their families, and in France they were not allowed to marry without permission. Everywhere higher wages were offset by the higher cost of living, so many immigrants felt they were no better off. Yet many of them did prosper. Their contribution not only made the economic expansion of the postwar period possible, it transformed Western Europe into a multiracial society.

ITALIAN WORKERS (ABOVE) *at this Vespa factory worked night shifts producing enough vehicles to satisfy the huge demand. The extra shifts increased the number of jobs available, bringing prosperity to more workers who could then also afford to buy more products for themselves.*

was able to afford something better than a motor scooter. Fiat were making a tiny car, the 500 cc model known as Topolino, Italy's name for Mickey Mouse. Gerardo Ciola and his wife went to buy one. 'When I went to get it from Fiat...I felt so emotional my legs were shaking,' he remembers.

Giovanni Lano also bought his first car in the early 1960s. It meant a great deal to him at the time. As he points out, 'To tell an ordinary person living in Turin in the 1950s that he would have a car eight years later was like telling someone in 1500 that you would take them to the moon.' Yet for millions of people all over Europe the fantasy was coming true. Only twenty years after the war, they were part of the new Western prosperity, and for many of them the car symbolized their new wealth.

The oil crisis

Oil and petrochemicals were vital to the new Western culture. They generated power for industry and provided the basis for the plastics and synthetic textiles of the new consumer products. And they fuelled cars. In the 1920s, when Henry Ford had made the dream of a car in every garage a realistic aspiration, his T-models and A-models drank American oil. By the 1960s, however, not only Western Europe but the United States as well had become increasingly reliant on imports of oil from the Middle East – a dangerous dependence on an unstable region. Support for the Palestinians, driven from their homes after the establishment of the state of Israel in 1947, led to repeated attempts by Arab countries to recover the Palestinians' homeland. The Israelis, backed by money and weapons as well as diplomatic support from the United States and its allies in Europe, were able to defeat these attempts.

By 1970 the Palestinian Liberation Organization was openly at war with Israel and its allies; in 1973 Egypt launched another war against Israel. Again the Israelis won. In their frustration the Arab countries drew on their most formidable resource: oil. Oil supplies from the Middle East were reduced month by month; by December 1973 world production was down by about 9 per cent. An embargo was imposed on all supplies of oil to the United States, the Netherlands (a staunch friend of Israel), and later, in order to please the Arabs' allies in sub-Saharan Africa, to Portugal, Rhodesia and South Africa. As a result the official price of oil, which in 1970 was less than $2 a barrel and by 1973 had risen only to $2.90, in the summer of 1973 reached $11.65; in practice, prices went even higher than that. Western governments, together with the major oil companies, did their best to maintain supplies from other sources, with the result that, over the whole period until the embargo ended in April 1974, oil supplies fell by less than 20 per cent. Even so, fatal damage had been done to the carefree economic climate of the 1950s and 1960s.

Many people in the West had begun to assume that their new prosperity would last for ever. The oil crisis shook their confidence. It precipitated recession, growing unemployment and an unprecedented combination of inflation and stagnation, and heralded the end of the boomtime era.

RUNNING OUT OF GAS
Gas stations in the United States struggled to supply their customers, who were shocked by the sudden shortage of the fuel on which the American way of life depended.

THE OIL WEAPON
(RIGHT) *The desert kingdoms of the Middle East, realizing how dependent on Arab oil supplies their Western customers had become, began to play a powerful new part in international affairs.*

13

Freedom Now

THE STRUGGLE FOR INDEPENDENCE

IN MILLIONS OF INDIAN HOMES families gathered round their radio sets on the evening of 14 August 1947 to listen to their new prime minister, Jawaharlal Nehru, as he formally announced India's independence from British rule. Among them was Birenda Kaur's family. She can still remember the occasion vividly. 'When the speech came on, I don't know if any of us actually heard the words or not, but the atmosphere was so emotionally charged…and when he said, "At midnight, when the world sleeps, India will awake to light and freedom," we forgot about everything else, and we all sat up that night. And then when the dawn came I just cannot describe to you how heady that feeling was. It was as though the world was new…you felt you could do anything, that we were free now colonial rule was at an end.'

In the morning Birenda Kaur was among the thousands of people who went to Delhi's Red Fort to watch the ceremony. 'First the Union Jack came down,' she recalls, 'and then the tricolour of India went up; it is my happiest memory.' There were celebrations all over India. Satpal Sainai, who was a farmer, remembers how that day 'a wave of joy went through the crowd. Everyone was very happy because until then we'd been under the thumb of foreign rule, but now we were free.'

People had high hopes that there would be a brighter future. 'The man in the street thought all would be well for him – there would be schools, hospitals and all the things he ever dreamed of,' Birenda Kaur explains. Satpal Sainai hoped 'that we would become prosperous, that our children would get the jobs in government and that all business would be in our hands.'

When India gained its independence, much of the rest of the world was also still governed by remote states far away in Europe. India's success offered an inspiring example to other subject peoples in the fight for control of their own destinies. It was the start of a process that would continue for the next thirty years. Nobody at the time could have predicted the pace of change. There were in 1945 some seventy independent countries in the world; by 1975 there were a hundred more.

SEEING THE WORLD ANEW *Jubilant citizens take to the streets to celebrate the dawn of independence in India.*

The road to independence

Before the Second World War a fifth of the world's land surface had been under imperial rule. Both the plantations and the diamond mines of the Congo, in the heart of Africa, were controlled from Belgium. The populations of the East Indies, in all their ethnic and religious variety and with their oil, tin, rubber and timber, as well as islands in the Caribbean, were governed by the Netherlands. Portugal ruled Macao on the coast of China, Goa on the coast of India, and three territories in Africa – Angola, Mozambique, and the Cape Verde Islands off the west coast.

The French colonies encompassed Indochina and Syria, islands in the Caribbean and the Pacific, and vast African territories from the green equatorial jungles and the savanna grasslands to the Sahara desert and the rich cities and farmlands of the northwest. The British also ruled territories across the globe, administering the largest empire of all: it stretched from Hong Kong and Malaya to Burma and the Indian subcontinent, through much of Africa, to the West Indies and across the Pacific to Fiji. Power over the lives and welfare of all their peoples was wielded by governments in Paris and London.

Imperial rule had brought certain benefits to India: a railway network, new industries, efficient administration. What it did not do was to relieve the country's heavy burden of poverty, which was worsened by its ever-growing population. Protests against British domination were ruthlessly suppressed. Eventually one man, Mohandas Gandhi, convinced the people of India both that their economic conditions would not improve until they were themselves politically free, and that more would be gained by peaceful non-cooperation and passive resistance than by violent rebellion. Gandhi's inspired leadership offered a vision of a new future. He led Indians in a mass protest against British rule, and during the 1930s millions of people followed the strikes and boycotts he organized. He was himself among the 60 000 Indians who were imprisoned as a result of these activities. Yet the British government did finally yield to their demands first for self-rule and then for complete independence.

INDIA'S MIGHTY ELEPHANT, *deftly guided by the frail but indomitable figure of Mahatma Gandhi, defies the British lion in a German cartoon of 1933.*

WOMEN SPEAK OUT *in 1930 in Bombay. Some of them were seriously injured when the police resorted to using their lathis (long batons) to control the crowd. Gandhi inspired several such campaigns, and urged people to take non-violent action whatever their status in society.*

INDIA'S INSPIRATION

'GANDHI WAS a national institution, an inspiration, by his own example. He was almost deified by the Indian public in the years leading to independence,' says John Lall, an Indian civil servant. 'I met him, and saw him as a very saintly figure. One didn't feel fit to touch the hem of his clothes, as the saying goes. He created that kind of aura, though he was a very human person...and he had a sense of humour. His creed of non-violence is still an inspiration to freedom movements all over the world.'

Indians called Gandhi the Mahatma, the 'great spirit'. This fragile-looking man, whose public image was reflected in the home-spun cloth he wore, became a symbol of moral authority over manifest strength, and fostered a new confidence in India's village origins. Gandhi believed that the country's problems stemmed more from the shortcomings of the Indians themselves than from the power wielded by British guns. His great aims were to free India from British rule; to alleviate the oppression of the 'untouchables', some sixty million people in the lowest class of the Hindu caste system; to improve the status of women and the poor; and to turn India back from the pursuit of modernization to its traditional values and practices. He sought to inspire unity among Indians – rich and poor, high- and low-caste, men and women, Hindu and Muslim.

Early in his career, Gandhi experienced racism and intolerance for himself as a lawyer in South Africa, where he campaigned for Indian rights through the principle of *satyagraha* or 'truth force': non-violent resistance as a method of social and political struggle. For this deeply spiritual man there was no place for violence, conspiracy or guerrilla war. He emphasized the moral qualities of *swaraj*, or self-rule, for individuals as well as for nations, believing that there was a close connection between political freedom and personal discipline, which he himself tested with long fasts and periods of solitude.

Gandhi returned to India in 1915. He quickly became the dominant figure in the Indian National Congress, which he transformed from a middle-class debating society into a mass movement rooted in small towns and villages throughout India. Anti-British activities during the 1920s led to Gandhi's imprisonment. In 1930 he organized his first campaign of civil disobedience against the government's hated salt tax, with the simple act of walking to the sea to make salt from sea water. Thousands of people joined him in what became known as the salt march.

During the Second World War Gandhi supported the 'Quit India' movement, but he shunned political power for himself. He strove to heal religious intolerance, but became a victim of it: he was assassinated by a fellow Hindu in January 1948, at a prayer meeting. Nehru, after announcing his death, broadcast to a stunned and grieving nation: '...the light has gone out of our lives and there is darkness everywhere... and yet...a thousand years later that light will still be seen... for that light represented...the living, the eternal truths.'

Gandhi's vision led India to independence, but not to peace. Freedom from empire did not mean freedom from bigotry and hatred. No satisfactory solution had been found to the fear that the minority Muslim population had at the prospect of being ruled within a majority Hindu state. As independence approached, plans were made to partition the subcontinent between Muslim Pakistan, in the northwest and northeast, and non-sectarian but overwhelmingly Hindu India. Millions of people found themselves on the wrong side of the new borders as old resentments flared up and hatred sought release in persecution. Altogether thirty million people – both Muslims and Hindus – fled from their homes, in what was perhaps the greatest forced migration in history. Some refugees travelled on foot, others went in convoys of bullock carts or crowded into and onto trains, clutching whatever belongings they could. The trains were often attacked, and thousands of migrants suffered from starvation or exposure.

The civil servant John Lall was posted to Delhi at the time of independence. He remembers that the atmosphere was at first 'absolutely delirious', but that 'the euphoria was very, very short-lived. The ugly fact was that killings were taking place in the newly created Pakistan and in India as populations moved back and forth from one country to the other. It was tragic. Whole trains would arrive from Pakistan that were empty. There was no one living left in them, no person alive in the whole train.' Hindus took revenge on Muslims, and when the Muslims fled they were treated with equal ferocity. During the weeks following Partition at least 200 000 people, perhaps as many as 500 000, were killed.

Rupa Gujeral grew up as a Hindu in Peshawar, in the heart of what is now Pakistan. It was a quiet town, with Hindus and Muslims living and working side by side. After Partition this changed. 'We could hear only murders, fires and noise. We were so scared. My family felt it would be safer to go away and come back when there was peace in the town again.' The Gujeral family's Muslim friends and employees escorted them to the station. An official who had been entrusted with some mail was a fellow passenger. Rupa Gujeral's mother was afraid of travelling with a single Muslim. 'But he said, "Don't worry, I am with you, and I have got a revolver," which as a child frightened me. When we reached Amritsar, it was his turn to be afraid. He said to my father, "Now you take care of me!"'

The tragedy of Partition was a very high price to pay for independence. But as Birenda Kaur recalls, 'I know there was the trauma of Partition: we lost a lot of property, other people lost a lot of relatives, lifelong friends became strangers overnight – but yes, it was worth it. You can't keep on being spoon-fed by some-body....Okay, we made mistakes, we will probably make bigger mistakes, but we are a country, not a colony.'

FREEDOM AND BLOODSHED *An Indian police officer receives help after violent clashes between Hindus and Muslims in the streets of Lahore in 1947. This one incident caused fifteen deaths and left 114 people injured. Partition intensified ancient Hindu–Muslim hostilities, and caused rifts between once peaceful mixed communities.*

"We could not sleep when we were in Peshawar because there was always noise. We could hear only murders, fires and noise."

RUPA GUJERAL

Freedom vote

INDIAN BALLOT PAPERS *carried symbols for each candidate, since the overwhelming majority of the population could not read or write. While all the images conveyed national progress of a kind, there was fierce competition among candidates for the most potent symbols. The Indian Congress Party was denoted by the twin bullocks, representing rural progress.*

THOUSANDS OF MUSLIM REFUGEES *seek sanctuary in the Purana Quilla Fort in New Delhi. At the same time Sikhs and Hindus make the journey south from the newly formed Pakistan. Millions of refugees from both sides fled to avoid becoming a beleaguered minority. The greatest forced migration in history was part of the price to be paid in forging the world's largest democracy.*

A BUYER'S MARKET
(ABOVE) *Farmers on the Gold Coast deliver sacks of cocoa beans and collect their payment at a bush station. While farmers like Anim Assiful (*TOP*) resented the British price controls, they had no alternative markets for their crops.*

An example to follow

Gandhi maintained that if India could break free, others would be encouraged to follow its example. The European powers thought quite differently: they planned to hold on to their empires. But the Second World War had brought great changes in the status of the imperial nations, shifting the balance of power across the world. Japanese victories in the Far East had destroyed the prestige and apparent invincibility of the Europeans there, and the countries that emerged the strongest after the war, the United States and the Soviet Union, were both strongly anti-colonial. By 1947, as India went its own way, other Asians in Indonesia and Indochina were also fighting for their freedom. Indonesia gained its independence from the Dutch in 1949, and Vietnam from the French after defeating them at Dien Bien Phu in 1954.

The European powers were most determined to keep their African colonies. European needs often came first: much of the best land was used to grow crops for export rather than food for the local people. In the Portuguese colonies 98 per cent of Africans received no education, and instead of being self-sufficient on their own smallholdings were forced to work as labourers on the cotton plantations for low cash wages. In the Congo, Belgians used harsh discipline – including amputations – on the men who mined diamonds, copper and gold on their behalf.

About a third of the world's supply of cocoa beans was produced in the Gold Coast, in British West Africa where Anim Assiful was a cocoa farmer. 'There were a lot of British companies involved in the cocoa industry at that time,' he remembers. 'They sent their agents out to buy cocoa from the villages. We didn't have our own scales for weighing the cocoa, so we were really cheated by these agents. We had to accept the prices the British gave us. We had no say – our hands were tied.'

It was the Africans who had fought in the British army during the war who now began to loosen the bonds. Geoffrey Aduamah fought against the Italians in East Africa in 1940. On the way there he stopped in Durban in South Africa, where he met troops from all over the British empire. 'The Indians were very

> "*Nkrumah came in his native clothes resplendent in his African attire, and he said, 'Africans should hold their heads up high'.*"

EDDIE FRANCOIS

SONS OF AFRICA, ARISE *The father of African independence, Kwame Nkrumah (centre), is given an enthusiastic reception. He became a socialist and started to dream of a free, united Africa while studying in Pennsylvania and London. As leader of the first modern independence movement in Africa, he inspired Africans throughout the continent to take pride in their identity and demand a role in their country's future.*

political. They said they thought we were coming to help them fight the whites. We said, "We are fighting for white freedom." So they asked us, "Are you yourselves free?" We said no. "Well, fight for your own freedom first." This made a very big impression on the Gold Coast soldiers, and on me especially....I am fighting against somebody I don't know, and the person who is using me to fight is the same person who is oppressing me.'

When veterans returned home the struggle for freedom in the Gold Coast accelerated. Dismissed back to civilian life without pensions, they felt betrayed. 'We came back and saw that they were not doing anything to help us to get re-established in life.' Like many others, Geoffrey Aduamah joined an ex-servicemen's union, and took part in the early protests against the British. These were turned into a mass movement by Kwame Nkrumah, who had returned after twelve years in the United States and Britain, where he met other Africans against colonial rule. A charismatic campaigner, he urged Africans to take direct action themselves, and founded a new political organization, the Convention People's Party (CPP). He also organized a general strike and a boycott of British goods. The British regarded Nkrumah as a dangerous fire-brand, probably under communist influence, and imprisoned him. But far from quelling the campaign for self-government as they hoped, this gave it new impetus.

Geoffrey Aduamah joined the CPP as 'it was the only dynamic organization at that time. Those who brought Nkrumah from Britain, they were all lawyers, doctors and high-placed people; they didn't feel for the ordinary man like me,' he remembers. 'One of them even called us "verandah boys", and they didn't respect us at all. But Nkrumah said, "I am also a verandah boy. I will sleep on the verandah with you".... So we realized this man could do better for us. Nkrumah wanted self-government *now*. Self-government in the shortest time, we don't understand that; but we do understand "Now".'

VOTING FOR ALL *Africans vote for the first black African parliament in elections on the Gold Coast. Men and women trekked long distances to exercise their new right. The election was part of a gradual process, first of self-government under the British and eventually complete independence.*

While Nkrumah was in prison the party was successfully run by his friend Komla Gbedema. The British agreed to a general election in 1951, hoping that the CPP would lose. The result was a landslide victory for Nkrumah's party, and he was subsequently released. Komla Gbedema was there to meet him. 'Apart from my own personal feelings of joy, I didn't see very much because I was driving him, but the crowds were tremendous. A large area in front of James Fort prison was filled with people. It was a slow march, orderly singing and dancing and shouting, all the way to the arena where we held our meetings.'

The feeling in the party was that 'we prefer self-government in danger to servitude in tranquillity. We had to do things the way we wanted without showing that we didn't know what we were doing. By and large I think we did well enough, because in three years the Colonial Office of the British government said, "If you give evidence of your ability to manage the economy and control your finances, we will hand over power to you".'

A THIRD WORLD VOICE

TWENTY-NINE COUNTRIES were represented at the international conference held in Bandung, on the Indonesian island of Java, in April 1955. What was extraordinary about this event was that there were no Western European, American or Soviet representatives – the world's most powerful states were excluded. For the first time in modern history, recently independent states proved that they were now a force to be reckoned with. No longer could they be treated as pawns in an international game played by the great powers.

The conference host was the president of Indonesia, Achmed Sukarno, who told the delegates that their nations had 'arisen from a sleep of centuries', and promised that their

peoples 'would be able to mobilize the moral violence of nations in favour of peace'. The leaders of many Asian countries and several of the newly emerging African states had gathered to discuss issues of interest to them all such as racialism, colonialism and national sovereignty; the economic and social problems they faced; how they could contribute to world peace; and how to make the voice of their people – the majority of the world's population – heard in a world increasingly divided into the capitalist Western and communist Soviet camps.

The conference was held at a time when world peace was threatened by the hostility of the Cold War, and American and Soviet spheres of influence extended across much of the

globe. The gathering at Bandung was partly an expression of protest against the powerful states' failure to consider the points of view of the Afro-Asian nations in affairs that affected their part of the world. They were particularly concerned with the tension between the new communist regime in China and the United States. One of the achievements of the conference was that fear of Chinese communism among its neighbours, particularly Burma and India, was reduced.

The Bandung Conference both demonstrated and reinforced the new self-confidence of the emerging nations, and showed that when they stood together, they were now able to play a part on the world stage that could no longer be ignored.

Independence or assimilation?

The changes taking place in the Gold Coast were watched closely both by the rest of Africa and by the other European powers, who had no intention of following the British example of granting concessions. The colonial policy of France had in some ways been different from that of Britain. While the French and the British attempted to create an educated African elite, British efforts also focused on giving a minimum of education to a wider group. French policy after 1945 aimed at incorporating the empire into a 'greater France', and instead of independence the French offered 'integration': Algeria was legally part of France itself. In Senegal those born in the four principal towns were also granted French citizenship, which included the right to elect representatives to the parliament in Paris. Those who were intended to be leaders of French-speaking Africa were educated at the William Ponti Lycée in the capital, Dakar.

The special and privileged status of 'assimilation' did not necessarily satisfy those who qualified for it. One of them was Majhemout Diop. 'Being an *assimilé*: it meant everything and nothing,' he reflects. 'Everything, because your whole social status depended on it, and nothing because for all that, you never really felt like a Frenchman. The fact that I was born in St Louis, one of the special communes in Senegal, was what made me a citizen – I didn't choose to be one. The French wanted to transpose their culture: they introduced the French language and provided a good education for some people. But it was natural that as human beings we should want our independence and our freedom. We felt sure there was something unjust about our colonization which we had to overcome.'

Amadou Baro Diene, one of a group of radicals in Senegal, thought the leaders were too compliant. 'They were for independence, but more slowly and in a united Africa, whereas we were young and hot-headed, and we wanted independence at any cost and whatever the consequences.'

*"**F**rom the cultural point of view, we were raised up to a higher level of development. But there were other sides to it, the sides of domination, of a foreign power in a foreign land.*"

MAJHEMOUT DIOP

SHOULDERING THE BURDEN *The united efforts of French and African troops in the First World War are commemorated in a memorial erected in St Louis, Senegal, the first French settlement in West Africa. Thousands of Africans fought side by side with their colonial rulers, but their shared experience did little to encourage a lasting sense of unity.*

Fighting for the land

Some African colonies had attracted almost no settlers; the only Europeans were government officials and businessmen. In others where the climate was more favourable, there were plenty of new opportunities for settlers such as the tobacco farmers of southern Rhodesia, the train drivers and mining supervisors in the copper belt of northern Rhodesia, and those who lived in the highlands north of Nairobi in Kenya. Here in East Africa self-government seemed an even more remote prospect in the early 1950s.

A young Englishman, Peter Marian, had joined the British colonial service in 1939 after leaving university. 'I wanted to be an administrator,' he explains. 'There was a sense of dedication that you wanted to do something with your life, and there was also a sense of adventure. Colonialism was far from being a dirty word at that time, and you just felt that you might be doing some good for a country and for other people.' After the war he returned to Kenya and bought a farm, where he grew coffee and raised cattle.

Peter Marian loved the land he farmed. So did the Africans who had lived and worked on the land – 1.6 million hectares (4 million acres) of it – taken by the European settlers, who used them as servants and labourers, and denied them even limited political rights. There were 30 000 white settlers in Kenya; they were determined that they should be recognized as paramount, both then and, in the future, in a new East African Federation. But 75 000 Kenyan Africans had fought for Britain in the Second World War, and while British ex-soldiers like Peter Marian were encouraged to take up farming, the returning African soldiers were confronted by the restrictions of the colour bar, pass laws, unemployment, poor housing, and taxes that could be paid only by working on the plantations. Once again it was young men back from the war who were determined things should change.

The heart of Kenyan resistance lay with the Kikuyu people, with their traditional attachment to the land. One of them, Jomo Kenyatta, took up their cause, first in London and then, after his return in 1946, as leader of what became a popular nationalist movement in Kenya itself. Achhroo Kapila, a Kenyan lawyer who trained in Britain and knew Kenyatta personally, remembers that 'He had a tremendous following...he made an instant impression

A COLONIAL FAMILY (ABOVE) *in Kenya take afternoon tea with their pet leopard. Many settlers in Africa led a life they never could have expected, or afforded, to lead if they had stayed in Europe.*

A SEA OF SUPPORT (OPPOSITE) *for Jomo Kenyatta, who took up the cause of the Kikuyu people, and then of all Kenya's Africans.*

ASSEMBLY AT GUNPOINT
(OPPOSITE) *Mau Mau
suspects wait to be taken to
detention camps. British
troops and civilian volunteer
police raided Kikuyu villages
and forest hide-outs for
suspected supporters of the
'land and freedom army'.
Women and children were
taken to reception camps to
await the result of the
investigations, which could
take as long as a month.*

as a leader.' Achhroo Kapila also remembers the restrictions the colour bar imposed. 'We were not allowed to stay in a hotel or even go to a restaurant to eat a meal.' When the settlers pressurized the British to put down African demands for independence, the Africans' response was to form a secret organization calling itself a 'land and freedom army' – better known as Mau Mau. It attracted many thousands of supporters.

Waihwa Theuri decided he would join the Mau Mau. 'It was because of hardships. The major problem was the fact that our land had been taken by white people. Before, we used to graze our goats in the settlers' farms and in the forest, but we were then informed that each family would be allowed to graze only fifteen goats. Then there was the question of education. The schools we used to go to started to be closed, and this is when people felt they had had enough of the persecution. We came together and took an oath that an African was your brother, but when you see a white man you should know that he is your enemy.'

The British used the police and army to round up suspects from Kikuyu villages. Like many others, Waihwa Theuri went into hiding in the forests. 'We were pursued, and we had no food, we had nothing. We could not go back to the emergency villages because we would be shot. To survive everybody had to work for himself...and there was nowhere else to run to. That's when we started to fight, attacking settler farms and stealing their cattle. We prayed to God for help because we didn't have the arms that the settlers had...we only had guns later, stealing them from the settlers.' The British dropped 50 000 tonnes of bombs to destroy the forest hide-outs. Waihwa Theuri was arrested, interrogated and tortured for being a member of the Mau Mau.

A LOADED RIFLE
*accompanies the bedtime
ritual for a white family in
Nairobi* (BELOW). *Night-
time raids by Mau Mau were
an ever-present and alarming
danger for settlers in Kenya,
especially those living in
isolated farmhouses.*

As the Mau Mau movement grew, fear became part of life for the settlers. Sylvia Richardson, who lived on a remote farm, remembers how she and her husband used to keep their guns with them all the time, and how their neighbours survived an attack. 'There was a bang on their door one night and this gang came rushing in. Kitty and Dot shot at these people and killed two of them....They shot a number of bullets, and one killed their dog.'

Jomo Kenyatta was among the many Africans opposed to the violence, but he was arrested and imprisoned for encouraging the rebellion. Altogether more than 11 000 Mau Mau rebels were killed and 80 000 suspects detained. Some 2000 loyalist Africans were killed by the Mau Mau. The terror they generated for white settlers, however, was not reflected in the death toll: just thirty-two whites were killed between 1952 and 1956.

The rebellion had a contradictory effect on Kenya's history. The violence alienated many Africans, including the Kikuyu, but by bringing in British soldiers to crush the Mau Mau the British

BRINKMANSHIP OVER SUEZ

When President Gamal Nasser announced the nationalization of the Suez Canal in July 1956, the Egyptian people greeted the news with delight. In both the Middle East and Africa his bold challenge to the Western powers was admired, while in the West there was anger and dismay.

The canal was one of the world's busiest shipping lanes. In providing a waterway across Egypt to link the Mediterranean and the Red Sea, it had shortened the distance between Mediterranean ports and Asia by as much as half. Intended both to serve and to profit from growing international trade, the canal had been opened in 1869 to all ships of all nations. At that time shares in the Suez Canal Company were held by Egypt and France; by 1875 the Egyptian shares had been sold to Britain.

Nasser's immediate reason for nationalizing the canal was to obtain for Egypt the revenue from tolls paid by ships using it. This would provide the huge sum of money needed to finance an ambitious national project to build a dam on the river Nile near the ancient town of Aswan. The dam would control the annual floodwaters, improve irrigation to boost agriculture, and provide hydroelectric power to support Egypt's industrialization.

The dam was originally to have been financed by the United States and Britain. But there were political strings attached to the promise of a loan, and as a result of improved relations between Egypt and the Soviet Union at the height of the Cold War, the West's offer was withdrawn. Nationalization of the canal would enable Egypt to go ahead on its own.

Britain and France were concerned that the canal would be closed altogether, cutting off Western Europe from access to vital oil supplies in the Middle East; they also feared Nasser's considerable following in the Arab world. To reinforce their own position, they secretly invited Israel (which had its own reasons to fear Nasser) to invade Egypt. Israel took action when its ships were prohibited from using the canal; a joint British and French invasion to 'protect' the canal against damage followed. However, the combination of Soviet threats, United Nations condemnation and United States disapproval forced the invaders to withdraw. Nasser had turned the tables on the European powers. Instead of being humiliated by them, he had inflicted humiliation on them.

Egypt's triumph for a time brought Nasser enormous prestige throughout the Middle East and in Africa. Nasser's bold initiative proved that new countries could outwit old masters on the international stage. It also showed that while the Soviet Union and the United States were world powers to be reckoned with, the European states were no longer to be feared. This realization boosted the determination of Africans fighting for an end to colonial rule.

THE SMOKING EMBERS *of Port Said, the Egyptian town badly damaged within a few hours by an Anglo-French bombing raid in November 1956.*

government had discovered how costly it could be to control the colonies, and its attitude was changing fast. Politicians of both parties became increasingly unsure that Britain could afford to maintain colonial rule, or that doing so could be justified.

There were European-born communities in French as well as British colonies. The largest community of white settlers – Italian and Spanish in origin as well as French – lived in Algeria, an overseas *département* administered as an integral part of France. In 1954 they too came under attack. Muslim Arab rebels took up the struggle against foreign control when a 1947 statute that would have allowed them a greater part in the political and social life of their country was not put into effect. Supported by the French army, the settlers resisted, and a terrible eight-year war followed. The military were given responsibility to deal with those who were involved in the rebellion, but extended their authority over the whole Muslim population. Their aggressive tactics against the villages and against their inhabitants increased support for the National Liberation Front (FLN).

As harassment and humiliation were stepped up, the rebels also became more violent, using guerrilla tactics that the army could not defeat. More than a million people died in the struggle, and millions more – both Arabs and Europeans – were driven into exile or suffered in the many other ways of civil war. It brought down the French government, and brought General de Gaulle to power. He was to preside over the dismantling of French colonialism, both in Algeria and in equatorial and West Africa.

SHOTGUN WAR *In Algeria women as well as men were recruited to fight for independence from France* (ABOVE). *This bitter colonial struggle, France's most costly conflict, lasted eight years and was a demonstration that the plan for 'integration' was unworkable. Soldiers of the French Foreign Legion often meted out harsh treatment to FLN rebels* (BELOW) *and supporters.*

The wind of change

The changes that were being so keenly resisted elsewhere were being put into practice in West Africa. The Gold Coast gained its full independence as Ghana in 1957, and Nkrumah was elected president. Komla Gbedema was there. 'We mounted a platform and we were all ready when the light went on at five minutes to twelve. Everybody was happy, cheering, there was total hysteria.' Nkrumah, moved to tears, declared: 'At long last the struggle has ended. At last Ghana, your beloved country, is free forever. From now on there is a new African in the world.'

Beatrice Quatey, who sold vegetables in the Accra market and was one of the traders who helped to maintain the Ghanaian economy, was thrilled that independence had been achieved. 'We were very happy...to elect a leader of our choice. When we heard that Nkrumah had won there was general merrymaking. We went on procession through the streets of Accra singing and dancing.'

WHIRLWIND CHANGES
The rush for independence in the 1960s in Africa was as rapid as the European scramble for territory had been in the 1880s, when frontiers were drawn up in Brussels, London and Paris. The colonial era left an indelible mark both on Africa's map and on its people. But as freedom arrived, expertise left and old tensions resurfaced; civil war and military takeovers followed in equally rapid succession.

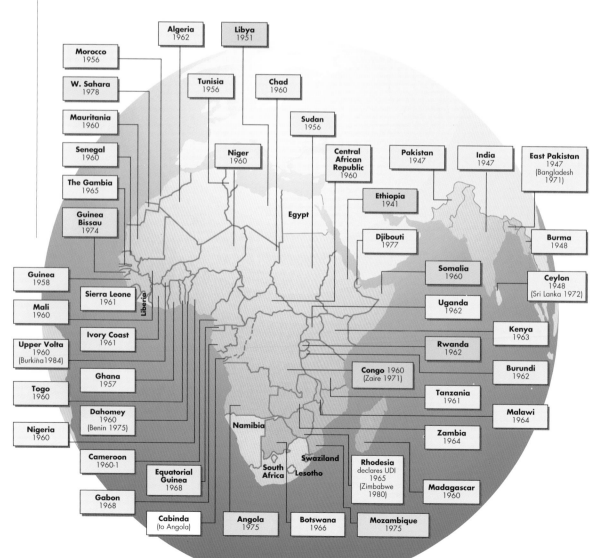

Algeria 1962
Libya 1951
Morocco 1956
W. Sahara 1978
Tunisia 1956
Chad 1960
Mauritania 1960
Sudan 1956
Senegal 1960
Niger 1960
Central African Republic 1960
Pakistan 1947
India 1947
East Pakistan 1947 (Bangladesh 1971)
The Gambia 1965
Egypt
Ethiopia 1941
Guinea Bissau 1974
Djibouti 1977
Burma 1948
Guinea 1958
Somalia 1960
Ceylon 1948 (Sri Lanka 1972)
Sierra Leone 1961
Liberia
Uganda 1962
Mali 1960
Kenya 1963
Ivory Coast 1961
Rwanda 1962
Upper Volta 1960 (Burkina 1984)
Congo 1960 (Zaire 1971)
Burundi 1962
Ghana 1957
Tanzania 1961
Togo 1960
Malawi 1964
Dahomey 1960 (Benin 1975)
Namibia
Zambia 1964
Nigeria 1960
Cameroon 1960-1
South Africa
Swaziland
Lesotho
Rhodesia declares UDI 1965 (Zimbabwe 1980)
Equatorial Guinea 1968
Madagascar 1960
Gabon 1968
Cabinda (to Angola)
Angola 1975
Botswana 1966
Mozambique 1975

Colonial territories and their dates of independence

- Belgian
- British
- French
- Italian
- Portuguese
- Spanish

TROUBLES IN INDONESIA

THE EXPERIENCE OF INDIANS AND AFRICANS struggling for independence was matched in other parts of the world. In Indonesia, which had been ruled by the Netherlands since the seventeenth century, independence also failed to free the country from its reliance on foreign powers, and presented new problems.

During their occupation of the Dutch East Indies in the Second World War, the Japanese had hastened the process of decolonization by undermining Dutch prestige there and by releasing Indonesian nationalists from prison. Among them was Achmed Sukarno, who in 1946 became president of a new, self-proclaimed independent state. The Dutch fought back until 1949, when they agreed to a negotiated withdrawal and Indonesia became truly independent.

Indonesia is a vast archipelago consisting of over 13 000 islands, and its people belong to many different ethnic, religious and language groups. The conflicts that emerged between them were heightened by a crisis-ridden economy. Despite the wealth in the country's valuable rubber plantations, tin mines and oil reserves, there was chronic inflation and poverty. After independence, millions of Indonesians joined political parties and organizations hoping to effect change.

The huge support for the communists disturbed the powerful military elite, which believed that the foreign investment needed to rebuild the economy would be denied to a communist country. By 1965 Sukarno was discredited, and the army took control under General Suharto. In an attempt to wipe out all communist activity, he instigated a programme of mass murder, terror and imprisonment. More than 500 000 people were killed, and thousands more were imprisoned. Indonesia's links with China and the Soviet Union were broken in favour of Japan and the United States.

Indonesia had behaved aggressively towards its neighbours under Sukarno, and now the violence spread. Irian Jaya, formerly also part of the Dutch empire, was annexed in 1969. In 1975, a week after East Timor had gained its independence after five hundred years of Portuguese rule, Indonesia invaded and unleashed a reign of terror upon the people of the island: more than 100 000 men, women and children were brutally massacred, and a further 300 000 imprisoned.

PUBLIC RELATIONS *A smiling President Sukarno poses with troops' families in 1958 after suppressing an uprising in Sumatra. His rule was marked by corruption and conflict, and he eventually alienated even his former allies, the army.*

'RAISE YOUR HATS *for the national anthem!' Komla Gbedema (*ABOVE, *second from left* AND LEFT*), at Nkrumah's side from the start, became Ghana's first minister of finance. He shares the pride and the glory as the newly elected president takes the podium on independence night. Fireworks and dancing followed in the old polo ground, where the song of the night was 'Freedom Highlife'.*

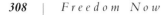

CALL FOR FREEDOM *Followers of nationalist parties wait with banners and flags for de Gaulle in Dakar, Senegal, during his 1958 tour of French equatorial Africa. Some demonstrators ran along behind the president's car, waving their placards and shouting 'Independence now! Independence now!'*

Stamp of statehood

SYMBOLS OF NEW IDENTITY *were an important element in the changed status of nations at independence. In Ghana a commemorative stamp was issued to celebrate Independence Day, 6 March 1957. On that day, in a ceremony that was to be repeated all over the continent, the colonial flag was lowered and the new national flag – red, gold and green – hoisted in its place.*

This was just the beginning. Most European governments had recognized that independence could not be stopped, and had realized that they must compromise. In 1958 President de Gaulle toured France's African territories. His driver in Senegal's capital, Dakar, was Babacar Ndiaye. 'We drove in a convertible with de Gaulle standing up all the way, taking the airport road via the Corniche, which was crowded with people shouting "Vive de Gaulle!" But by the time we got to the Medina things had changed. People threw leaflets into the president's car, clamouring for independence. De Gaulle wasn't very pleased.'

Amadou Baro Diene, inspired by the activities of leaders fighting for independence elsewhere in Africa, was in charge of the placards for the demonstration. On the day of de Gaulle's visit, he remembers that 'Things were very tense. But we'd taken the precaution of hiding our placards. The moment de Gaulle arrived, we came forward.' De Gaulle's impassioned speech pleading for unity in the city square had little effect, and independence soon followed. By 1960 all twelve African members of the French Community had become independent republics.

In February 1960 Britain's prime minister Harold Macmillan also toured Africa. He told the South African parliament that 'the wind of change is blowing through this continent, and whether we like it or not this growth of national consciousness is a political fact.' Only eight months later Nigeria, the most populous state in Africa, was independent. In August 1961 Jomo Kenyatta was freed; within two years he had won a sweeping victory in a general election and was well on his way to power as president of an independent Kenya. Within less than three years, a total of twenty-five countries celebrated their independence.

The jubilation as new countries emerged was moderated by an awareness of the difficulties still to be faced. There were few administrators trained to run the new nations, and unity was hard to achieve with borders drawn up to suit Europeans rather than the distribution of different peoples and languages. For some countries the colonial legacy proved to be a bitter one.

Each of the main European powers had dealt with colonial power in Africa in a different way. The Belgians and Portuguese were the most reluctant to yield it, and bitterly resisted to the end;

the Portuguese held out in Angola and Mozambique until 1975.

The Belgians had kept the Congo as isolated as possible from the wind of change. While its mineral wealth, particularly in the province of Katanga, was vigorously exploited, most of the country was left virtually untouched by Belgian rule, and it was ill prepared to rule itself. In this huge territory of fourteen million people there were in 1959 only 137 Africans with a secondary school education, and just sixteen university graduates – only three among 1400 civil servants. Faced with violence, the Belgians got out as quickly as they could. With independence in 1960 came chaos, mutiny in the army, civil war, massacres and the secession of Katanga. Order was restored by a United Nations peacekeeping force, with the United States convinced that the troubles were the result of a Russian plot. Patrice Lumumba, the Congo's first prime minister, was dismissed, then arrested and murdered by the army. In 1965, the year after the United Nations left, Joseph Désiré Mobutu, with United States support, seized the presidency. His highly nationalist policies included the requirement that citizens take African names, and his one-party state was renamed Zaire.

WAR-WEARY REFUGEES (ABOVE) *in the Belgian Congo leave for home in the villages of Kasai province after staying in a refugee camp. The civil war following independence led to displacement, disruption and losses for many people.*

BATTLE FOR POWER (BELOW) *Soldiers of Colonel Mobutu's forces with Patrice Lumumba, former president of the Congo, shortly after his arrest. He was made to eat his words when the paper claiming his right to rule was forced down his throat.*

DIVIDED PEOPLES

THE STRUGGLE BETWEEN PEOPLES in countries seeking independence did not take place simply between the rulers and the ruled. Some of the societies over which Europeans imposed imperial domination had already been deeply divided before the Europeans arrived. In the Indian subcontinent, for example, a Muslim Mughal empire had ruled over a population still overwhelmingly Hindu. At independence India's Muslims insisted on creating their own state, Pakistan, because they did not trust the Hindu majority. Many Sikhs and Parsees in India, who had been persecuted before colonization, supported British rule, and other religious and ethnic minorities turned to the Europeans for protection.

During the colonial period the ruling powers had sometimes sent people from one part of their empire to work in another. Thousands of Indian labourers were sent to work on sugar plantations in the Pacific islands of Fiji, where they made their homes and brought up their families. By the time Fiji gained its independence in 1970 Indians made up nearly half the population, and there was considerable rivalry between the Indians and the indigenous Fijian people. In Guyana, on the northern coast of South America, colonial policy resulted in two different groups of foreigners, descendants both of African slaves and of Asian Indian labourers, dominating the nation's population; the original Amerindian people mostly lived in remote villages.

The colonial powers also relied on troops recruited from minorities or from abroad to help them govern: Sikhs from the Punjab and Gurkhas from Nepal were deployed in British India; Sikh police worked in Hong Kong and Shanghai; Indian troops were used in the British Middle East and black African troops in French North Africa. In Algeria a substantial proportion of the Muslim population joined the French army; after independence many thousands of them were killed for having done so.

The 'divide and rule' policies of the colonial powers were reflected during the independence process. In the newly independent nations many minority peoples continued to be exposed to the hostility of a more powerful majority – a bitter legacy of conflict and mistrust.

THE HUMAN TOLL *of civil war reached epidemic proportions in Nigeria in the conflict between the Hausa and the Ibo people of the Eastern Region, who attempted to secede as Biafra. Between 1967 and 1970 three million starving children were reduced to this pitiful condition.*

New hopes, new fears

Despite the difficulties they faced, many African countries began their life as independent states with high hopes. The Ghanaian cocoa farmer Anim Assiful remembers what Nkrumah helped them to achieve. 'We had very high expectations, and these were met immediately after independence. For example, he helped us in our cocoa industry, he gave us free education. Look at some of the facilities like dams, roads, hospitals, education. We realized that Nkrumah was living up to his promises.'

The changes that took place were particularly important for people in rural areas. Eddie Francois was assistant chief engineer in the public works department responsible for roadbuilding, and he too remembers how much Nkrumah was admired. 'He tried to unify all the various sections of Ghana. And he made sure that the women were a part of the political structure...in the early stages everything was just going right...he said Africans should hold their heads up high....I think his failing was economics.'

Like most of the new African governments, Ghana believed a socialist system and central planning could best improve life for its people. Nkrumah called his version 'scientific socialism'. But too much was attempted, too soon. A giant dam on the river Volta was planned that would produce enough electricity to supply the entire country. Huge silos were built to house the cocoa crop, but were not used. Eddie Francois became critical of the grandiose roadbuilding schemes that went far beyond the country's needs, but he was advised to keep his views to himself. There was also suspicion of corruption. 'The usual thing that was bandied around was that 10 per cent of every project went to the party. We supported independence movements everywhere in Africa – not just verbal support but

A VILLAGE WORKSHOP (OPPOSITE) *At independence Ghana had a thriving economy in which women played an important part. Their prosperity was threatened by more grandiose enterprise schemes.*

NO MORE IDEOLOGY *Young people from the Institute of Journalism lead a protest against President Nkrumah, former hero of independent Ghana, whose 'scientific socialism' gave way to autocracy, self-idolatry and repression. Ghana underwent several attempted coups in less than a decade, and the president was finally overthrown by his own army in 1966.*

financial support...until we actually went broke.' Beatrice Quatey explains how disillusionment set in. 'We started getting fed up with Nkrumah when he passed a law to declare a one-party state, and he introduced some socialist ideas. For example, he decided no one was going to get paid. Everyone was going to work for the state, and he organized points where you could get food to eat.... You were spied upon and bugged. Anything you said against Nkrumah, they would come and arrest you, and just send you to prison, and if you are there you die, you die.'

Nine years after the triumphant celebration of independence in Ghana, Nkrumah was overthrown in a military coup, which led to further changes. As Anim Assiful recalls : 'The soldiers neglected us completely. All they did was look after themselves. We were afraid to confront them or complain because they had the guns. You could be arrested or shot, so we just had to keep quiet and watch as they were amassing wealth and we were getting poorer and poorer.' Despite this, he is convinced that independence was worth while. 'When the British were here they did nothing....In anything you are beginning to do you are bound to have problems, and despite the problems it was very good because the local people also had opportunities to take things into their own hands.'

Many of the new African states experienced difficulties in the years after independence. Ghana's setbacks were repeated across the continent. Coup followed coup as armies claimed that only they could bring stability to countries in chaos. Most of the new dictators were cruel and corrupt, and for many Africans one kind of repression was followed by another. After all the suffering and the struggle to gain freedom from colonial rule, there were further freedoms they needed to gain: freedom from hunger, from poverty and from oppression. Peace and prosperity often seemed a distant prospect. Yet, as the Indian farmer Satpal Sainai points out, 'The price had to be paid. Who wants to be a slave? Everyone wants to be free in his own house.'

RULE BY THE BOOK
Holding aloft a copy of the Koran, Idi Amin is sworn in as military head of state in Uganda in 1971 after leading a coup. Eight years of notoriously brutal dictatorship followed. Amin was deposed by forces from the neighbouring state of Tanzania, which invaded Uganda in 1979 in retaliation for the Ugandan invasion the year before.

STATUES OF LIBERTY
(RIGHT) *Jakarta's extravagantly costly monument to freedom, a man breaking free of his chains, presents a stark contrast to the continuing poverty endured by many Indonesians. Despite this, many people here and elsewhere believed that independence was worth almost any price.*

Acknowledgements

Television

Executive Producers
Peter Pagnamenta (BBC)
Zvi Dor-Ner (WGBH)

Archive Producer
Christine Whittaker

Programme Producers
Archie Baron, John Bridcut, Daniel Brittain-Catlin, Graham Chedd, Jennifer Clayton, Mark Davis, Jim DeVinney, Sally Doganis, Bill Jones, Jonathan Lewis, Angus Macqueen

Assistant Producers
Harry Gural, Isobel Hinshelwood, Lisa Jones, Marcus Kiggell, Kathleen Kouril, Dominic Ozanne, Liana Pomeranzev, Jonathan Smith, Tony Stiker, Amy Tarr, Sarah Wallis, Armorer Wason

Film Researchers
James Barker, Alex Cowan, Alexandra Crapanzano, Deborah Ford, Hilary Goldhammer, Jill McLoughlin, Alison Smith, David Thaxton, Jeanette Woods

Film Editors
David Berenson, Graham Dean, Margaret Kelly, Roderick Longhurst, Chuck Scott, Guy Tetzner

Supervising Film Editor
Steve Sampson

Series Manager (London)
Carol Harding
Production Manager (Boston)
Kathy Shugrue

Core Team
Laura Azevedo, Sheoko Badman-Walker, Alexandra Branson, Jim Dobel, Jill Flippance, Alison Lewis, Sue MacGregor, Fiona Mellon-Grant

Publishing

People's Century was produced for BBC Worldwide Publishing by

B·C·S Publishing Limited, Chesterton, Oxfordshire

Editorial Director
Candida Hunt

Art Director
Steve McCurdy

Editors
Deena Daher, Jo Newson, Clare Ramos, Jenny Roberts

Assistant Editors
Tabitha Jackson, Helen McCurdy, Rebecca Simor

Picture Research
Alexander Goldberg and James Clift of Image Select (London), David Pratt

Index
Sarah Ereira

Illustrations
Julian Baker

Picture credits

10 Topham Picture Source, 12 Popperfoto, 12/13 Hulton Deutsch, 13 (top) ET Archive, 13 (bottom) Roger Viollet, 14 (top) ET Archive, 14 (bottom) Ann Ronan at Image Select, 15 Range/Bettmann, 16 (top) Range/Bettmann, 16 (bottom) Range/Bettmann, 17 (left) Ellis Island, 17 (middle) Yetta Sperling, 17 (right) Ellis Island, 18 (top) Amy Sears, 18 (bottom) Mary Evans Picture Library, 18/19 Ann Ronan at Image Select, 19 Hulton Deutsch, 20 (top) Elmie Steever, 20 (middle) Elmie Steever, 20 (bottom) Range/Bettmann, 21 (top) Arthur Whitlock, 21 (middle) Army & Navy, 21 (bottom) Ulster Museum, 22 (bottom) Cadbury Ltd, 22/23 Range/Bettmann, 23 Hulton Deutsch, 24 (left) Hulton Deutsch, 24 (right) Hulton Deutsch, 25 Ann Ronan at Image Select, 26 Australian War Memorial, 28 Hulton Deutsch, 28/29 ET Archive, 29 Image Select, 30 (left) Bayerisches Armeemuseum, Ingolstadt, 30 (right) AKG Berlin, 30/31 Robert Harding Picture Library, 31 Australian War Memorial, 32 (top) Albert Powis, 32 (middle) Albert Powis, 32 (bottom) Robert Harding Picture Library, 33 ET Archive, 34 (top) Image Select, 34 (left) Peter Newark's Military Pictures, 34 (bottom) AKG Berlin, 36 (top) Ernst Weckerling/Julian Baldwin, 36 (bottom) Ernst Weckerling, 36/37 Image Select, 37 (top) Image Select, 37 (middle) Walter Hare, 37 (bottom) Norman Tennant, 37 (inset) Norman Tennant/Julian Baldwin, 38 (top) Tela Burt/Tony Mayne, 38 (middle) Tela Burt, 38 (bottom) Image Select, 40 Peter Newark's Military Pictures, 40/41 The Bridgeman Art Library/Imperial War Museum, 42 (left) Andrew N. Gagg ARPS, 42/43 (top) Mary Evans Picture Library, 42/43 (bottom) ET Archive, 43 (top) Walter Hare/Julian Baldwin, 43 (middle) Walter Hare, 44 (top) Peter Newark's Military Pictures, 44/45 Topham Picture Source, 45 The Trustees of the Imperial War Museum, 46 (top) Imperial War Museum, 46 (bottom) Bettmann Archive, 46/47 Popperfoto, 48 AKG Berlin, 49 AKG Berlin, 50 Archiv Gerstenberg, 52 (top) David King Collection, 52 (bottom) Novosti (London), 53 David King Collection, 54 The Bridgeman Art Library, 54/55 Alexander Briansky, 55 Alexander Briansky, 55 David King Collection, 56 (top) Archiv Gerstenberg, 56 (bottom) Novosti (London), 57 Department of Politics, Glasgow University, 58 Archiv Gerstenberg, 58/59 David King Collection, 59 Archiv Gerstenberg, 60 (top) Novosti (London), 60 (bottom) David King Collection, 61 (top) David King Collection, 61 (bottom) Novosti (London), 62 (left) Ella Shistyer, 62 (right) Ella Shistyer, 63 (top) Novosti (London), 63 (bottom) Novosti (London), 64 Novosti (London), 65 Archiv Gerstenberg, 66 (bottom) Novosti (London), 66/67 Roger Viollet, 67 Roger Viollet, 68 David King Collection, 69 David King Collection, 70 (bottom) Boris Yefimov, 70/71 David King Collection, 71 David King Collection, 72 David King Collection, 72/73 David King Collection, 74 ET Archive, 76 (left) US National Archives, 76 (bottom) Imperial War Museum, 77 Hulton Deutsch, 78 (top) Topham Picture Source, 78 (bottom) Culver Pictures, 79 AKG Berlin, 80 Mary Evans Picture Library, 80/81 Topham Picture Source, 82 Topham Picture Source, 83 (right) US National Archives, 83 (bottom) *The Tacoma Daily News*, 84 Hulton Deutsch, 86 Edimedia, 87 (top) Kobal Collection, 87 (bottom) Topham Picture Source, 88 Ann Ronan at Image

Select, **88/89** Hulton Deutsch, **89** Peter Newark's Military Pictures, **90** *(top)* Peace Pledge Union, London, **90** *(middle)* Donald Soper, **90** *(bottom)* Hulton Deutsch, **90/91** Topham Picture Source, **91** Robert Harding Library, **92** *(top)* Karl Nagerl, **92** *(bottom)* Karl Nagerl, **93** Hulton Deutsch, **94** Karl Nagerl, **95** *(top)* Geffrye Museum, **95** *(bottom)* AKG Berlin, **96** *(left)* ET Archive, **96** *(right)* Peter Newark's Military Pictures, **97** Hulton Deutsch, **98** Ford Motor Company, **100** *(top)* AKG Berlin, **100** *(bottom)* AKG Berlin, **100/101** Range/Bettmann, **102** *(top)* Ford Motor Company, **102** *(bottom)* Range/Bettmann, **103** *(top)* Ford Motor Company, **103** *(middle)* Archie Acciacca, **103** *(bottom)* Range/Bettmann, **104** Fiat, **105** Mary Evans Picture Library, **106** Fiat, **106/107** Popperfoto, **107** Les Gurl, **108** Ford Motor Company, **108/109** Ford Motor Company, **109** Range/Bettmann, **110** AKG London, **111** *(left)* Range/Bettmann, **111** *(top)* Espedito Valli, **111** *(bottom)* Espedito Valli, **112** AKG London, **112/113** Range/Bettmann, **113** *(right)* Paul Boatin, **114** Steven Richvalsky, **115** Range/Bettmann, **116** Fiat, **117** Range/Bettmann, **118** *(top)* Zenaide Provins, **118** *(bottom)* Zenaide Provins/Archie Baron, **119** *(top)* Range/Bettmann, **119** *(bottom)* Range/Bettmann, **120** Range/Bettmann, **121** Range/Bettmann, **122** Caruso, **124** Mary Evans Picture Library, **125** *(left)* Hulton Deutsch, **125** *(right)* Hulton Deutsch, **126** *(top)* Joe Liguori, **126** *(middle)* Joe Liguori, **126/127** Range/Bettmann, **127** *(top)* JL Charmet, **127** *(bottom)* Range/Bettmann, **128** Hulton Deutsch, **128/129** Hulton Deutsch, **129** *(top)* NBC, **129** *(bottom)* Sidney Garner, **130** Hulton Deutsch, **130/131** Hulton Deutsch, **131** *(top)* Diego Lucero, **131** *(middle)* Diego Lucero, **131** *(bottom)* Allsport, **132** *(left)* Caruso, **132** *(right)* Caruso, **132** *(bottom)* Hulton Deutsch, **133** *(top)* Baseball Hall of Fame, **133** *(bottom)* Range/Bettmann, **134** *(top)* Anna Freund, **134** *(middle)* Anna Freund, **134** *(bottom)* Range/Bettmann, **135** NBC, **136** Hulton Deutsch, **136/137** Mirror/Telegraph Newspapers, **137** Mary Evans Picture Library, **138** Hulton Deutsch, **138/139** Range/Bettmann, **139** Range/Bettmann, **140** Range/Bettmann, **141** NBC, **142/143** Edimedia, **143** *(top)* Helen Stephens, **143** *(middle)* Range/Bettmann, **143** *(lower middle)* Allsport, **143** *(bottom)* Baltimore Afro-American, **144** NBC, **145** Range/Bettmann, **146** AKG Berlin, **148** Popperfoto, **149** Range/Bettmann, **150** *(top)* Edimedia, **150** *(bottom)* Waddingtons, **150/151** Edimedia, **151** Edimedia, **152** Edimedia, **152/153** Edimedia, **154** Hulton Deutsch, **155** *(top)* Hulton Deutsch, **155** *(right)* Range/Bettmann, **157** *(left)* Range/Bettmann, **157** *(top)* Chilean Biblioteca Naçional, **157** *(bottom)* Chilean Biblioteca Naçional, **158** Humphrey Spender, **159** *(top)* Con Shiels/Archie Baron, **159** *(middle)* Con Shiels, **159** *(bottom)* Hulton Deutsch, **160** Hulton Deutsch, **161** Edimedia, **162** *(left)* Tore Alespong/Archie Baron, **162/163** *(top)* Swedish Labour Movement Archives,

162/163 *(bottom)* Tore Alespong, **163** *(top)* Göta Rosén/Archie Baron, **163** *(bottom)* Göta Rosén, **164** *(left)* Edimedia, **164** *(top right)* Bill Bailey/Archie Baron, **164** *(right middle)* Bill Bailey, **164/165** Range/Bettmann, **166** Range/Bettmann, **166/167** AKG Berlin, **167** DC Comics, **168** *(top)* Mancil Milligan/Archie Baron, **168** *(bottom)* Mancil Milligan, **169** Range/Bettmann, **170** Photofest, **172** BFI, **172/173** Image Select, **173** Range/Bettmann, **174** *(top)* Range/Bettmann, **174** *(middle)* Image Select, **174** *(bottom)* Danny Patt, **175** *(left)* AKG London, **175** *(right)* AKG London, **176** AKG London, **177** Peter Aprahamian, **178** *(top)* Image Select, **178** *(bottom)* The Bridgeman Art Library, **179** Range/Bettmann, **180** Range/Bettmann, **180/181** Range/Bettmann, **181** AKG London, **182** *(bottom)* Range/Bettmann, **182** *(top)* Image Select, **183** Range/Bettmann, **184** *(left)* BFI, **184** *(right)* Rajam Ramanathan, **184** *(bottom)* AKG London, **185** Image Select, **186** *(left)* Cy Locke, **186** *(bottom)* Range/Bettmann, **186/187** Popperfoto, **187** *(top)* Image Select, **187** *(bottom)* Range/Bettmann, **188** *(top)* Robert Opie, **188** *(bottom)* Popperfoto, **189** *(top)* Walt Disney/Mirror Syndication International, **189** *(bottom)* Popperfoto, **190** O. Winston Link, **191** Image Select, **192** Hulton Deutsch, **194** Hulton Deutsch, **196** *(top)* AKG Berlin, **196** *(bottom)* AKG Berlin, **197** *(left)* AKG Berlin, **197** *(right)* AKG Berlin, **198** Hulton Deutsch, **198/199** Hulton Deutsch, **199** AKG Berlin, **200** *(top)* Imperial War Museum, **200** *(middle)* Reinhard Spitzy/Jonathan Lewis, **200** *(bottom)* Reinhard Spitzy, **201** AKG Berlin, **202** *(top)* Bundesarchiv, **202** *(bottom)* Pressens Bild, **203**, AKG Berlin, **204** *(top)* Gerda Bodenheimer/Jonathan Lewis, **204** *(middle)* Gerda Bodenheimer, **204** *(bottom)* Hulton Deutsch, **204/205** YIVO Institute for Jewish Research, New York, **206** Hulton Deutsch, **207** *(left)* Anna-Maria Ernst, **207** *(right)* Ann-Marie Ernst/Jonathan Lewis, **207** *(bottom)* Bundesarchiv, **208** Wiener Library, **208/209** Niedersächsische Tageszeitung Hannover, **210** *(top)* Hulton Deutsch, **210** *(bottom)* AKG Berlin, **212** Edimedia, **213** *(top)* AKG Berlin, **213** *(middle)* Hans Margules, **213** *(bottom)* Hans Margules, **214** *(top)* Edimedia, **214** *(bottom)* The Jewish Museum, Prague, **215** Edimedia, **216** Hulton Deutsch, **217** AKG Berlin, **218** Hulton Deutsch, **220** *(top)* Hulton Deutsch, **220** *(bottom)* Hulton Deutsch, **220/221** *(top)* Range/Bettmann, **221** *(middle)* Hulton Deutsch, **221** Imperial War Museum, **222** *(top)* Hulton Deutsch, **222** *(bottom)* AKG Berlin, **224** Hulton Deutsch, **225** AKG London, **226** Hulton Deutsch, **227** *(top)* Mary Evans Picture Library, **227** *(bottom)* Hulton Deutsch, **228** *(top)* Sid Newham/Lisa Jones, **228** *(middle)* Sid Newham, **228** *(bottom)* Hulton Deutsch, **229** *(top right)* Margarete Zettel/Lisa Jones, **229** *(bottom right)* Margarete Zettel, **229** *(left)* Hulton Deutsch, **230** Hulton Deutsch, **230/231** Victor Cole, **231** *(left)* Victor Cole, **231** *(middle)* Victor Cole, **231** *(bottom)* Edimedia, **232** *(top)* AKG

London, **232** *(bottom)* Hulton Deutsch, **233** *(top)* Edimedia, **233** *(bottom)* Kieko Saotome, **234** *(top)* Leonid Galperin, **234** *(bottom)* Leonid Galperin, **235** *(top)* Edimedia, **235** *(bottom)* Novosti London, **236** Edimedia, **236/237** Novosti London, **237** Edimedia, **238** *(top)* Hulton Deutsch, **238** *(bottom)* Hulton Deutsch, **239** Hulton Deutsch, **240** Hulton Deutsch, **240/241** Hulton Deutsch, **242** US National Archives, **244** Bettmann, **244/245** AKG Berlin, **245** *(left)* Anatoly Semiriaga, **245** *(right)* Anatoly Semiriaga, **246** *(top)* Range/Bettmann, **246** *(middle)* Topham Picture Source, **247** *(left)* Bettmann, **247** *(right)* Bettmann, **248** Hulton Deutsch, **249** University of Canterbury, **250** School of Slavonic Studies, **251** Edimedia, **252** *(top)* Gail Halverson, **252** *(middle)* Gail Halverson, **252** *(bottom)* Bettmann, **253** AKG Berlin, **254** *(top)* Tamara Banketik, **254** *(bottom)* Tamara Banketik, **255** Novosti London, **256** *(left)* Alexei Kozlov, **256** *(right)* Alexei Kozlov, **257** Hulton Deutsch, **258** *(top)* Manny Fried, **258** *(middle)* Manny Fried, **258** *(bottom)* Manny Fried, **258/259** US National Archives, **259** *(left)* Kobal Collection, **259** Bettmann, **260** AKG Berlin, **261** Bettmann, **262** AKG Berlin, **262/263** AKG Berlin, **263** *(left)* Hulton Deutsch, **263** *(right)* AKG Berlin, **264** *(top)* Anita Möller, **264** *(middle)* Anita Möller, **264** *(bottom)* AKG Berlin, **265** Hulton Deutsch, **266** Advertising Archive, **268** Popperfoto, **269** *(top)* Topham Picture Source, **269** *(bottom)* Topham Picture Source, **270/271** Topham Picture Source, **271** Edimedia, **272** *(top)* Raymond Jolivet, **272** *(bottom)* Raymond Jolivet, **273** *(top)* SAIS Bologna School, **273** *(bottom)* Popperfoto, **274** Popperfoto, **275** *(top)* Advertising Archive, **275** *(bottom)* Range/Bettmann, **276** *(left)* Advertising Archive, **276/277** Popperfoto, **277** *(bottom)* Topham Picture Source, **277** *(right)* Bettmann, **278** *(top)* Advertising Archive, **278** *(bottom)* Gamma, **279** Bettmann, **280** *(top)* Bill Braga, **280** *(bottom)* Range/Bettmann, **281** AKG Berlin, **282** *(top)* Ludwiggsen Associates Ltd, **282** *(bottom)* Popperfoto, **283** Popperfoto, **284** Edimedia, **285** *(top)* Edimedia, **285** *(bottom)* Farabolafoto, **286** *(top)* SAIS Bologna School, **286** *(middle)* Gerardo Ciola, **286** *(bottom)* Gerardo Ciola, **288** Popperfoto, **289** Camera Press, **290** Hulton Deutsch, **292** *(top)* Mary Evans Picture Library, **292** *(bottom)* Popperfoto, **294** Hulton Deutsch, **294/295** Popperfoto, **295** Indian Press & Information Bureau, **296** *(top)* Anim Assiful, **296** *(bottom)* Popperfoto, **297** Hulton Deutsch, **298** Hulton Deutsch, **299** Popperfoto, **300** Magnum, **301** Popperfoto, **302** Popperfoto, **303** Popperfoto, **304** Popperfoto, **305** *(top)* Hulton Deutsch, **305** *(bottom)* Edimedia, **306/307** Popperfoto, **307** *(left)* Komla Gbedema, **307** *(right)* Popperfoto, **308** Hulton Deutsch, **309** *(top)* Popperfoto, **310** *(left)* Popperfoto, **310/311** Popperfoto, **311** John Hill Agency Ltd, **312** Popperfoto, **313** Popperfoto

The publishers would like to thank all the people who took part in the making of the programmes and kindly lent their own photographs for use in this book. Also special thanks to; Ian Blackwell, Anna Calvert, Mohammed Lounes, Helen Menzies and Dawn Ryman.

Index